Writing a Research Paper in Political Science

Third Edition

SAGE was founded in 1965 by Sara Miller McCune to support the dissemination of usable knowledge by publishing innovative and high-quality research and teaching content. Today, we publish more than 750 journals, including those of more than 300 learned societies, more than 800 new books per year, and a growing range of library products including archives, data, case studies, reports, conference highlights, and video. SAGE remains majority-owned by our founder, and after Sara's lifetime will become owned by a charitable trust that secures our continued independence.

Los Angeles | London | Washington DC | New Delhi | Singapore | Boston

Writing a Research Paper in Political Science

A Practical Guide to Inquiry, Structure, and Methods

Third Edition

Lisa A. Baglione

Saint Joseph's University

Los Angeles | London | New Delhi
Singapore | Washington DC | Boston

Los Angeles | London | New Delhi
Singapore | Washington DC | Boston

FOR INFORMATION:

CQ Press

An Imprint of SAGE Publications, Inc.

2455 Teller Road

Thousand Oaks, California 91320

E-mail: order@sagepub.com

SAGE Publications Ltd.

1 Oliver's Yard

55 City Road

London EC1Y 1SP

United Kingdom

SAGE Publications India Pvt. Ltd.

B 1/I 1 Mohan Cooperative Industrial Area

Mathura Road, New Delhi 110 044

India

SAGE Publications Asia-Pacific Pte. Ltd.

3 Church Street

#10-04 Samsung Hub

Singapore 049483

Printed in the United States of America

Library of Congress Cataloging-in-Publication Data

Baglione, Lisa A.

Writing a research paper in political science: a practical guide to inquiry, structure, and methods/Lisa A. Baglione. — 3rd ed.

p. cm.
Includes bibliographical references and index.

ISBN 978-1-4833-7616-5 (pbk.: alk. paper)

1. Political science—Authorship. 2. Political science—Research. I. Title.

JA86.B24 2015
808'.06632—dc23   2011025074

This book is printed on acid-free paper.

Acquisitions Editor: Sarah Calabi
Senior Development Editor: Nancy Matuszak
Editorial Assistant: Davia Grant
Production Editor: Libby Larson
Copy Editor: Jim Kelly
Typesetter: C&M Digitals (P) Ltd.
Cover Designer: Anupama Krishnan
Marketing Manager: Amy Whitaker

MIX
Paper from
responsible sources
FSC® C014174

16 17 18 19 10 9 8 7 6 5 4 3 2

About the Author

Dr. Lisa A. Baglione is professor and chair of the political science department at Saint Joseph's University. Her major fields of study are international relations and comparative politics. Dr. Baglione has published works exploring post-settlement peace building; the arms control decision-making process in the United States, the Soviet Union, and Russia; and the research paper–writing process and has coauthored articles on the transformation of the Russian polity and economy in the early postcommunist period. Currently, she is researching the determinants of contemporary Russian foreign policy. At Saint Joseph's, Dr. Baglione teaches two courses—Writing in International Relations and Sophomore Seminar in Political Science—in which she develops and tests the ideas, advice, and techniques offered in this work.

To Jack Moran
The consummate teacher-researcher-friend

Contents

List of Features

Figure

Tables

Boxes

Recipes

Preface

A s I write this preface, I am preparing to speak at a memorial service for my dear friend, Jack Moran, the long-time head tutor at Cornell-in-Washington's (CIW) internship and public policy program for undergraduates. My commitment to the importance of teaching research paper writing and this book originated in my experiences there and are very much a result of my interactions with Jack. For those of you who notice that the dedication of this edition is different from the previous one, the reason is not related to any change in my status but as a way to honor my friend, who taught me so much as a graduate student and who, over the ensuing two-plus decades, engaged in numerous conversations with me about teaching research methods and how to engage students in the research process. I was not an early believer that requiring political science undergraduates to undertake a journal-style research article was a good idea. The instructors who are picking up this book likely have heard these criticisms and more: such an endeavor puts students under too much pressure, is too specialized when a liberal arts education is not intended to produce academics, and is too much work for faculty and students alike. In my time at Cornell and then with even more fervor as a faculty member at Saint Joseph's University in Philadelphia, I became a convert, and Jack was central to helping me arrive at that transformation. I firmly believe that learning how to conduct research and effectively communicate ideas in the form of an academic paper not only teaches students invaluable writing, research, logical, and analytic skills but, perhaps most compelling, *empowers* them to become critical consumers of information and, therefore, better citizens in a democracy. Today Americans and people in liberal polities the world over must assess arguments, weigh evidence, and consider the appropriateness of cases, data, and comparisons as they decide whose policy positions appear best suited to contemporary challenges and whose inclinations and worldviews seem capable of handling unforeseen opportunities and dangers.[1]

Jack Moran was the consummate teacher, who knew how to expertly guide students through the research process and, over his career, oversaw more than a thousand undergraduate public policy theses, ranging in length from about 60 to 100 pages. Weekly, he would meet individually with his students after having read their drafts, intellectually poking and prodding them to sharpen their ideas, encouraging, laughing, and challenging them to do their best. He shaped so many students and gave them an unbelievable experience that was more than an intellectual one, because Jack was not just a teacher but a mentor. He lived in the CIW complex with these students, and he gave them his all. Also remarkable about Jack was how much time and energy he spent on the graduate students who were teaching at CIW. For this program to succeed, the Cornell Center needed a group of tutors to work with the under-grads, but most of the time, graduate students—despite being in the early stages of writing their own dissertations—had had very little training in the research process. And the majority certainly didn't know much about teaching research paper writing. Jack took the tutors under his wing, helped them master the art of teaching at CIW, and encouraged them through their own theses, often giving useful advice on how to overcome methodological challenges and writing blocks, and aiding countless tutors in finishing so that they could move on to their faculty appointments. The puzzle of Jack for some of us was that he never completed his own dissertation, when he certainly could have; thankfully, he was not regretful. The joy of his interaction with students and colleagues, his wonderful life filled with friends, politics, art, music, culture, and great food, and living in Washington, D.C., with ample time for travel, was enough. Why wouldn't it be? Most of us look at his life and say, indeed, it was a life *very* well lived. Jack was a remarkable individual who changed lives and was such a good friend to so many.

Thus, I dedicate this book to Jack Moran. Future generations of Cornell undergraduate and graduate students are much deprived by his loss, and CIW will never be the same without him. I will miss his laugh, his friendship, and his willingness to discuss research challenges and design issues. This dedication is a small token of my appreciation of him as a mentor to those embarking on policy and political research, as well as an effort to mark the enormous contributions he has made to the development of discerning citizens through his service at Cornell's Washington Center.

In addition to honoring Jack, I want to thank some people for their help, encouragement, and generosity as I have worked on this book. First and foremost, I must give an enormous thank you to my students at Saint Joseph's University, who constantly challenge me to find better ways to teach about the research paper writing process and who, every semester, are willing to go along for the research paper ride (or marathon) with me. I hope they know how much I appreciate their hard work and that I do realize how much effort, concentration, and pure determination their research papers take. Second, I'd like to express my gratitude to my colleagues, who have humored me over the years and accepted my belief in the importance of research paper writing. While not all of them are as convinced as I, they have supported the course as a major requirement for almost fifteen years. I want to single out Graham Lee, who undertook this effort with me at the outset; Kaz Fukuoka, for his commitment to the research paper in the senior seminars; Becki Scola, for her devotion to data analysis and empiricism that always keeps me on my toes; Rick Gioioso, for his ability to question "old ways"; and Susan Liebell, for her discerning mind and overall commitment to student learning and writing. You have all influenced this book in multiple ways, and I am grateful to have you as colleagues. Third, I want to thank friends who have been supportive and provided me with excellent feedback over the years. I especially appreciate Marissa

Martino Golden of Bryn Mawr College for her ideas and friendship and for leading me to one of my student contributors. Mary Malone at the University of New Hampshire has again been enormously positive and someone whose instinct and judgment on research and teaching I always seek. And, of course, my husband Steve McGovern, at Haverford College, is the greatest sounding board and the person who helps me—the comparativist and international relations specialist—be confident that I am doing a decent job when I make a foray into American politics.

I owe an enormous debt of gratitude to the students who have allowed me to share their work with you in this book and on the Web site. Yes, Zoe Colman is a real (and highly impressive) person who recently graduated from Bryn Mawr College. Not only do I greatly admire her senior thesis, but I am extremely thankful that she has allowed me to share it with you in segments in this book and in full on the Web site. Mary Korchak of Saint Joseph's University has also given me permission to provide her semester-long paper, written as a sophomore, on the Web site. Finally, two other students, Kevin Black and Rachel Sellers, are the composite of "Kevin" in my text, with Kevin inspiring the discussions about being torn between case studies and statistical analysis in studying the 2011 Arab uprisings and Rachel providing the research question and some of the actual text for the example of qualitative analysis. Thanks so much to all of you for your generosity in sharing your work with me and future students.

I am also very grateful to Dr. Kim Logio of the Saint Joseph's Sociology Department, who has had numerous conversations with me in the past about teaching research methods and using SPSS with students and helped bail me out at a crucial time when a computer crash rendered my software unusable.

The team at SAGE/CQ Press has been just great, again. I was thrilled when Charisse Kiino asked me to move forward with the third edition a year ahead of schedule, and Sarah Calabi and Nancy Matuszak have been fabulous to work with. At key times during the revising process, they provided me with valuable guidance to help make this edition a great product. They also found me fifteen anonymous reviewers, who deserve my thanks for the time and effort they put into the feedback that makes this book not only more current but better, serving student and faculty needs more appropriately. To the reviewers, thank you for the positive comments, recommendations, and criticisms. I hope that you can see your influence on this third edition, and I apologize here for those ideas I left behind. Please know that I did not ignore them, but rather considered what I could do in the space allotted with my purpose and talents. Jim Kelly is an extraordinary copyeditor, unbelievably organized, patient, and with a great sense of humor. Thank you, Jim! Finally, I extend my gratitude to Libby Larson who moved the work expertly through production, and to Allison Hughes for all her efforts on the web resources. I am very lucky to have had such a great staff helping me every step of the way.

As usual, the remaining flaws are all my own, and I hope there are far fewer in this edition, so that this book can be worthy of my friend, Jack Moran. Dear Jack, already you are sorely missed, and you will never be forgotten. You touched so many, many people in such meaningful ways.

NOTE

1. My colleague Susan P. Liebell has made an excellent case for the importance of teaching science to prepare a democratic people. See *Democracy, Intelligent Design, and Evolution: Science for Citizenship* (New York: Routledge, 2013).

chapter 1

So You Have to Write a Research Paper

L et's be honest. When many students look at a new course syllabus and view the assignments, seeing that the professor has assigned a research paper typically brings one of two reactions. A first possible response is one of horror. Many students dread the assignment because they don't know how to write a research paper. Students with this viewpoint may drop the course because of this requirement, be panicked about it all semester, or just ignore the assignment until the last moment (as if it might somehow go away) and then turn "something" in. An alternative response is, "No problem, I'll just write a *report* on something I'm interested in." Neither reaction is productive, nor are the strategies mentioned for dealing with the dreaded assignment fortunate. The goal of this book is to teach you how to write a research paper so that you (1) won't respond in either fashion and (2) will realize why the typical reactions are so problematic.

First, a research paper can be intimidating because—and this point is very important to remember—few secondary schools and institutions of higher learning bother to teach how to write one anymore.[1] Yet many faculty assign research papers, as if knowing how to write one were an innate ability that all college students possess. Research paper writing, however, is a set of skills that needs to be developed. These skills can be taught and learned, as well as used throughout a college career.[2]

Second, research paper writing is so daunting because the task seems unbounded. Where do you start? What is a good topic? How do you know where to look for information? What does the text of such a paper look like? How do you know when you're done? This concern with boundaries is obviously related to the general ignorance about what constitutes a research paper. But another problem here is recognizing that writing, whether for a research paper or some other assignment, is discipline specific.[3] Faculty often forget to make that point explicitly, and students typically conceive of writing skills as consisting of only grammar, usage, and paragraph construction. While those skills are certainly important, they are not the only ones students need to develop for writing good research papers, particularly in political science.

Political science has its own conventions (which are similar to those of the other social sciences and in some instances even related to those in the natural sciences) for paper writing that students must learn. Just because you earned an A in freshman English does not mean that you are ready to garner an equally excellent mark on your political science research paper. You not only must learn to speak a new language (the vocabulary of political science) but must adopt the conventions, values, and norms of the discipline.[4] Here again, faculty have so successfully internalized these norms that they forget that students need instruction. This book, however, will teach you to write a research paper in political science, demystifying the structure and the process. Developing this set of writing skills will be useful to you in a number of ways: not only will it help you write more effectively in this discipline, but it will allow you to see more easily the conventions that apply to other fields of study. In addition, once you know the style and format for any subject, your reading comprehension skills in that discipline improve, and understanding even the densest academic tome will become easier. Why? Because scholars use this structure themselves, and once you know what to expect from the form of an article or book, you will be better able to distinguish the argument from the evidence, the logic from the information, or the normative claim from the underlying principles.

Third, knowing how to write a research paper is something that will be useful to you throughout your life. You might find that statement funny, thinking to yourself that you are writing research papers only to get your degree, but thereafter, you intend to be working in the corporate or nonprofit world. (My apologies to those of you out there who see an academic career in your future.) Well, if you were amused, you need to stop laughing and recognize that you likely will spend much of your career writing, and a good portion of that writing will be persuasive communication that (1) surveys a number of opinions or studies on a particular problem, (2) assesses logically the strengths and weaknesses of the various approaches, and (3) uses evidence from a case or cases of particular interest to you, your boss, and/or your clients to determine what the best approach to this problem is for your purposes. In effect, then, you will be performing the types of analysis involved in writing research papers for your living, no matter what you do. So why not learn how to do it now and develop the aptitude, so that you will be in a better position in your future?

Some of you might be skeptically reading this introduction, believing that as a more advanced student of political science, you have already developed the skills, knowledge, and ability to write an excellent research paper. With no disrespect to your accomplishments, experiences of scores of faculty from around the country, at the best institutions, suggest that even the most capable readers of this book have something to learn, because you have never before been asked to put your ideas together in such a systematic way to perform a rigorous assessment of the literature, assert a thesis, create a fair test for evaluating evidence related to your contention, perform systematic analysis, and present your results in a standard fashion. So, even if you think you have little need for this book, I counsel you to read on. You are not the first to have doubts, and virtually all of your predecessors have come away finding value in these pages.

Others of you might simply not want to "waste your time" reading a book about writing, as well as inquiry, structure, and methods. In some ways, this book is like the oft-overlooked instructional manual that comes along with your newest electronic device. Most of us prefer to ignore that text and play around with our new toy to figure it out on our own. Your professor, however, does not want the trial-and-error approach here and believes that you will benefit enormously from this book. An instructor doesn't make decisions about texts lightly, as faculty recognize your constraints—the amount of money that is appropriate to spend on course resources and the number of pages you can read in a week—and yours has decided that this book will help you arrive at the desired end point of writing a high-quality research paper in political science. So, respect your faculty member's knowledge and assessment of your needs. Besides, the chapters are relatively short and the reading is easy. Your time investment will not be enormous, but the pay off will be great.

Importantly, the return will not be confined to this particular course, as the book will help you acquire skills that will empower you in multiple ways. By learning how to write that research paper, you acquire expertise—skills of reading comprehension, writing, research, and analysis—that will enable you to do well in all of your classes. Moreover, these are all talents you will use in your future career, whether you are an attorney, a CEO, an activist, a public servant, a politician, a businessperson, or an educator. Such professionals are frequently asked to evaluate information and provide recommendations. For instance, imagine you are working at the Department of Health and Human Services and are asked to determine the impact of the Patient Protection and Affordable Care Act. At the outset, you will to need to find the legislation itself and then define what *impact* means. You also will need to justify your definition and explain from where and why you selected your information. Once you have some data, you must analyze them and then write up your findings in a form that will impress your boss. You will learn all of the skills required to do an excellent job on such a project in this book.

WHAT IS A RESEARCH PAPER? A FEW HELPFUL METAPHORS

Most students think that a research paper in political science is a long, descriptive report of some event, phenomenon, or person. This is a dangerous misconception that focuses on determining facts. Numerous texts on the methodology and philosophy of science explain that true facts are often elusive because researchers interpret what they see or because they report only what they deem important, knowingly or unknowingly, failing to provide a more complete picture.[5] While we will return to the topic of data collection later in the text, the problem I am raising here is the one that characterizes so many papers: conceiving of them as "data dumps," or all the information you can find on a particular topic. Descriptive reporting is only one element of a political science research paper. It is an important part, and having a chance to learn about politically relevant events, persons, or phenomena is probably why you are a political science major. But knowing about politics is not being a political scientist. For political scientists, details are important, but only if they are the right ones, related to either the logics or the norms you are exploring or the precise evidence required to sustain or undermine an argument. Facts for the sake of facts can be boring and distracting.

Two metaphors help explain the balance you should seek. The first is that of a court case. In writing your research paper, you are, in essence, presenting your case to the judge and jury (readers of the paper). While you need to acknowledge that there are other possible explanations (e.g., your opposing counsel's case), your job is to show that both your preferred logic and the evidence supporting it are stronger than any competing perspective's framework and its sustaining information. Interesting details that have nothing to do with the particular argument you are constructing can distract a jury and annoy the judge. Good lawyers lay out their cases, connecting all the dots and leaving no pieces of evidence hanging. All the information they provide is related to convincing those in judgment that their interpretation is the correct one.

If you find the analogy of the courtroom too adversarial, think of your paper as a painting. The level and extent of detail depends on both the size of the canvas and the subject to be painted. Too few details in a landscape can make it boring and unidentifiable, whereas too many in a portrait can make the subject unattractive or strange. The goal here is to achieve the "Goldilocks" or "just right" outcome.[6]

I will use two other metaphors throughout this book to help you (1) maintain the appropriate long-term perspective on the project (the marathon) and (2) know exactly what you need to do as you proceed through the paper (the recipe). Like running a marathon, the research paper is the culmination of great efforts. Just as the typical person cannot expect to get up on the morning of a race, go to the starting line, and run for more than twenty-six miles, a student needs to go through preparatory steps before completing a research paper. While runners stretch, train, get the right nutrition and rest, and prepare mentally for years, months, and days before the big race, students need to practice their writing and develop their theses, create plans for evaluating those contentions, find the right kinds of information, evaluate the data, and work on presenting their claims and the evidence as accurately and effectively as possible. All of these tasks require time and energy. Only with adequate preparation do the marathoner and the student finish the race and the paper successfully.

While few of us are likely to run a marathon, everyone who reads this book will write a research paper. My point in writing is to show you that if you follow the advice spelled out here, you will not only finish your paper but turn in something of which you feel proud. Too often I have seen students rushing at the end just to get their papers done, without really caring about quality. Their feelings are at times understandable. They didn't know how to approach the project, haven't asked for or received any guidance, and are having a totally unsatisfying time working on their research papers. When this is the case, not only is the end result poor, but the exercise itself is a failure as an assignment.

To avert such negative outcomes, this text serves as a kind of cookbook, with a recipe at the end of each chapter that suggests the supplies and steps to take to write an excellent paper. For some of you and in some sections of the text, these recipes might seem a bit simple, as they set out the basics. When that is the case, like any experienced cook, you should free to modify, adding the spices and flourishes that might fit your tastes. But your final product won't be satisfying if you ignore the basics, and thus the recipe provides those essentials for you.

In addition, this textbook comes with a companion Web site, http://study .sagepub.com/baglione3e, that includes many resources designed to help you master the materials presented so that you can write an excellent paper. Most chapters have corresponding handouts or guides, as well as exercises for practicing the skills that are the subject of the chapter, calendar reminders, and checklists that you can customize (based on the recipes) designed to serve as rubrics that clearly state exactly what you need to accomplish. Flashcards on the site provide definitions to the key terms appearing in italics throughout the book.

The most important insights of this guide to research paper writing (and ones you would do well to internalize) are that you can have a rewarding and satisfying learning experience if you devote time to the process, recognize that you have something to learn from this book, regardless of how many political science courses you have already taken, and conceive of the research paper as consisting of smaller, definable tasks. Each piece can be accomplished on its own, and the parts can then be assembled and reworked to create a coherent and significant whole. In effect, then, the tasks are like the marathoner's efforts to prepare before a race or a cook's steps to create a delicious multicourse meal. Each performs on the appropriate day but succeeds only after days and weeks of preparation.

In fact, continuing with the running analogy, I am asking you to consider the fable of the tortoise and the hare: slow and steady will win this race. While some people have natural talent (whether as runners or as writers and researchers), individuals finish marathons and write research papers because they are determined, diligent, and skilled. The hare may be the more naturally gifted and the faster runner, but the tortoise industriously persists throughout the course to win the race. Be the tortoise![7] Work on your paper slowly but surely throughout the writing period, and you will produce a fine final product.

WHAT RESEARCH PAPER WRITING ENTAILS

This book seeks to teach you the basics of writing a research paper in political science. Each chapter is devoted to a particular section of that thinking and writing process and the skills you need to develop to make that part a good one. The whole effort can be broken down into eleven distinct but interrelated tasks,[8] which map into different sections of the paper as specified in Table 1.1. Because institutions use different-length terms (semesters, trimesters, and quarters), and some students using this book might even be writing theses of longer duration, I'm providing a suggested calendar in relative terms. By setting out deadlines along the way, I am underlining the notion that you cannot write a research paper in a matter of days or hours. Moreover, while I stress that you frequently will be rethinking your drafts, you do need to put ideas on paper—thus the suggested deadlines. The timing here, however, is provisional, and you should look to your instructor's guidelines as you work on your project.

Each of the following chapters will identify precisely what you need to do to write the different sections of a paper. In the text that follows you will find instructions and examples of actual student efforts. At the end of every chapter, I will provide a practical summary to guide you through accomplishing the goals and a recipe designed to make your tasks crystal clear. Please remember, research paper writing takes time: to develop a question, find appropriate sources, read and understand them, write, think, plan your research, conduct it, reflect on its significance, and finally, revise and edit it. While the task chart makes the process appear to be linear—you work through one task, complete it, and then move on to another—do not be fooled: the quality of your writing improves as the clarity of your ideas does. A better picture of how you proceed is not a straight line but a spiral whereby you are constantly looping back, adding insights, information, and sophistication because you have rethought and sharpened what you have understood and written before. A guiding assumption here is that your paper benefits from reconsideration and iteration, and by coiling (picture a spring) back through some ideas while you are also pushing forward, you make progress on completing your goal. To stay in one place to perfect that section might give you a brilliant and polished early part of your paper but won't lead to a finished product, which is a key goal. So, get started, work steadily, follow the deadlines your professor provides for finishing each section, and do not be ashamed to rethink and change earlier thoughts. Keep thinking of that spiral, and remember, "First thoughts are not best thoughts. They're just first."[9]

Essential to springing forward is having some work to reconsider. Thus, this book asks you to begin thinking and writing as soon as possible. This recommendation may seem counterintuitive. "How can I write when I am still learning about a subject?" most students ask. The response is that writing is part of the thinking process, and you cannot make adequate intellectual advances without putting your ideas on paper at the outset. By the end of the process, you will have a draft that looks very different from the first one you wrote, but that final version that you put forth is a product of the thinking and learning you did throughout the entire project. This book encourages (and in fact demands) that you write your research paper in pieces, beginning with the first substantive parts of the paper and revising as you proceed. Insisting on writing from the outset makes clear a distinction that most students don't recognize: *revising* and *editing* are different processes. Revising entails rethinking and major rewriting, whereas editing consists of fixing grammatical errors and format mistakes and varying word choice. We all know the importance of correcting those silly errors, but many of us aren't aware of just how important rethinking and reconsidering our early ideas are. In fact, ask any researcher and you will find that she or he is constantly drafting, and that the redrafting process is primarily concerned not with editing but with perfecting the argument, sharpening the concepts, amassing better evidence, and adapting the structure to best suit the researcher's purposes. Thus, like a researcher, revising will be essential for you to create the excellent finished product you seek.

BLUEPRINT OF THE BOOK

In the paragraphs that follow, I will briefly explain the contents of each chapter of the book. I recommend that you read this now to gain a better general understanding of the research paper–writing process. If you like, come back to these discussions prior to reading each chapter as a way to help you focus on the main tasks to be accomplished in that section.

In chapter 2, we take up the challenge of determining a good Research Question (RQ). Posing a question that is interesting and important to you, scholars, policy makers, and the average citizen is the key to a good choice. As you will see, coming up with an interesting query is one of the hardest and most important parts of the project. It sets the stage for the whole research paper. As we consider what makes a compelling question, we will note the diversity of kinds of research in which one may be engaged as a political scientist. And you will meet four students whose interests and research topics will reappear at different points in the book. You will even see excerpts of some of these students' efforts to give you examples of how others like you have handled the distinct tasks involved in writing a research paper.

After identifying an RQ, you are ready to look at how others, namely scholars, have answered similar queries.[10] In chapter 3, you begin work on the second phase of your project: determining and understanding the academic debate. At this point, you need to discover how experts answer your RQ in both its general and specific forms. You will begin this process by working on the Annotated Bibliography and, if you like, using some source management software to help you keep track of your materials. In chapter 3, you will learn about finding good, scholarly sources—both books and articles—and using these

Table 1.1   Research Paper: Tasks to Be Accomplished, Sections, and Suggested Calendar

Tasks	Sections/ Assignment	Suggested Calendar
(1) Develop a "good" topic or, more accurately, a good Research Question and find excellent, related scholarly sources.	Annotated Bibliography	At the outset, refine over the first third
(2) Identify, classify, explain, and evaluate the most important scholarly answers to that Research Question, and (3) assert a thesis.	Annotated Bibliography Literature Review	By the end of the first third, add sources, revise ideas throughout the process, having a polished Literature Review by the midpoint
(4) Develop a Model and Hypothesis (if necessary, given your Research Question) that follow directly from the thesis.	Model and Hypothesis	By the end of the first half of the course, sharpen your argument and assertions throughout
(5) Revise and (6) edit.	All sections	Throughout, with an intense effort in the last phase
(7) Plan the study, with attention to defining and selecting appropriate cases for analysis, creating usable operational definitions of concepts and strategies for their knowing values, identifying data sources, developing instruments for generating data (if necessary), and explaining methodology. In addition, justify this plan and recognize its potential flaws.	Research Design	About midway to two thirds through
(8) Evaluate the hypothesis or thesis across the chosen cases; present evidence in effective ways so that you and the reader can easily follow why you have reached your judgments on the applicability of your argument for your cases.	Analysis and Assessment	Start about two thirds of the way through (earlier if possible)
(9) Write a Conclusion that reminds the reader of the findings, discusses why these results emerged and where else they might be applicable, and suggests paths for future research; (10) an Introduction, with the thesis clearly stated, that both explains why this question is interesting and important to multiple audiences and provides an overview of the paper; and (11) a title that conveys your argument and your findings in a brief and inviting way.	Conclusion Introduction Title	Final phase

works to lead you to others. In addition, I will introduce you to a variety of citation forms and discuss the difference between paraphrasing and plagiarizing. Sources are good ones if they provide answers to your RQ; your goal here is to uncover the commonalities and differences in the works of scholars. By the end, you should be grouping the arguments of your books and articles into schools of thought—common answers to the RQ that are united by a similar approach, such as pointing to a particular factor as the key cause or sharing a methodology.

Then, in chapter 4, you continue the process of finding, summarizing, and categorizing excellent scholarly arguments by preparing a Literature Review (LR). This is the first section you actually write; in essence the Annotated Bibliography provides you with the notes and framework for the LR. This section presents the different answers to your RQ and assesses their strengths and weaknesses. You conclude your LR with a *thesis*, your preferred answer to the RQ.

For certain types of empirical research, this thesis must be developed further to guide you through the rest of the project. Chapter 5 then helps you translate this thesis into a *model* and a *hypothesis*. A model is a kind of flow diagram that identifies the cause(s)[11] and effect(s) as concepts and asserts graphically that $X \rightarrow Y$ (where X leads to Y). While the model helps you focus on the key factors you will need to study, it does not specify exactly how they are related. Does Y increase if X decreases? Because you cannot tell from the model, you need the hypothesis. The hypothesis identifies the ways in which these factors are related and is typically stated as, "the more of X, the less of Y," if you are positing a negative relationship between two continuous variables. (If you were expecting a positive relationship, the sentence would read, "the more of X, the more of Y").[12]

Before proceeding further, the text acknowledges that all good writers take an enormous amount of time to revise and edit their work. You will too. At this stage, in chapter 6, you focus on how to revise and edit, as your paper is satisfactorily done only when it is polished. Producing an excellent final work requires you to check to make sure that each section accomplishes what it should; that the paper is well written and has no silly typographical, grammatical, or spelling errors; and that you have followed all of the formatting instructions your professor has specified. Chapter 6 provides details on the revising and editing process, and to be successful, you should return to its advice every time you have drafted something and think you are about ready to turn it in.

Once you have a sense of what you want to assert and which factors are essential in your argument, you are about halfway through this project, at the equivalent of mile 13 in this marathon. Chapter 7 walks you through writing the Research Design (RD), which is your research plan and your justifications for it. In this section, you design your evaluation or test of your hypothesis, and this undertaking is multifaceted. Here you determine which set of cases you need to study to conduct a fair assessment. You also explicitly state how you will translate the concepts into identifiable or measurable entities. Locating sources and data is important now too, and you will see how the kind of information you need at this stage is very different from what you relied on earlier. Finally, you explain exactly how you will generate your information, for example, identifying how you will know which values your variables take on or providing a sample survey if you plan to administer one.

Throughout this section, you acknowledge any weaknesses and profess any compromises you had to make in designing your project because of difficulties in finding the best case, determining more precise measures for a concept, or obtaining the data you wanted. As you will see, designing a perfect project is often impossible. Thus, every researcher must make tough choices and explain both why these decisions are warranted and what their potential effects are. If you have good reasons, you understand the possible drawbacks, and the problems are as limited as possible, your instructor will be willing to allow you to proceed.

In his classic textbook on methodology, W. Phillips Shively noted with tongue in cheek that political science is not rocket science. Natural scientists and engineers have verifiable physical laws that have been shown to hold and describe the situations in which they are interested, as well as instruments that can precisely measure the phenomena they are investigating. In political science, we have few laws, difficulty translating key concepts into measurable entities, and trouble collecting or getting access to good data. Thus, as Shively noted, political science is not rocket science—it's much harder![13]

In chapter 8, you learn how to analyze and assess the hypothesis. Using the plan you developed in your RD, you analyze the values of your concepts across your cases to assess how well the data support your contention. Does the evidence confirm your hypothesis? How can you best convey your information to show your reader why you have reached your conclusions? This is the part of the paper about which students are most excited; it is also what most students conceive of (prior to learning what a research paper really is) as the only important part of the paper. However, as I hope to show throughout this book, the Analysis and Assessment section of the paper cannot stand alone. It makes sense and carries weight only after you have performed the other tasks. Moreover, by surveying the literature, developing a thesis and then a Model and Hypothesis, and carefully designing the research, you are in a better position to write a focused and convincing assessment of the evidence, principles, and/or logic that can sway a reader to hold the same view that you do.

Once you have determined how well your hypothesis reflects reality, you are ready to wrap up your paper. Using the running analogy, you are at mile 22 here, done with the hard part, and now all you need is the stamina to complete the race. Chapter 9 provides instructions to help you finish the two essential bookends for your project—your Introduction and Conclusion—and assists in revising your title. Perhaps surprisingly, you turn to the Conclusion first, because you need to know what you are concluding when you write the overview in your Introduction. Just like the marathoner, you cannot simply give up in the last few miles, limp to the finish line, and feel satisfied. You need to complete the race/paper strongly, with an effective Conclusion that ties the whole project together, reminds the reader of what you have achieved, explains why these accomplishments are important, considers both the limits of the research and whether this project provides insights that are applicable to other situations, and poses questions for future research. This section is particularly important if you believe that the compromises you had to make in the RD had a negative impact on your findings. If appropriate, you should explain your continuing confidence in your hypothesis, as well as discuss what you have learned about the choices you made and what might be more productive paths to pursue. Remember, regardless of whether your hypothesis was confirmed or rejected or the jury is still out, if you have proceeded in the fashion recommended, you should be pleased with your findings. The whole point is to learn something in the research process, not to be right.

Upon completing the Conclusion, you turn to the Introduction and then to devising an excellent title. A good Introduction communicates the question and thesis of the work and entices people to read the paper. In addition, the Introduction provides the writer and reader a road map or snapshot of the whole work. Academic writing in political science is very different from mystery or even most fiction writing: readers don't like surprise endings. Think for yourself how difficult reading an article is when the author isn't clear about her or his query, thesis, or how that contention is linked to the literature, methodology, cases, and findings. Each of these essentials should be communicated clearly and effectively, with minimal jargon. In addition, writing the Introduction provides an opportunity for refining the paper's title. A good title will, in a few phrases, convey your question, argument, and cases.

Finally, you have a completed draft. Hooray! A first full draft is occasion to celebrate—but not too much. Even though you have been spiraling through this process, refining and rethinking as you go along, spending the time at the end to consider the whole work is especially important. Remember to consult chapter 6 again so that you can use all the recommendations provided to turn in a polished and beautifully written paper.

Now that I have specified the tasks to be completed and the parts of the research paper to be written, what is involved in writing this work should be much clearer. Whenever you find yourself getting foggy about the process and the goals, you can (1) turn back to Table 1.1 and (2) remind yourself,

> To write this research paper, I have to accomplish eleven tasks, and I have to write six distinct sections. Each of these sections has a definite purpose and a set of tasks I can accomplish. And after I finish each one, I can check it off as a "completed section draft," realizing that I will continue to think about and improve on each part as I continue.[14] Moreover, in the practical summaries and recipes at the end of the chapters, I have precise recommendations regarding what

I have to do to finish each section. I also have additional worksheets, calendars, and checklists available at the companion Web site. Thus, every part of the paper becomes manageable, particularly if I work on this project over a period of time. By following the directions and the advice spelled out here, I can turn in a paper that is compelling to any reader and of which I will be proud. In effect, then, if I am the tortoise and proceed slowly and steadily, I will win the race!

NOTES

1. National Commission on Writing in America's Schools and Colleges, *The Neglected R: The Need for a Writing Revolution* (New York: College Entrance Examination Board, 2003), http://www.collegeboard.com/prod_downloads/writingcom/neglectedr.pdf.

2. Marijke Breuning, Paul Parker, and John T. Ishiyama, "The Last Laugh: Skill Building through a Liberal Arts Political Science Curriculum," *PS: Political Science and Politics* 34, no. 3 (2001): 657–61.

3. For an excellent discussion of the peculiarity of writing for each field, see chapter 4, "Writing in Academic Communities," in Thomas Deans, *Writing and Community Action: A Service-Learning Rhetoric with Readings* (New York: Longman, 2003). Deans advances the concept of a "discourse community"—"a group of people who are unified by similar patterns of language use, shared assumptions, common knowledge, and parallel habits of interpretation" (p. 136). Such a term certainly applies to academic disciplines such as political science.

4. Ibid. Throughout this chapter, Deans develops the metaphor of writing in a particular discipline as being a traveler, a visitor to "strange lands." He does so by including two interesting works: an essay by Nancy Sakamoto and an article by Lucille McCarthy. Sakamoto examines the differences in the ways Japanese and Americans conceive of and carry on conversations, while McCarthy explicitly uses the phrase "Stranger in Strange Lands" in the title of her paper examining how one particular student fared when trying to write across the curriculum during his freshman and sophomore years.

5. Some works question whether any true facts actually exist. See, for example, Paul Rabinow and William M. Sullivan, eds., *Interpretive Social Science: A Reader* (Berkeley: University of California Press, 1979). Postmodernists will be disappointed with my discussion of the research process, because much of what I ask students to do will seem consistent with "brute data approaches." For that terminology, see Charles Taylor's piece in Rabinow and Sullivan, *Interpretive Social Science*, titled "Interpretation and the Sciences of Man," (pp. 25–71, especially pp. 53–54). I would argue, however, that the process of how intersubjective understandings come about can be modeled, that we need ways of putting forth contentions about social reality that are systematic, and that one's conclusions can be evaluated by others. Thus, I ask those of you who are skeptical of social scientific methodology because of its inattention to constitutive processes to bear with me to see whether

I am able to deliver a guide that works for the kinds of studies you would like to see performed.

6. Of course, some artists have had great success with these extremes that I am calling inadequate. Yes, I am a political scientist and not an art critic.

7. In working on this book, I learned that Eviatar Zerubavel, in his well-respected work, also uses Aesop's famous fable to explain the approach one should take to writing. See his *The Clockwork Muse: A Practical Guide to Writing Theses, Dissertations, and Books* (Cambridge, MA: Harvard University Press, 1999), 12.

8. In their first presentation, these tasks are put forth in a simplified manner. I will explain and develop the complexities in the ensuing chapters.

9. See Telequest, *Across the Drafts: Students and Teachers Talk about Feedback* (Cambridge, MA: Expository Writing Program, Harvard University, 2005).

10. Some undergraduate papers in political theory may not include literature reviews of secondary sources. Look to your instructor for guidance about whether and how she or he wants you to handle the task of identifying and classifying different perspectives.

11. Some will take exception to the notion of causation in the social sciences (especially univariate), and others would prefer to consider correlation. I assert that for certain types of arguments, encouraging students to think in terms of causation or driving forces helps them consider more clearly the processes they are investigating. As students become more sophisticated methodologically, I encourage them to consider the arguments against causation, but at this early stage in their careers, I emphatically believe that thinking about causes is both useful and appropriate.

12. The alternative is if the variables are noncontinuous or discrete (also referred to as category variables, which can come in unranked versions called *nominal*—such as sex or religion—or ranked versions called *ordinal*—such as educational achievement of primary, secondary, some college, college graduate, or postgraduate). With discrete variables, the basic hypothesis would read something like the following: "If X is A, then Y is B, but if X is C, then Y is D." Please note that we will discuss types of data—nominal, ordinal, and interval—in more detail in chapters 5 and 7.

13. W. Phillips Shively, *The Craft of Political Research*, 5th ed. (Upper Saddle River, NJ: Prentice Hall, 2002), 17.

14. If you are writing these as formal drafts for your instructor to review, you will be receiving excellent feedback to help you write a great paper. Be sure to address and respond to the questions and comments your reader makes, and don't hesitate to consult your professor during the process. In addition, whether you have a faculty reader or not, you can also benefit from the feedback of a friend, classmate, or member of your institution's writing center. Find a reader, and realize that criticism is useful; comments help you sharpen your ideas and improve your skills.

Getting Started

Finding a Research Question

Starting a research project is truly a formidable task. It is challenging because good research topics are usually very specific and, in fact, not topics but rather questions or puzzles. In this chapter, I will define the characteristics of a good research question and walk you through a variety of ways of finding one.

Some of you may wonder why you need a question at all, given that there are many interesting topics to investigate. There are three main reasons for locating a query. First, topics are too broad and contain within them many subissues. For instance, to acquaint yourself with everything related to either campaigns and elections in the United States or democratization around the world is a huge undertaking. You want a manageable challenge! Second, a question links you to a controversy and allows you to become engaged in the scholarly and/or policy debate by both interacting with the ideas being contested and examining some information to evaluate the veracity of those claims. Thus, a good question gives you focus and puts you in the thick of one controversy (not many). Moreover, it allows you the opportunity to develop your analytic skills as you weigh both theoretical perspectives and evidence that relate to the arguments. Third, a question gives you a reason to write: you must provide an answer. Having a question therefore helps propel you forward to the response and gives you a clearer indication of when you're done—when you have offered and evaluated an answer.

CHARACTERISTICS OF A GOOD QUESTION

All great research questions share five qualities, and you can use these criteria to help you generate a topic and then transform it into a question for study. Research questions are *interesting* and *important* to you, scholars, the public policy community, and, ideally, ordinary citizens. A good question is also *short* and *direct*: if you need multiple lines or sentences to state your query, then you still have some work to do to refine it into one that captures people's attention and concisely identifies a question. Finally, your research must be *doable*. In other words, you need to pick a question you can actually answer with the resources available to you. As we will see in chapter 7, there are many creative ways to find evidence and perform studies, but you will want to keep in mind some potential informational limits (a strange thought, but a real one, in our connected world) and consider adjusting your question accordingly.

There is a sixth criterion—that the question be puzzling. Political scientists love these types of queries because they investigate the counterintuitive and promote our understanding of theory. Finding a puzzling question is not always possible, although sometimes you can pick instances to study that will make your query a puzzle. Typically, however, your professor will agree that an interesting and important question that is concise, direct, and doable is fine.

FIND SOMETHING INTERESTING

OK, great, I've given you criteria, but now how do you satisfy them? You need to recognize from the outset that finding a good research topic and question takes effort. The right ones won't simply pop into your head, and often, when students hastily choose, they end up dissatisfied later on in the process. Unfortunately, by then they have already committed too much time and too many resources to change. Thus, you want to work at the outset on satisfying that first criterion: start by asking what is interesting to you. Some students are really excited about a topic, and for them, picking a general area of research is relatively easy, but not effortless. For others, this task is more of a challenge, but here are some strategies to help. A first method is to write down what motivated you to become a political science major. In addition, thinking about your career aspirations and extracurricular activities can be inspirational.

Let's use the experiences of some students to illustrate these approaches. The first is Gabriela, who became interested in politics as a girl watching the 2008 election. The seeming "star power" of both Barack Obama and Sarah Palin attracted her, and by 2011, she was volunteering on local campaigns, which made her believe that politics was her calling and political science should be her major. A Latina from California, Gabriela was interested in immigration and even spent the fall 2013 semester interning on Capitol Hill. There, the polarization and seeming incivility in American politics made her job extremely frustrating and gave her pause. Despite the need to deal with big issues like immigration reform, politicians shut the government down and Senate Democrats infuriated their Republican colleagues by voting to end the use of the filibuster on executive and judicial branch (excluding the Supreme Court) nominees. Gabriela wondered why and when politics became so nasty and whether American political elites will ever find ways to address the issues of citizen concern. She also began to question whether politics was the career for her and began considering law school instead. At least a jury or judge ultimately solves legal bickering; Gabriela wasn't sure she could survive the petty infighting and lack of accomplishment in contemporary politics. Perhaps she could work to advance political causes as an attorney instead?

Another student, Kevin, chose political science because he is a political news junky who is fascinated by the coverage and loves to write. Given his interests, he got involved in the school newspaper to hone his journalistic skills. Coming of age in an era when social networking sites like Facebook and Twitter have become such important political tools, Kevin was already predisposed to see their value in politics. And then, in an introductory political science class, his professor played the PBS video *Revolution in Cairo*. Kevin vaguely remembered hearing about the so-called Arab spring in 2011, when citizens in many countries in the Middle East and North Africa revolted against their authoritarian leaders. This film made the argument that new media played an important role in allowing citizens of repressive regimes to organize, propagate and hone their messages, and challenge these regimes. Kevin was intrigued. He had previously thought of new media as a political and social tool in the United States only, but this video opened up many ideas and possibilities about the role of Facebook, Twitter, and other sites in different contexts around the world. While journalism still remained appealing to him as a potential field, he began considering varied career options (both in substantive and geographic terms) in the media, communications, and public relations and their links to politics.

Last in this set is Max, who came to his major because he was always interested in the world. At a very young age, he started poring over maps, examining flags of the world's nations, and learning about different regions. Max was also an excellent athlete, and he enjoyed watching the Olympic Games, when he would see his two interests—countries of the world and sports—come together. Moreover, he loved hearing stories from his parents about how the Olympics were such political *and* sporting events during the cold war. Max was also fascinated by the various elements of the U.S.-Soviet rivalry. Not surprisingly, then, his favorite tales were about the Soviet men's basketball victory in 1972 and the U.S. men's hockey gold medal in 1980. Surprising as it might sound, Max missed the cold war and its effects on athletic competition and wished for something like the U.S.-Soviet rivalry again on the rinks, fields, and courses of the Olympics. In the lead up to the winter 2014 competition, Max remembered how spectacular China's 2008 "show" was and also recalled that there had been some sort of international incident during those games. Didn't Russia and Georgia have a small war then? These remembrances and the concerns about the 2014 games—Would there be a terrorist attack on the Olympic spectators or athletes? How would Russia respond to lesbian, gay, transgender, or bisexual (LGBT) activists if they demonstrated or just visited Sochi? Why was Russia seemingly provoking Ukraine?—filled his mind. Clearly, politics remained in the Olympics after all, and perhaps these reflections on the games could help him find something to research in political science. He could consider the politics of the games, or he could look more deeply into Russian foreign policy. Why was President Putin doing what he was doing? These thoughts gave Max something to ponder for the purposes of his course. His ideas weren't necessarily going to inspire his career (which he did hope would be related to sports, and he could also imagine being a social studies teacher and a coach), but he was happy for the purposes of his class paper to be homing in on issues that interested him.

Using academic and political passions, extracurricular activities, and interests and aspirations, our three hypothetical students might create the lists provided in Table 2.1.

A fourth way of picking a topic is to think about which courses you enjoyed or which segments of your favorite courses you liked best. We've already seen that strategy affect Kevin a bit, as a course video piqued his interest. Locate your syllabi, books, and notes from those classes[1]; if you don't have them, you've made a mistake, because you should always keep the materials from your major courses. A syllabus is more than a schedule with assignments; it sets out the logic, topics, and questions (and often competing arguments) for

Table 2.1 Finding a Topic: Students with Clear Passions, Activities, Interests, or Aspirations

	Gabriela	**Kevin**	**Max**
Why the major	Fascination with charismatic politicians Volunteering on campaigns	News junky	Early geography buff Cold war rivalry, superpower conflict
Career aspirations	Elected official (?) Attorney	Media or communications professional	Sports management Teaching, coaching
Extracurricular activities	Partisan politics Service (working with immigrants)	School newspaper Debate	Athletics[a]
Interesting topics	Polarization in American politics Immigration reform	Media and elections in the United States New media in the United States and around the world Arab spring	International sporting events Pride and identity in world politics Russian domestic and foreign policy

a. Being involved in organizations or activities often brings politics or political issues to the fore. No matter what they are, they can be good sources for questions, so tap into any and all of your experiences to find topics of interest to you.

the course, and you can benefit greatly from thinking carefully about what your professor assigned and why. Regarding books, I know the refund is tempting, but often you get relatively little money when you sell your books back, and these are excellent resources for the rest of your academic career. Hold on to your notes as well. Your faculty members use their time to provide you with the information they believe is essential for mastering a subject. Do not just throw this wisdom away at the end of the term. Remember, particularly in your major, you are supposed to be accumulating knowledge and skills throughout your college career—expanding on what you have learned before—and your books and notes are the foundations from which you build. If you were a foreign language major, you could not survive a literature class without first achieving language proficiency. So too, you should think about your own field of study as a cumulative endeavor. Your political science courses are building on one another; you are not simply learning a set of discrete facts about different countries, institutions, time periods, public policies, political philosophies, or interstate interactions. So keep your books to consult as you take advanced courses in the major. If you have no textbooks now, however, go to your library and check one out (or as a last resort, go to your professor and see if you can borrow one). Textbooks and readers are extremely useful sources not only for question generation but for the next stage of the research process: determining how different scholars have studied your puzzle. At this stage, use the table of contents, photos, illustrations, and tables to point you in the direction of interesting topics. After you've narrowed your interests by rereading the text in places, use the source lists and recommendations for further readings to help you find out more about your potential topic.

Now let's turn to our final student, Zoe. As long as she can remember, she's been interested in female political leaders and was intrigued as a girl by Hillary Clinton's 2008 campaign for president and surprised by the treatment Hillary received in the media and from the public. Not surprisingly, Zoe greatly enjoyed her Introduction to American Government and her Gender and Politics in the U.S. classes. In both, she was particularly interested in representation, both how elected officials should represent their constituents and who (with respect to gender, class, and race) were these elected officials. She especially remembered pictures and tables in her books that showed how male, wealthy, and white our national legislative bodies have been, and she was interested in both why that was and whether the gender composition in particular made a difference in terms of representation. Did the policy outcomes reflect the desires of all citizens or simply some? Do racial or religious minorities and white women—when they are elected to office—represent their constituents and "their" issues (i.e., minorities' and white women's) differently? Using these ideas, Zoe filled in the worksheet shown in Table 2.2.

Another way to find inspiration for a topic is to think about something that is important to you personally; as many activists and scholars have

Table 2.2 Finding a Topic: Using a Favorite Course

Interest	Zoe
Favorite course	Introduction to American Government
	Gender and Politics in the U.S.
Favorite part of courses	Congress
	Representation
Links to current events	Gender and politics
	Women as political leaders
Interesting topics	Which theory of representation best accounts for the way legislators act and vote
	How race or gender affects the way legislators legislate

learned, the personal is political! We have seen that strategy with each of our students, actually. Gabriela knows many people in her community who have relatives who are still undocumented immigrants, Kevin's interest in and enjoyment of social media are pointing him in a research direction, Max's fascination with sports stimulated his thinking about topics, and Zoe, too, is pursuing a long-standing interest in gender and politics. For those of you who are still looking for inspiration, recent issues of newspapers, journals of opinion, and radio, TV, or online news coverage can be great as sources, and they can also sharpen your focus. You might be able to use insight gleaned from reading newspapers as a jumping-off point for studying an incident. Perhaps what is most useful about contemporary media is that high-quality outlets will identify the "big stories," and from there you can think about more general issues. For instance, the recent coverage of the problems between Israel and Palestine brings to mind broader concepts such as "conflict," "terrorism," "occupation," "conflict management," or general topics related to this violence that you might find compelling. In consulting news sources, try to use the best. If you're interested in international or national news, examine recent issues of the *New York Times, Washington Post, Los Angeles Times,* or *Wall Street Journal.* You will want to look at not only the main news articles but also the editorial pages, where you can see what the papers' editors think about controversial issues as well as read what outsiders (typically scholars, practitioners, and other important people) have to say in the op-ed ("opposite the editorials") essays. Also consult the Web versions of BBC News, National Public Radio, PBS, and CNN; and, of course, there is a plethora of great political sites that exist wholly online, the most popular of which you can find listed at http://www.ebizmba.com/articles/political-websites. These sources, unlike news sites, often explicitly assert political positions, as do talk radio, shows on Fox News, MSNBC, and Comedy

Central (if you consume this news source, realize that it is comedy!), and journals of opinion—publications, typically in magazine format, that have a clear
political bent to their articles. Some of the best ones are, on the right, the
National Review and *Weekly Standard*; in the center, the *New Republic*; and on
the left, *The Nation* and *American Prospect*. When consulting sources that have
ideological positions, what seems to help students most is to access ones with
which they are *least* likely to agree. That strategy tends to increase motivations
to explore and debunk the contentions advanced and can help excite you about
a research project.

Not all good topics are about national or global issues; in fact, particularly
for original empirical work, there are many excellent questions to pursue that
hit close to home. To explore local issues, pick the most important relevant
paper and consult its metro section; also, look for free papers, sites, and blogs
from your chosen place. If you're interested in San Francisco or the Bay Area,
start with the *San Francisco Chronicle*; if it's Philadelphia policy and politics,
check out the *Philadelphia Inquirer* or *Philadelphia Daily News*. Look for the
papers and places where local issues are most knowledgeably covered.

Some of you might be wondering why, in thinking about topics, I am
encouraging you to explore news sources that reflect on and explore primarily
contemporary events and controversies. I have three reasons. First, in my experience, students, particularly those who do not have specific issues in mind, do
not have much detailed knowledge of the past. Therefore, to sift through history to find something compelling is very hard. Second, one of my goals for you
is to inspire you to perform some original empirical work. That means I want
you to investigate a political issue or policy as no one has done before. Now,
doing an original study does not mean that you must work on contemporary
topics. In fact, excellent research is always being done in history, political science, and sociology (and other disciplines) that reexamines the past. However,
I have found that when *students* choose a research paper topic about something
in the past (typically that they know a lot about), they fall into what I call the
"report trap." Students then seek to describe everything they have learned from
others' research. Usually, they also split the difference between the two prominent competing explanations, arguing that the best way to understand their
issue is to somehow combine the main existing views. This approach is flawed
methodologically and is not a reflection or exercise of your analytic or intellectual capacity. Finally, I want your research to ask a question for which you
need to know the answer (and you have not already settled on an explanation
because of a past course you've taken, reading you've done, and what you "just
know"). Being compelled not by your professor but by some internal spark is a
great motivator. Finding contemporary debates, then, and entering into them is
my way of encouraging students to identify the kinds of topics that are interesting, important, and even puzzling: those good-question criteria. Of course,
sometimes those contemporary debates lead us to reconsider issues of the past.
But now you understand that if you do reexamine an event or issue, you will be

doing original research and not, for instance, finding two good books and combining their arguments in some way. No, in the research paper–writing process, you will learn to be the scholar or policy analyst and assess your argument with information that you interpret. Don't worry; you aren't going to do this alone. In chapter 7, on research design, you will learn how and when to lean on the work of others and the conditions under which you can generate your own information. But these issues are a much later concern, and I must ask you to trust me and your instructor that if you follow this method, your paper and study will be successful and compelling.

In sum, while there are many ways to get you started finding a research topic, nowhere will you find a flashing neon light that says, "Here's a great topic; take it!" Instead, you need to follow any or all of the methods described here—considering (1) why you chose your major, (2) what your extracurricular activities are and how they might be related to politics and political issues, (3) your career aspirations, (4) your favorite classes, (5) your personal concerns, and (6) current events and debates.

There's one last exercise I'm going to ask you to engage in: you should acknowledge explicitly why these topics are interesting to you. In addition, consider why a topic might be interesting to *scholars*, *policy makers*, and *citizens*. Each of these three groups has different priorities. Scholars tend to be most interested in explaining or interpreting events in light of larger academic debates. Often they seek to show that their argument or theory is better at explaining or predicting politics or behavior than others. In your early political science courses, you have probably been best exposed to these debates in your Introduction to Global Politics class, where you can see the "dueling paradigms," with adherents of realism, liberalism, and constructivism—among others—arguing about the best way to account for global developments. All of the subfields have similar overarching debates (though perhaps not as prominent as the one in international relations), and no matter what question you pick, you can be sure that scholars will be on opposing sides of your query and thus would find your exploration interesting. While academics are interested in explaining the real world, for policy makers—politicians, bureaucrats, and practitioners—solutions are all important. They want to fix the problems they identify in society; thus, their interests tend to be practical and applied in nature. Some will also be interested in ideology and the philosophical underpinnings of policies. Finally, although citizens are sometimes also policy professionals and scholars, we often imagine ordinary people to care about how issues directly affect their lives. So ask yourself, How might my topics affect people's pocketbooks, their ability to plan for the future and go places, and even their moral sensibilities? How does my research speak to citizens' concerns?

As you start the research process and begin to identify a topic, I recommend that you engage in self-reflection and fill out the "Finding a Topic" chart (on the next page and on the Web). You don't have to fill in every space, but the more you do now, the more certain you will be of your choice. You'll notice that I ask you

Table 2.3   Finding a Topic: Using Various Techniques to Find a Topic That Is
Interesting to Multiple Audiences

Technique	Your Answer
Why did you choose your major?	
What are your career aspirations and why?	
What are your extracurricular activities and why do you enjoy them?	
What was your favorite course and why?	
What was your favorite part of that course and why?	
Which current events are most interesting to you? Why?	
What are your personal concerns about politics?	
What political debates or issues do you like to read about? How, if at all, are any of these relevant to your interests, activities, career hopes, and concerns?	
What issues have you identified as interesting to you by searching through various sources (newspapers, news Web sites, journals of opinion, and others)?	
Why are these topics interesting to you?	
Why are these topics interesting to scholars, policy makers, and citizens? To which concepts and theoretical or ideological debates do they relate?	

not only to offer a question but to start thinking about its appeal. On one hand, basic self-reflection is important to dig deep into your intellectual interests, but it is also extremely helpful to think hard about what you already know from previous political science classes as you analyze your responses. Can you link your answers to concepts or theoretical and policy debates you have studied before? At this point, seek to have a few (no more than three) candidate topics. In the next stage, we'll start to translate topics into research questions and then give you criteria for choosing the best query. Because each topic can lead to multiple questions, you are OK with even one subject that you are enthusiastic about. But don't simply settle on the first idea that pops into your head, or you may regret it in the future.

DETERMINING WHY YOUR TOPIC IS IMPORTANT

Along with being interesting, your Research Question should be important to you and a larger community of scholars, policy makers, and citizens. You may doubt that your particular interest—Facebook as a political tool for Kevin or the Olympics for Max—could be important, but you will be pleasantly surprised to learn that many people share your curiosity. To identify the level of scholarly interest, your tendency might be to "Google" or search in another Web browser your issue. Although we can find an enormous amount of information by looking directly on the Internet (and I will encourage you to search this way at another stage in the research), look first in an *online database* of academic articles. Why? If you Google a term, you might find articles to which you don't seem to have free access or for which you can't be sure of their quality. Library databases, available through your institution's login, provide access to millions of scholarly pieces, all free of charge. In addition, if works are available in these sources, then you know that they have gone through a review process to be selected for publication in a journal. Some excellent databases for your purposes include Academic Search Premier (from EBSCOhost's research databases); Journal Storage: The Scholarly Archive, more popularly known as JSTOR; Project MUSE; and ProQuest Research Library. There are certainly others, and they are also useful. These main ones can help you locate articles in the premier journals in political science as well as related fields such as economics, history, sociology, and various area studies.

As you start your investigation of your research topic, you may want to begin by reading several book reviews or article abstracts to get a better sense of why academics find this subject important. These activities also help you see what the big controversies are and the many ways academics think about your issue. Once you have found a good source in your search, note the subject terms associated with this article or book. Use these to search for more; alternatively, in several of the databases, you have the option to find "more articles like these" with a click.[2] Take advantage of this shortcut.

Students are too willing these days to rely exclusively on sources they can read on or print from their computers. While digital materials are wonderful, there's a wealth of knowledge you can acquire in the library. First of all, books are extremely important repositories of knowledge, and you typically cannot get access to full-length scholarly works online free of charge. In addition, older and sometimes more recent issues of some journals might not be available electronically. JSTOR, in particular, can have a relatively long lag time before a publication is posted. Moreover, databases index different subsets of journals. You may have chosen a database to search that doesn't include one of the most important journals for your topic. So be sure to use your library's online catalog to find books and the major journals concerned with your topic. In addition, go to the library, and actually poke around. If you find a good book or journal, chances are that shelved near that source you will find several other interesting and useful ones. And of course, you should let the first sources you identify lead you to other ones. Look at what the authors cite as key works and be sure to read those books and articles too. I can't tell you how many times students fail to take advantage of the information they have. The articles they find can lead them to often even more important works they should consider. Learning to use your sources to find new ones is an important skill; identifying who the "big voices" are in the field is also essential. These are the authors whom various works discuss. When you see a scholar being cited by many others, you must read her or his most relevant works, too. Your sources will tell you what these important pieces are, if you only look at the citations!

For some help determining whether and why your topic is significant to ordinary people, you can brainstorm and come up with reasons on your own. You can also consult news articles and opinion pieces on these subjects. While scholarly sources are much more important later on, these popular pieces give you a useful perspective at this very early stage. Journalists write with the general reader in mind and explain the importance of the news to members of the community. Editorial writers and columnists also make the case for the larger significance of events or policies. How do you find these types of articles? Here you can search using LexisNexis (a legal resources and news database) as well as Academic Search Premier or ProQuest Research Library. Notice that in any of these databases, you can often specify the magazine, journal of opinion, newspaper or type of paper, and type of article (news, editorial, op-ed) along with the subject you are searching. When using these news sources, be aware of both the audience for whom the authors are writing and any ideological leanings. For instance, you will find different political perspectives in the *Weekly Standard*, *New Republic*, *American Prospect*, and *Economist*. You will also find varied coverage from newspapers that see themselves as national—that is, the *New York Times*, *Washington Post*, or *Wall Street Journal*—versus local—the *Columbus Dispatch* (Ohio) or *Times-Picayune* (New Orleans). All kinds of sources are valid for discovering the significance of your topic, but you need to be mindful of the intended audience and ideological leanings of the publication.

After you have done some research on why your issue is important, add what you have discovered to the "Finding a Topic" chart you started (see Table 2.3). If you are taking an idea from another writer, be sure that you note all the bibliographic information you will need to cite the source of that point, in case you use it in your paper.[3] Moreover, the more work you do, the more likely it is that you will be able to start narrowing in on one particular issue. While I don't want you to make that decision too quickly, you also need to realize that time is limited and you need to start deciding exactly what you will study. Typically, your professor will define a process for approving your topic and then question. Particularly if there is no formal process and you are unsure, go in and have a conversation with your instructor about how you are proceeding. In ten minutes of talking, you can resolve issues that on your own might seem impenetrable.

IF POSSIBLE, IDENTIFYING A PUZZLE

So let's imagine you have found a topic that is interesting to you and that you know is important to others. At the outset, I mentioned that you also may be able to find something puzzling, and puzzles are especially good questions from the perspective of theory building. But what could be puzzling about politics, or what is a puzzle in political science? I'm not talking about a jigsaw puzzle or Rubik's cube but rather an event or development that doesn't seem to make sense *given what we know*. Another way of thinking about this kind of intellectual dilemma is that either it lacks obvious answers, or the conventional wisdom appears to be incorrect. Finding a puzzle typically means linking something *empirical* (something that has occurred and is observable) with your issue or concept of interest. Sometimes, identifying a real puzzle can be very hard and is closely related to your decisions about which cases (e.g., events, years, people, policies) you will study.

Again, locating a puzzle means that what has happened is surprising given our current theories. So perhaps for Gabriela, the increasing polarization and hardening of the American party system is surprising, because citizens seem so evenly divided, and many of them tell pollsters that they hold moderate views.[4] In particular, immigration reform has support among voters at large, Republican voters, and many important Republican-leaning interest groups (like the Chamber of Commerce), yet even with a crisis on the U.S. southern border in the summer of 2014, with children from Central America showing up alone and in great numbers, Congress has been unable to pass a bill the president will sign.[5] Why is immigration reform being held up when majorities support it? Why has this become such a partisan issue when support for a solution seems widespread? One of our other students, Kevin, wonders why Tunisia, of all the countries in the Middle East and North Africa (MENA), has had more success with its transformation away from authoritarianism and why attempts at seemingly liberal political change in Egypt have seemed instead to harden its anti-democratic politics. Both of those thoughts also reflect potential puzzles, as few scholars would have predicted, with what they know about democratization, that Tunisia would be best suited for liberal political change. Regarding Egypt, scholars might have been more sanguine about the possibility of an uprising there, but knowledgeable insiders and policy makers are still somewhat surprised by the course of events. Thus, both of these queries lead Kevin in good and "puzzling" directions.

STARTING WORDS FOR QUESTIONS

Sometimes you know enough about theory to inspire a puzzling question, but even if you don't, your current topic, while compelling, is likely too broad. You need to narrow it down further, and in this process, you will find a question. My recommendation to narrow your scope likely seems strange. Typically, students are worried about finding enough information for their papers, so they think they need an expansive subject for which they can gather lots of facts. Here again, the misconception that the paper is purely a descriptive report is misleading students. Your paper is not a story about the *who, what, where,* and *when* of politics; your paper is an analytic effort that (usually) answers questions of *why, how, to what extent,* or *under what conditions. What* can work, as long as you aren't interested in simply *what happened* but, in addition, what that development means or tells us about politics or *what was really going on*; in other words, we might think we know the story about some issue, but in fact, events unfolded differently or mean something different from the standard interpretation, and you will explain *why*. Remember, the goal is to engage in research that enlightens not just you but many others. So, while you might not know, for instance, in which MENA regimes there were uprisings in 2011, this information is easily knowable with a few searches. However, your interest in this topic could lead you to ask a question about why these uprisings occurred, how the responses of state leaders affected the course of the challenges, and to what extent (if any) these revolts succeeded in achieving the goals their initiators hoped to attain. In answering any of those questions (and note the "good" interrogatory words at the outset), you will learn what happened, but additionally, you will be investigating and understanding so much more.

Selecting the right starting word for your question is actually quite important. Sometimes if you force yourself to ask queries you would like to answer, you can derive a good question. For instance, students often want to pose and then respond to questions that begin with "should," "ought," or "what should or ought." Gabriela, in fact, might start out by asking, "Shouldn't Congress do something about immigration given that the majority of American voters say they support its reform?" or "What should immigration reform in the United States entail?" Questions that start this way are excellent ones for identifying the issue(s) you find compelling. Their answers, however, are likely not to be settled on the basis of empirical evidence but rather on ethical, ideological, or even political arguments. In addition, they are in some ways speculative, and for your research paper, I ask you to avoid seeking to predict the future. Instead, for this project, you must (1) use some theoretical or conceptual material to develop a claim and then (2) evaluate it on the basis of evidence. Both parts—the theory, primarily the concern of the Literature Review and Model and Hypothesis sections—and the evidence—planned and justified in the Research Design section and presented and evaluated in the Analysis and Assessment section—are equally important to the success of the paper. So if Gabriela goes back to my recommendation about beginning question words ("why," "how," "to what extent") and her issues (polarization and immigration reform), she might come up with these questions: Why is the United States so polarized now compared with other times? What are the policy consequences of that polarization? Why is immigration reform so hard to achieve in the

United States in 2014, when it hasn't been at other times? (This last question is more specifically focused.)

In addition to starting the question off well, keeping your preferred answer out of the query is important from the outset. So for Gabriela, in the second variant, she puts her answer, "polarization," into the first question. Because one of the next steps in writing the paper will be to uncover multiple responses, it's best not to include an answer in your question. Perhaps polarization isn't that important to immigration reform; then, Gabriela would have posed a less-than-desirable question. Better to ask the question generally and then see what answers emerge from your research. Similarly, Kevin might want to ask, "How did social media affect the revolutions in MENA in 2011?" Here again the question, in a sense, asserts the best response, but scholars and others have posited many other possible answers, too. Thus, you can use your hunch or your interest to pose a first question, as Gabriela and Kevin did, but ultimately shift your focus at this point from your preferred answer to the big concept at stake. For Gabriela, the issue might be either polarization itself or the policy of immigration reform (she still has to decide), and for Kevin, this concept is revolution. Asking generally why (or how or to what extent) will lead to all kinds of great sources on this subject and help you have a broad and excellent understanding of the phenomenon of interest. It will lead you to multiple ways of thinking about your subject and answering your question, and ultimately, you may believe that your first insight is right. But your early research will show you that there are other plausible arguments out there. So the *why* question leads you to specific and different answers. For instance, why has polarization become worse? Well, you might not know, but you can bet that scholars and analysts provide multiple responses. Similarly, if Kevin examines how social media affected the 2011 uprisings, he is assuming at the outset that they did have an effect, which he will then trace. But what if he is pursuing an argument few people think is plausible? As an insurance policy for high-quality research, you are better off taking your answer out of your question initially. You may come back to it and focus on that factor (polarization making immigration difficult or the reason for polarization for Gabriela, social media enabling revolution for Kevin), but taking the step back and rephrasing the question helps you distinguish between the concept at stake and the explanation you want to assert. Understanding the difference between the two is very important as you proceed through the project.

Another way students often want to start their questions is by asking what will happen. For instance, Max might ask, "What will Putin do next?" or "Will Putin annex eastern Ukraine or other parts of the former Soviet Union?" These questions are ones you can see answered in the op-ed pages of major newspapers as well as in quality blogs or journals of opinion, but they are not appropriate for your research paper. In asking those questions, Max is trying to understand what motivates contemporary Russian foreign policy, particularly toward the post-Soviet states. So, without focusing on predicting the future—which is something that he can't do, because he can't subject his assertions to validation based on evidence. Max can ask, "What seems to be the most important factor motivating Russian foreign policy in the Putin era?" or "Why does Russia act as it does toward the former Soviet states?" Max might even wonder, "Is Putin's foreign policy different from that of Yeltsin?" and in asking that question, he is asserting that there is something different about the leader or era that might affect Russian external behavior. In investigating the two earlier and more general questions, Max might have insight into why the policies of the 1990s were different from more contemporary ones, but I would counsel him to wait to determine whether to focus his question in that way. And of course, what Max finds—that power or opportunity drive Russian behavior, that domestic political concerns are most important, or that leaders have particular visions of Russia's role in world politics that they enact in their policy—will help him make some predictions about future actions. Forecasting the future is handled very briefly in the Conclusion of your paper, once you have some confidence that you have appropriately understood your concept and can use your logic and research to assert that you understand how the future (in a limited sense) will unfold.

In sum then, a research paper in the form I'm suggesting needs to be both theoretical and empirical (observable, factual) in nature. Your work may have *normative* implications—in other words, it might provide insight into behaviors or policies that are morally superior—but this is work in political science, not ethics. For this reason, I discourage students from asking "should," "ought," or "what should or ought" questions, because they tend to focus on the normative side only and instead push students to use these normative queries as inspiration for formulating new ones that can fulfill the requirements of being both theoretical and empirical. Second, your answer can provide insight into future behavior as part of your concluding comments. Thus, Gabriela might use her findings to predict when immigration reform might be more propitious, Kevin might be poised to assert under what conditions successful revolutions will occur again, and Max might be able to tell Russia watchers what to expect from that country in the near future and why. But each of these speculative discussions is brief, found in the Conclusion, and couched in circumspect language, such as "Given that these findings are valid and that conditions in the future do not deviate greatly from what is apparent now, Russia is likely to. . . " Still, recognizing that your research is designed to give you power to understand the future or provide insight into similar cases is important and is something I will stress later as you write your Conclusion. Important to remember here is that you may be able to find inspiration from thinking about what will happen next. Last, a good research question has a particular form: It starts with the "right" kind of word, and it omits the answer or preferred approach from that query. In doing so, the goal is focusing on some big concept in political science (and not your answer). The reason for this focus will become clearer in chapter 3, but trust me for now: if you can ultimately determine a phenomenon you're interested in—polarization, congressional action, revolution, Russian foreign policy—you will have an easier time than if you focus on the factor you want to pursue—polarization (for the immigration question),[6] social media, Putin. Moreover, you may say to your instructor, no, actually I am more interested in what you're calling "my specific," for instance "polarization" or "social media" or even "Putin." So perhaps you do want to "bump" this aspect up to the key status in your question, and you do want to ask why U.S. politics is so polarized in 2014 (and the immigration debate starkly highlighted the importance of polarization), or you might want to investigate which social media strategies are more successful than others in mobilizing people to participate in political action or why Putin has seemingly been able to dominate the international agenda in 2013 and 2014. These are also valuable questions, and you need to choose which conceptual focus is right for you.

TYPES OF RESEARCH AND QUESTIONS

Clearly, the question you ask has a big impact on what type of research you do, and we can divide research into three kinds: *theory advancing, public policy*, and *conceptual*.[7] Each of these types is both theoretical and empirical. Theory helps the researcher frame the answer in the first place, but the test of that theory—the ultimate judgment—results from holding up its contentions to the real world. Three factors distinguish the kind of research: (1) whether there's a posited underlying causal relationship or correlation, (2) the extent to which the research helps solve a particular problem, and (3) the nature of the evidence. Theory-advancing research and public policy research typically are based on an insight that asserts that some effect varies with some other factor. These elements could change simultaneously, that is, be *correlated* without any direct connection, or they could be *causally* linked, meaning that changes in the first lead to modifications in the second. Theory-advancing and public policy research differ, however, according to how applied they are. Applied research is intended to solve real problems, such as how to design a "good" political system in a certain cultural setting or how to create a "good" city school system in the United States. Public policy research is applied, and it typically asserts that "better ways" exist to solve problems. Thus, there is a normative link here, and public policy researchers often set out their values— how they are determining that one outcome is better than another—at the outset. So for one set of applied researchers, a good political system guarantees an improving economy, while for others it could be one that protects individual rights. Regarding school success, one might be perceived to be more successful because graduation rates are higher, while another plan might seek to ensure that a larger percentage of its students go on to additional training or education after graduation. Public policy questions can be ways of transforming normative questions into empirically researchable questions. Theory-advancing work seeks to move our conceptual understandings of a particular concept forward, identifying weaknesses and strengths in existing approaches. It explores why politics is the way it is and often tries to take a stand in a debate between scholars—which answer is better or best on the basis of logic and evidence. Similarly, conceptual research is not applied but aims to arrive at better knowledge of fundamental concepts. While there may be practical applications for theory-advancing or conceptual research, the ultimate policy spin-offs are not what motivate these inquiries.[8]

Finally, regarding evidence, theory-advancing and public policy research find their empirics in real-world phenomena, such as election outcomes, effects of state-run health care systems, preconditions for democracy, the impact of micro-financing, or causes of war, to name a few. In contrast, conceptual papers investigate the meanings and implications of the works of great political thinkers or of theoretical positions by engaging the ideas and looking to texts for clarification. Examples here might be investigating whether Thomas Hobbes was actually a forefather of liberalism or determining what peace actually means.[9] While events often inspire this work, the real-world content is neither as substantial nor as logically important to the project. Instead, ideas, clarifying concepts, and improving understandings of theories or theorists are central. The data here are the words or writings of those involved in the discussion, and claims about the meanings or definitions are evaluated on the basis of logic and texts.

So as you work to transform your topic and your questions into doable ones, remember that your preferred type of query will vary depending on the course for which you are writing this paper or the purpose of the research. For most empirical courses, you will be encouraged to write theory-advancing or public policy research papers, and for theory classes, you will engage in conceptual research.[10] As you ask your question—with the appropriate starting word—remember that you need to strike a balance (depending on the type of research) between theory and evidence. Typically, you should avoid a broad theoretical question (How do we account for the nature of the international system?). Instead, you're looking for what Robert Merton dubbed "middle-range" questions[11]: in other words, questions inspired by phenomena of importance in the real world that require you to use theory and evidence to answer them. I have been guiding you toward these types of questions throughout this chapter, so if you follow the advice, you should develop appropriate ones.

USING THE ADVICE TO GENERATE QUESTIONS

Table 2.4 shows how Gabriela and Kevin are proceeding with their searches for a question.

As you look at Gabriela's and Kevin's early questions, there are a few important points to acknowledge. First, their normative instincts helped them get under way. Second, they used the appropriate starting words. Third, they did

Table 2.4 Generating Questions and Identifying Their Type

Self-Consciously Transforming Topics into Different Types of Questions	Gabriela	Kevin
Interesting topics	Polarization/incivility Immigration reform	Media and elections in the United States New media in the United States and around the world Arab spring
Why interesting to multiple audiences?	Political scientists debate whether the country is polarized, how uncivil we are, and what are the impacts of polarization and incivility. Policy professionals wonder if anything can be accomplished in a time of great problems. Citizens may be disillusioned with politics, and this dissatisfaction is arguably impeding the quality of democracy, as fewer citizens seek to participate in politics, and American lack respect for political leaders of all stripes. In 2014, the United States was arguably facing an immigration crisis on its southern border because of the difference between the way non-Mexican child immigrants are handled versus all adults and Mexicans. A policy fix seems in order, but it is not happening. Scholars of public policy would be interested in understanding this failure, practitioners are all trying to find a way to use these developments to their advantage in the upcoming elections, and citizens have a variety of concerns that include doing what's right, job prospects, costs of U.S. policies, and the nature of American society.	With respect to the American context, scholars debate the importance of the media in suppressing turnout and mobilizing the base. Because of the importance of money in elections, perhaps the new media—which are free in some regards—can help level the playing field. Scholars and policy makers would be interested in understanding that balance, as scholars seek to explain and campaign professionals hope to win their races. Most American citizens dislike the negative nature of advertising, and yet it has seemed to work on them, and they have tuned to outlets in line with their views. Regarding the Arab spring, are the new media the big difference? Did having these communication systems allow citizens to circumvent the power of the authorities, organize, and overcome the fear that regime opponents had that they were alone in their disgust with the system? For theorists, these questions illuminate fundamental questions about why revolts happen and how citizens mobilize. Activists and authoritarians want to know what works to bring people out to challenge a regime so that they can promote such behavior or thwart it. Finally, citizens of these countries are likely wondering how it all happened (and how things could be so different now), and people around the

Self-Consciously Transforming Topics into Different Types of Questions	Gabriela	Kevin
		world love their devices and connections and may be interested in thinking more deeply about their potential.
Why important to multiple audiences?	Again, for these topics—polarization and immigration reform—there are both big scholarly debates and issues to resolve, so the theory and policy professional find these topics appealing. Many citizens are angry at our politicians for not being able to compromise and worried about conditions in this country. If nothing is accomplished, what impact will that have on the future and U.S. democracy?	These lines of research suggest new ways of affecting politics, getting certain people elected (U.S.), and removing others from office (Arab spring). These topics are interesting to scholars of campaigns and elections in the United States as well as to specialists on authoritarianism, social movements, and political change around the world. They are especially important to scholars of the media. For citizens, thinking about the potential political impact of their phones and social networks might be fascinating.
Public policy questions	Why has immigration reform not passed, when the majority of voters favor it and many powerful interest groups do too? Why was immigration reform possible in 2008, when it seems impossible in 2014? What are the policy consequences of polarization?	What types of social media strategies have succeeded in unseating incumbents in U.S. elections? How did activists learn from past protesters and activists around the world as the events of 2011 were unfolding?
Theory-advancing questions	Why is U.S. politics so polarized now? To what extent is U.S. politics more polarized now than it was in the past? Given polarization, how did President Obama achieve some key legislative successes in his first two years, and why have these been so hard to come by in the first years of his second term?	Under what conditions do challengers win congressional seats in contemporary politics? Why did the Arab spring occur in 2011? Why was Algeria, which had suffered significant unrest and opposition to its authoritarian regime throughout the 1990s, relatively calm during the 2011 uprisings, while its neighbors were not? Why has Tunisia's revolution been more successful then Egypt's?

(Continued)

(Continued)

Self-Consciously Transforming Topics into Different Types of Questions	Gabriela	Kevin
Puzzling?	The first two public policy questions are puzzles. In the first case, the big factors that affect congressional behavior—voters' attitudes and the positions of powerful interest group—seem to be arrayed in favor. In fact, most observers also say that Republicans need to do something to court Latinos if they are ever going to win the White House again. So why aren't they acting? And why would the Republicans have been able to act in 2008 with an unpopular and lame-duck President at the helm and facing a tough election bout? Why was the logic different then? The last two theory-advancing questions are also puzzles in the sense that they address a change or a difference in two time periods that Gabriela can't easily and obviously account for. Perhaps further research will show that the variations are obvious, but perhaps not, and finding those differences among seemingly like events is a good strategy for finding a puzzle. Your instructor will have a good sense of whether the events you are juxtaposing are similar enough to be worth pursuing, so don't hesitate to check out your question with her or him.	The first public policy question asserts that social media are what made the difference in unseating incumbents (which is very hard to do). If that is the case, then Kevin has a genuine puzzle. However, this contention might turn out to be factually wrong, so Kevin has to find out whether this is true in general or whether he can find, for instance, two similar cases in which the difference (incumbent loss) seems to come down to social media. Of the questions related to 2011, the last two in the theory-advancing category are potential puzzles. Here we see the kind of surprise in which cases that seem comparable did not turn out the same. Again, Kevin would be wise to consult his instructor to see whether she or he is impressed that these cases are appropriately comparable.

not ask questions that would require them to know what is happening in the future. As we have seen, while good theory helps us predict the future, we should avoid research papers that are wholly future focused. For instance, Gabriela would likely not receive approval from her professor for a research paper that asked, "Will Congress pass immigration reform legislation by 2016?" That might be an interesting think-piece essay, but the empirics would not be available. However, often when analysts wish they could know the future, they look to other cases to give them insight. So, once Gabriela knows, for instance, what has caused the increase in polarization today, she would be able to think about what is likely to happen in the future and what impact that would have on polarization. The bulk of their work is then on another case or cases, but their research gives them some knowledge about the situation that motivated their question. Last, only one of the student questions so far poses a puzzle.

You should also notice that Gabriela and Kevin have begun to justify their topics. This work is part of their insurance policy—confirming that they have picked issues that others, especially their professor, will care about; ensuring that they will be able to find information, both theoretical and empirical, on their topics; and making a kind of down payment on future writing assignments. As you will see, your paper's Introduction will explain why your topic is interesting, important, and perhaps puzzling to multiple audiences. Doing this work now means that Gabriela and Kevin will have an easier time at the end of their writing projects when they need to draft their Introductions.

STATING YOUR QUESTION CONCISELY AND DIRECTLY

When you can state your Research Question with the appropriate starting words and can justify why scholars, practitioners, and citizens would be interested in it, then you, too, are on your way to a good paper. But you're not done yet. Have you ever gone to a public lecture and noticed that a questioner takes too long in posing her or his query to the speaker? Are you often frustrated listening to that audience member go on about her or his issue before stating the question? If you answered yes to these two queries, then you have an instinctual understanding of the fourth characteristic of a good research question: it is short and direct. You want to identify a question and ask about it as briefly and straightforwardly as possible. For instance, notice the differing impact of two questions that Max could ask:

Example Question A: Vladimir Putin has impressed people all over the world with his tough talk and gruff style. He has been enormously successful in helping Russians feel pride again in their country, and

(Continued)

(Continued)

important to that pride was Putin's successful hosting of the Olympics in February 2014. Many people thought the Olympics would be a disaster, that there would be terrorist attacks, that the facilities would be inadequate, that LGBT competitors and spectators would be harassed or arrested, and that protests would mar the games. Instead, the games were a wonderful spectacle, but instead of ushering in the peace the ancients had hoped would arise from these competitions, Putin used this time to foment greater unrest in the Ukraine. As a result of Russian efforts and those of separatists in Crimea and eastern Ukraine, about a month after the Olympics' end, Russia had annexed that peninsula and had designs on the east. While all this happened, the West simply stood by. Did Putin simply think he could get away with taking parts of Ukraine for Russia? How did the Olympic Games affect Russia's behavior, and does it account for Russia's aggression toward Georgia in 2008 too? Do these territorial grabs mean that Russia will continue to expand and take land from other post-Soviet states?

Example Question B: Why did Russia intervene in 2008 and 2014 in the disputes between separatists and the leaders of post-Soviet states (Georgia and Ukraine)? Is the Olympic similarity merely coincidence or of some importance?

In the first example, Max spends too much time explaining the background logic for his question and actually gets sidetracked into details that are interesting and may even be related to his question, but need to be investigated further for their relevance. Yes, some of this information will likely appear in his paper in some form, but at this early stage, being able to state the question concisely is important (having a focused explanation for the question is relevant too, but Max isn't there yet). The questions in B are focused and they don't require Max to get inside Putin's head (as in the first example). Clearly, Max is interested in Russian foreign policy not only because of what happened but because of what may occur, but he needs to realize that he won't be able to predict the future. In B, Max focuses on two cases of intervention that occurred during different Olympic Games. Perhaps the world competition is relevant, perhaps not. As Max continues his research on Russian foreign policy, he may adjust this question somewhat so as to achieve more of a puzzle (Why such decisive behavior regarding Crimea and much less clear action on eastern Ukraine? Or why challenge Ukraine in February and March 2014 but not earlier?). But even still, this second set of questions is preferable because they are brief, use appropriate starting words (at least for the first query), don't contain the answers in the questions, and are actually doable.[12] The lessons for you from Max's question asking are to seek that crisp question and recognize that you will have plenty of time later in your Introduction to explain why your query is interesting, important, and maybe even puzzling. Most important now is to structure your question succinctly, with an appropriate starting word and without your answer appearing in the query. And if Max did pursue question B, what kind of research would he be doing? Why, theory-advancing research, of course. Max wants to understand what motivates Russian foreign policy, and he plans to examine some cases of Russian interventionism to do just that.

Pushing yourself to ask an appropriate question and taking some time to refine it are enormously important, because a well-phrased query makes your life much easier as your proceed. Remember that our fourth student, Zoe, came to her project with a kind of knack for question asking that may be a result of her research acumen, background in the field, or just plain luck. Her interests in gender and representation have led her relatively quickly to an excellent set of interrelated questions: How different are female legislators from male ones? Do they pass women's-issue legislation more often than male legislators do? Zoe's first question could be rephrased in a more general way (removing her answer from the question), to ask what determines how legislators vote or why legislators vote as they do. Her query assumes that gender is the main factor, but you will see (or perhaps you remember) that specialists on representation posit multiple factors for explaining the behavior of legislators. Still, that first query contains a theory-advancing element—Is gender an important determinant of legislative behavior?—as well as an important public policy one—If we seek policies that are female friendly, are we better off supporting female candidates regardless of their ideology or party or other factors that might affect a representative's policy preference? Note, again, that Zoe's questions are short and direct. Her second question, although it seems to be a yes-or-no question, will be sufficiently answered only when she analyzes the differences between what women and men accomplish in legislatures and considers the importance of gender as a predictor of behavior. Still, Zoe has a great start on her research with these excellent questions.

One final word. You may have noticed by now that I have a preference for why or how questions. In general, I think they lead you most clearly to the kind of research query you will find easy to answer, because they assert the basic concept you will need to research and they demand multiple, conceptually distinct (not just different intensity) answers. My advice is to do your best to push yourself into an appropriate why or how question. They are, in many ways, the "gold standard" of starting words for your research journey.

PRACTICAL SUMMARY

In this chapter, you have learned about what makes a good research question and the different kinds of research in which political scientists typically engage. Excellent research questions are interesting, important, brief, and doable.

Sometimes they are also puzzling. They start with an appropriate interrogatory, and while a certain factor might have inspired you to be interested in your question, be sure to take your answer (that factor) out of the question as you proceed. Once you state a question, check it again for its brevity and appropriateness. Also consider the type of research (theory advancing, public policy, or conceptual) as you are thinking about possible research questions. The type of query you pose is often not dependent on the topic but on the course or the purpose for which you are writing the paper. In other words, you can develop many different kinds of research questions from one topic. You want to be sure that the question you have posed will let you investigate concepts and events or developments that are actually interesting to you. So, think through the implications of your questions carefully. You may even want to talk through your question with your instructor before you move on.

This chapter has also provided several methods for generating research questions. We met four students (who will return in other chapters as we work through different stages of the research process) who are learning how to discover interesting topics and transform them into actual questions. Finding such a query often takes some effort, but it is not impossible, especially if you follow the advice outlined here. Perhaps the hardest part in determining the question is uncovering a source of inspiration. I have suggested several: (1) why you are majoring in political science, (2) your extracurricular activities, (3) your career ideas, (4) topics you enjoyed in earlier classes, (5) your personal concerns and hopes, and (6) contemporary issues and controversies.

To guide you in this process, the best advice I can give you is to fill out the matrices, just as some of our students have done, and work hard on actually stating a question that conforms to my advice. Your effort in generating your Research Question will be very worthwhile, as getting off to a good start is essential for your future success. Once you have some good candidate questions, try to decide which one would be most fun, interesting, or possible for you to do. You should also consider which one will satisfy your professor's criteria for the assignment best. Remember that your question will likely be refined as you proceed (again, the research process is not simply a linear one, but rather iterative), but without a start you have nothing to improve upon. With the question stated, you are on your way.

RECIPE 1: THE RESEARCH QUESTION

INGREDIENTS

- Tables 2.3 and 2.4 from the text and as blanks (supplied in the online materials: "Finding a Topic" and "Generating Questions")
- Access to Max's two attempts to state his question and Zoe's questions

INSTRUCTIONS

1. Using the work of the four students and the techniques explained here, develop your own question. This will require you to fill in Tables 2.3 and 2.4 for yourself and spend time refining your question so that it achieves the desired characteristics—in addition to its broad-based appeal, that it is short, direct, and potentially puzzling; has an appropriate starting word; and does not contain an answer within the question. If you are stuck, do either of the exercises below to help you.

2. Subject your question to further tests for "doneness." Ask yourself (and write down): What concept is the fundamental focus of my question? Will I be investigating events that have already happened? Will this question lead me to public policy or theory-oriented research? (If you can't identify a concept of importance or be sure that you are investigating events that have happened, you need to go back and revise until you can answer affirmatively.) Question posing takes time. This chapter is designed to walk you through the process, although in this recipe, I am skipping the early steps, hoping that simply reading along has gotten you thinking about your interests. Some of you, though, might need to go back and fill in Tables 2.1 and 2.2 for yourself before you can make progress. I will say, though, that if you have been trying but you are not able to achieve "doneness," you should bring what you have written down (and if you haven't written anything down, then you haven't tried sufficiently, so go back and make some efforts) to your instructor. Your thinking about what will be appealing to you and your instructor's skill at asking good questions will help you solve this challenge in no time. *Bon appétit!*

EXERCISES

1. Pick up a recent newspaper. Develop a research question based on a news article or editorial selection. Identify the type of question (theory advancing or public policy), and be sure your query starts with an appropriate word, is concise, and is doable. Explain why others—scholars, practitioners, and citizens—would find your question compelling. Remember that they each will have different reasons for liking your question.

2. Consult one of your introductory textbooks. Develop a research question with its help. Identify the type of question (theory advancing or public policy), and be sure your query starts with an appropriate word, is concise, and is doable. Explain why others—scholars, practitioners, and citizens—would find your question compelling. Remember that they each will have different reasons for liking your question.

NOTES

1. You can probably find some things still posted online on Blackboard or your school's equivalent.
2. You'll find a more complete discussion of searching in chapter 3 when you have to get very serious about finding the best quality sources for your research.
3. I'll discuss citations, as well as citation management tools like Zotero, Mendeley, and EndNote, and the importance of giving credit to sources and avoiding plagiarism in more detail in chapter 3.
4. Morris P. Fiorina with Samuel J. Abrams, *Disconnect: The Breakdown of Representation in American Politics* (Norman: University of Oklahoma Press, 2009).
5. Jennifer Rubin, "Immigration Polling Tells Congress to Act," *The Washington Post* (July 9, 2014), http://www.washingtonpost.com/blogs/right-turn/wp/2014/07/09/immigration-polling-tells-congress-to-act/.
6. Like some of you, Gabriela is initially interested in polarization both as an effect (Why is the United States so much more polarized now?) as well as a cause (How is polarization impeding immigration reform?). In political science, many concepts can play both roles. Ultimately, Gabriela and you will have to choose which factor is her major interest that she will investigate.
7. These terms come (with adjustments in nomenclature) from W. Phillips Shively. He identifies four kinds of research—normative philosophy, formal theory, engineering (what I call public policy), and theory oriented (here, theory advancing)—divided along two dimensions—nonempirical versus empirical and applied versus basic. For most undergraduates, formal theory papers are beyond their interest and the scope of their training, so I will not deal with them explicitly here. Discussions with political theorists and reflections on my own subfields have made me realize what political theorists share with others in the field, as all types of political scientists may write conceptual papers that make assertions about the state of the literature or engage in debates about concepts and definitions. Also, the renaming of types of research, I hope, will help reduce the confusion some students have had between Shively's terms of political theory and theory-advancing research. W. Phillips Shively, *The Craft of Political Research*, 5th ed. (Upper Saddle River, NJ: Prentice Hall, 2002), 4–6.
8. Ibid.
9. For instance, Richard Boyd, "Thomas Hobbes and the Perils of Pluralism," *Journal of Politics* 63 (2001): 392–413; Oliver P. Richmond, "Critical Research Agendas for Peace: The Missing Link in the Study of International Relations," *Alternatives* 32, no. 2 (2007): 247–74.
10. For assignments less than the full-fledged research paper in American, comparative, and international politics, you will often write conceptual papers.
11. Robert K. Merton, *Social Theory and Social Structure*, enlarged ed. (New York: Free Press, 1968). Merton was discussing the types of theories, but a middle-range question will lead to developing middle-range theory.
12. At some point, Max will likely determine that the Olympic connection (in his second question) is related to one of the possible answers, so that one will drop out.

Learning Proper Citation Forms, Finding the Scholarly Debate, and Summarizing and Classifying Arguments

The Annotated Bibliography

We are like dwarfs sitting on the shoulders of giants. We see more, and things that are more distant, than they did, not because our sight is superior or because we are taller than they, but because they raise us up, and by their great stature add to ours.[1]

While the last chapter stressed that you are going to be performing original empirical work, you will be building heavily on the ideas and approaches of previous scholars and analysts. In fact, you cannot do a good job if your effort is not well situated in the field's understandings of the key concepts and theories at stake in your question, events and issues, and methodologies. The Annotated Bibliography (AB) is the first step in finding the giants on whose shoulders you will be sitting. What is crucial is to (1) uncover those authors who and sources that are the most important, (2) become satisfied not after finding one behemoth but after locating multiple *competing* arguments, and (3) understand precisely the implications of the differing claims. All of this work is an essential and critical foundation of your paper. Just as with a physical structure, if your conceptual framework is inadequate, your paper risks falling apart. The AB is where you begin the foundation on which you will base the Literature Review and Model and Hypothesis sections.

Now that you have a Research Question (RQ) (although you will likely refine your query as you work through the AB and the next part, the Literature Review), your next task is to begin finding the scholarly answers to it. Before turning directly to that endeavor, you need some prior skills. I want to address the nuts and bolts issues of understanding the bibliography and the information you need to collect in this early stage, avoiding plagiarism and properly citing sources, and learning how to take notes on materials. Providing this information first will ensure that you keep track of all the information that you need, understand the care required in using sources, and develop the skills necessary for grouping your materials. Thereafter, you will locate, understand, and classify the participants in the debate and their most significant works.

WHAT ARE BIBLIOGRAPHIES, AND WHY DO WE BOTHER WITH THEM?

Each scholarly paper contains a list of works, sometimes called a *bibliography*,[2] that provides all the sources that contributed to the work. Over the years, particular forms for displaying this information have come into being, and you are obligated to choose one style for documenting your sources and providing other information (e.g., citations and styles for headings and title pages). Proper documentation of these materials is essential in a research paper. You should be prepared from the beginning of the writing process to keep track of the sources you use and the precise places in the text where these authors have influenced your work. That means that you must choose a particular format, such as the American Political Science Association (APSA), American Psychological Association (APA), or Chicago (*Chicago Manual of Style*) form. In political science, any of these formats is acceptable, but your professor may have a preference for one in particular, so check before you choose. Typically, getting access to these rules is easy; many introductory writing classes assign writing manuals that contain these guides, so you may already own one, your library often has these materials online, and you can find them through an Internet search. Please remember that you do not have to memorize the format, but you should neither make up your own style as you go along nor change the one you use as you proceed.

Once you have chosen a format for documentation, you need to keep careful track of where and how different works influence you. Many of you have had access to NoodleBib or some other similar source and citation management software in middle and high schools. In college, you may want to use one of the other tools designed for more advanced work; these include EndNote, Zotero, and Mendeley. What this software does for you is help keep track of all your sources (complete with copies of the sources), help you create your reference list in the appropriate form, and allow you to pick and choose which sources should be in your bibliography. One of the great advantages of these types of software is that they can produce a reference list of precisely the sources you want, and, depending on the assignment, they can change the format you need. One weakness of which to be aware is that sometimes these programs do not produce citation lists accurately, so you should check over the types of mistakes they tend to make in your required format and fix them accordingly. Another enormous benefit is that they allow easy access back to any of these electronic files. As one of the lessons I am trying to emphasize is that your work in political science is cumulative, these devices underline that point. You can go back in any future semester to these sources, access them, and create a new bibliography for an entirely new paper.

Choosing among these tools is often a matter of taste, although some disciplines and some faculty have preferences. Zotero and Mendeley are free (and your institution might have free access to EndNote), so they tend to be particularly popular. There can be an additional cost for extra online storage space, but for the purposes of a semester paper, that should not be an issue. You can use both programs on- and offline, they allow you to share files with others, and you can save materials on your local computer but also access them from others.[3]

Of course, you can also make a citation list the old-fashioned way. If that is your choice, I recommend that you open a new document and build your bibliography as soon as you start your research, just as you would with a citation manager. That way, you won't have to type all of your sources in when you are frantically trying to finish. Also, you'll understand exactly which information you need from the outset and won't be in the position of not having a date or page numbers when you need them. Last, because you will be turning in an AB, amassing the source information is necessary for your first assignment.

In working with students, I have found that many don't understand why authors use reference lists and what the components of each entry mean. Because demystifying the bibliography helps you conduct research, let me enlighten you. Authors include source lists to show where they found their information and to help provide legitimacy to their work. While the quality of one's sources doesn't guarantee that a paper will be great, understanding a topic is very difficult if you haven't consulted the recognized giants. So the bibliography communicates something of the quality of the work. In addition, when beginning a research project, the sources' bibliographies are potential gold mines, telling you who the experts are and whose work you need to understand. Bibliographies can also contain information about excellent data sources for your topic. In other words, these lists lead you to important works that you must read to do a good job on your project, both at this point, when you're focusing on concepts and theory, and later, when you need data and evidence. Thus, the bibliography is a kind of treasure map, making your detective job of finding good materials much easier. Similarly, your bibliography will be a reflection of the research you did and will show others what helped you.

No matter how frequently I encourage my students to use the bibliographies of their sources to find additional resources, only the best ones seem to heed my advice. One of my conclusions (which also follows from watching them struggle when they have to produce a reference list without using software) is that students ignore me because they don't understand how to read a citation. So, let's look at some references (from different formats) to try to understand what they are communicating.

APSA Form:

Fiorina, M. P., with S. J. Abrams. 2009. *Disconnect: The Breakdown of Representation in American Politics*. Norman: University of Oklahoma Press.

Chicago Manual of Style Form:

Goldstone, Jack A. "Understanding the Revolutions of 2011." *Foreign Affairs* 90, no. 3 (May 2011): 8–16. http://search.ebscohost.com/login.aspx?direct=true&db=aph&AN=9204680&site=eds-live.

APA Form:

Toal, G. (2014). *Could Crimea be another Bosnia?* Retrieved from http://www.opende-mocracy.net/od-russia/gerard-toal/could-crimea-be-another-bosnia-republika-srpska-krajina

Wolff, S. (2012). Consociationalism: Power sharing and self-governance. In S. Wolff & C. Yakinthou (Eds.), *Conflict management in divided societies: Theories & practice* (pp. 23–56). New York: Routledge.

Regardless of which citation style the paper is using, you should be able to figure out the author, the kind of source and its title, and how you would go about finding it. Among the works I have listed above, I have four different types of sources. Can you identify them? The first is a book, which is arguably the easiest one to see. The citation is rather simple, with the author's name (notice, always last name first—unless there is no author—because a source list is alphabetized by last name, no matter what form you use and what type of source you have), the book's title, and information about who published the book, where, and in what year. In some styles, publication year comes after the author (as in this example of APSA form), and in other instances, it goes with the details about the publisher. But the point is, you can see that this source is a book, and if you decided you wanted to find it, you would go to your library or use interlibrary loan (ILL) to access it.

The final source comes from a book but is not the whole work. It is an article in an *anthology* (an edited book of related essays), and as you can guess, in order to locate this work, you need the name of the chapter *and* the name of the book. In addition, knowing the author, the editors, and the publication information helps. That's why there's so much more in this citation, in addition to the pages of the chapter.

The middle two entries are electronic. The one about the revolutions of 2011 is from an online database that indexes the journal *Foreign Affairs*. I would hope that many of you know that *Foreign Affairs* is a journal; even if you didn't, though, you should recognize that volume and issue numbers are included, with a season or month and year, and the fact that a URL is listed demonstrates that this source comes from a journal in a database. The second electronic source is from a Web site that publishes scholarly works. Both these entries include the author's name, title, and other publication information. Notice that for journals and Web sources, you don't see places of publication; instead what is important for tracking a work like this down is knowing its volume and issue numbers, as well as pages, or simply the URL or the digital object identifier (DOI), an alternative to the URL that some databases use to locate their works.

One last point to note: the different forms use different capitalization norms. Be sure to follow the appropriate one.

I hope that all of you now understand what these entries are communicating and will be more able to use citation lists to help you find useful sources. In addition, working with multiple style forms and different kinds of sources allows you to recognize what is similar and different among the styles and that moving between them is not difficult.

PLAGIARISM VERSUS PARAPHRASING

Another important reason for keeping track of your sources and exactly how they influence your thinking is to protect yourself from plagiarism, the academic offense of improperly borrowing another's ideas or words and trying to pass them off as your own. Remember, in college, your professors are impressed when you show that other, particularly high-quality, sources influence you, even in a think-piece essay, so they want to see citations. When you're writing a *research* paper, your instructor can't imagine that you can write one without many excellent outside sources; the name of the assignment, "research paper," *means* that you will be consulting others (as well as doing independent empirical work) to write this work. So, celebrate your citations and your reference list! The more you have and the higher their quality, the better off you are! (Within reason, of course. You don't want citations simply for the sake of sources, and you should cite only works you used.)

You might be surprised to learn that you must cite ideas, not simply quotations and figures, and that accounting has to be done at the appropriate place in the text. This point is so important that I'll repeat it: *No matter which citation form you choose, you must attribute* ideas *and* information, *not simply quotations and data, to their original authors.* If you do not, you are plagiarizing.

Plagiarism is an extremely serious academic offense, the equivalent of a scholarly crime. The plagiarist steals another's prized possessions—her or his thoughts and hard work—and passes them off as her or his own. It is analogous to driving around in a beautiful, but stolen, car. Most institutions of higher learning punish plagiarists severely, putting them on academic probation or throwing them out of school. Once you have been identified as a plagiarist, you can often forget about postgraduate education, especially law school. The lesson is never to plagiarize, either intentionally or accidentally. Keep careful track of the works that have contributed to your intellectual development, and learn how to cite and paraphrase properly.

While one way to avoid plagiarism is to provide complete quotations (properly cited) from your sources throughout your paper, this method is not the most effective. Think back to some of the works you have read for classes or while developing your RQ. How many of them contained large numbers of direct quotations? I am confident that none did. Instead, these authors used proper *paraphrases*, restating in their own words the sense of others' arguments and citing the original sources. Your goal, then, is to minimize direct quotations but maintain, even maximize, the references. Typically, mentioning the author's name in your text to associate her or him with the ideas is appropriate, but you need to find your own way of expressing those ideas. Making your version different enough from the author's can be difficult, especially if you have the work open in front of you and/or you are trying to capture the sense of a particular sentence or a small amount of text. My recommendation is that you take the time to ruminate on the author's words and close the book, journal, or electronic file and not look at it as you try to explain these ideas. You will also have an easier time avoiding plagiarism if you are distilling a larger chunk of text into a smaller one. If you're trying to condense a chapter into one paragraph, you simply cannot use the precise words, because you won't have the room. Do not consult the abstract or any summary paragraph you may find when writing this type of summary; you will run a grave risk of plagiarizing by not making your text significantly different from the author's. In addition, do not use another writer's discussion of this work without giving that person credit. Box 3.1 provides some insight into proper paraphrasing and plagiarism.[4]

The bottom line here is to use your own words but still cite the source. It was the writer's idea, and your reader is likely to know that. You will impress the reader by showing that you know the literature and can express in your own words the ideas of the scholar. If you find, however, that you simply cannot independently communicate this author's arguments, then use a direct quotation. The direct quotation also requires its own footnote, of course. Whether you've conveyed the ideas or used a direct quotation, you need to include in the citation the page number from the text from which either came.

As I am discussing plagiarism here, I'm assuming your good intentions, that you are doing your research and you are trying to include some great ideas from sources that you found. As I'm sure you know, there are malevolent versions, where some people lift the work of others—maybe a paragraph, a page, a section, or even a whole paper—from someplace. These are published pieces, papers purchased online, the work of a friend, or recycled papers from previous courses that the person submitting the new paper has written. In ways, I see these violations as far more egregious than improperly paraphrasing, because the student is being intentionally devious and lazy. In terms of the definition of plagiarism, however, these offenses are the same, and both will land you in trouble (although some faculty or institutions might impose even higher penalties for the more duplicitous variant). The only thing I can say is that plagiarism is truly a terrible act that can ruin your life! Passing off another's work as your own is highly dishonest, and plagiarists never regain the trust of others. Another problem is that the risk for getting caught is high, but also the issue is that college is not simply about getting through your courses (although I know everyone feels that way at some point) and getting your "piece of paper." The point is that having the experience of writing, researching, thinking, and writing again is what allows you to be able to handle complex research, analysis, and writing assignments in the future. You are involved in this major and this project to develop skills for the long term, and you won't accumulate any benefits from cheating by using someone else's work or recycling your own.

BOX 3.1 **Paraphrasing and Plagiarism: Knowing the Difference**

Immediately below is an excerpt from Mickey Edwards, *The Parties versus the People: How to Turn Republicans and Democrats into Americans* (New Haven, CT: Yale University Press, 2012), 4. After that, I've provided examples of paraphrasing and plagiarism, documented in APSA form. Can you tell which is which?

ORIGINAL SOURCE

While it's true that parties came into being early in the nation's history, they were nothing like the ones we have today; their members were united on some major issues, but not on everything all the time. Ironically, there is diversity within Republican and Democratic ranks in today's Congress, too, but the system in which they are forced to operate enforces conformity, not independent thinking. As Alan Abramowitz of Emory University points out, our system of government was not designed to function with the kind of partisan division that exists today; instead the Founders saw political parties as "dangerous fomenters of conflict."[a] Today we have become accustomed to seeing straight party-line votes on everything from tax issues and spending issues to judicial and executive branch appointments. It is not the existence of parties but the excessive loyalty member of Congress feel to the parties they belong to, and the great power we have given parties over our elections and our governance, that have led us to the crisis we are in today, unable to come together even on the most urgent questions, and even with the nation's well-being at stake.

1. According to Mickey Edwards (2012, 4), while American political parties came into being early in the nation's history, they do not closely resemble today's political organizations.

2. Mickey Edwards (2012, 4) contends that something has gone terribly wrong with American political parties since they emerged in the early Republic. In the old days, members of Congress would at times vote with their partisans, but at others they would cast their ballots with members from the other grouping. As the Founders predicted, overly ideological and united parties have become an enormous problem for U.S. democracy, and Edwards asserts that we are at a crisis point today because of this partisanship.

(Continued)

(Continued)

3. Parties themselves aren't the big problem. The issue is the extreme loyalty which elected officials have toward their parties and the enormous authority those organizations have over selecting our representatives and deciding our policies.

ANSWERS

1. **Plagiarism:** Although the author and page numbers are provided, the student uses some of Edwards's words verbatim, and in the rest, the sentence construction and language are far too close to the original.

2. **Paraphrasing:** The student has captured the sense of the paragraph in his own words. He gives the author credit in the citation and provides the page number.

3. **Plagiarism:** The student uses the same sentence construction and words very similar (with some synonyms) to Edwards's. In addition, the student fails to give the author any credit (either in the text or with a citation). (Even if the student had provided a citation here, it still would be plagiarism, because the sentence structure is too similar to Edwards's.)

[a]Alan Abramowitz, *The Disappearing Center: Engaged Citizens, Polarization, and American Democracy* (New Haven, CT: Yale University Press, 2010).

ANNOTATING THE BIBLIOGRAPHY

Now that we understand what a bibliography is and why it is important, as well as what plagiarism is, how serious an offense it is, and how to avoid it, we turn to annotation—what is it and why do it? In writing an AB, you are providing a list of the works (so that you will have a jump on your final bibliography), but you are adding something else to it. Underneath each entry, you write a paragraph or more that contains a summary of the *arguments of the work as they relate to your Research Question*, as well as key information about the topics the author discussed in making the argument and the research findings. Please note that to yield useful information, you must summarize the argument, not just discuss the topic. For instance, if you were like Gabriela, searching for works on polarization, and you were discussing only the topic, you would be writing, "This work is about political polarization in America" for each source. Well, of course! So train yourself to *never again* write "This work is about" but instead to record "The author argues/asserts/contends/insists"—pick your favorite verb and vary it as you write your summaries. In other words, for the AB to help you—and all of the tasks presented in this book are designed to assist you, not simply to make extra, unnecessary work—you have to think about (and capture in your writing) that piece's thesis (which is likely closely connected to how it answers your RQ); how the author defines concepts that are crucial to your topic, what instances, cases, or data sets the work uses to assess its argument; and what the findings (or conclusions) are.

In reading these sources, remember that a scholar will write her or his book or article in a form similar to the one you are learning about here for research papers. So you should be able to find the thesis up front in the preface and the introduction, as well as what is motivating the piece. Typically, authors write because they believe that existing approaches are wrong or they have superior policy solutions. Again, this information is a gold mine for you, because the author is telling you who and what other arguments are out there! In a more detailed literature review section, you can discover how that author divides the field into schools of thought.[5] The writer will also tell you who are the most important proponents of each view and what the essential works to read are. Thus, early on in reading a source, you are on your way to unlocking the scholarly debate on your question and finding other excellent sources to consult for your own paper. You still must use care, however, not to accept someone else's assessment of the field at face value. Each author has a particular argument she or he is making, and while you may agree with it, you cannot be sure until after you have read other principal works too. Thus, you should read a few scholarly works or literature review sections carefully to help you have an idea of the debate and the major players in it.

IDENTIFYING THE KEY CONCEPTUAL ISSUES

Now you know what you need to do and why, but how should you get started? Your first job is to find good sources, and the best place to start is your question and the concepts you identify in it. Those concepts will lead you to the issues political scientists are debating. Because you need to uncover the scholarly answers to your question, you will be looking for scholarly sources, that is, the work of academics. While journalists and commentators may provide interesting answers and insights into your question, they should not be the authors you are searching for at this stage, although early on in the question stage, newspapers and journals of opinion were important for helping inspire you. These works may make their way into your AB, but you need to supplement them. You need to find recognized experts in the field, but who are they and where can you find their work? Generally, these experts are scholars who tend to be professors (working at universities or colleges) or people employed by think tanks and public policy and governmental institutes. These people usually publish their work in books (often, but not exclusively, ones that are published by university presses, textbook publishers, and think tanks and under certain imprints of large publishing houses) and in what are called peer-reviewed journals, periodicals with policies of sending any piece that comes in for consideration out to other experts to review and approve. Academic journals publish varying numbers of issues a year but aren't weekly, like *The Economist* for instance. Scholarly journals tend to have footnotes and bibliographies. More policy-oriented journals (e.g., *Social Policy*, *Foreign Affairs*, or *Current History*) may lack the list of sources, but the articles that appear in them can be extremely relevant and are peer reviewed.

With the need for scholarly sources in mind, we will turn to the task of finding some. Let's start, as mentioned, with an examination of some of the questions our students suggested. To move us forward, I have created Table 3.1, which highlights the key concepts on which the research will focus and includes the hunches our students have (if they have any) for answering their questions.

Table 3.1   Questions, Concepts, and Hunches

Student	Question	Key Concept(s)	Hunch(es)
Gabriela	Why is U.S. politics so polarized now, and what are the policy consequences of polarization?	Polarization Effects of polarization	??? not sure
Kevin	Why did the Arab spring occur in 2011?	Revolution, uprisings	Social media
Max	Why did Russia intervene in 2008 and 2014 in the disputes between separatists and the leaders of post-Soviet states (Georgia and Ukraine)?	Intervention Explaining the external behavior of states	??? not sure
Zoe	Why do legislators vote as they do? Do female legislators seek and achieve women's issue legislation more frequently than their male counterparts?	Legislator voting behavior Legislating	Gender

Notice that a well-formulated question leads straight to a concept the student can use to search for information and link back to the work that she or he has done in previous courses. You should try to identify a concept or set of them around which your question revolves.[6] Although some students (Kevin and Zoe) have guesses about what the answers are, they are not necessarily in a better situation than the others. At this stage, keeping an open mind about the possible responses to your question is very important, because the goal, which I will turn to next, is to find competing or alternative answers to your query.

SEARCHING FOR SOURCES

Once you have identified the key concepts at issue, go back to your materials from related courses (textbooks, anthologies—edited volumes that contain collections of articles written by different authors—and electronic reserves and course packs). Also look at the sources you found when working on your question. Some of these authors might be scholars whose academic works you can find. Notice what I have not suggested: I have not recommended that you perform a Google (or other Internet search engine) search. Your goal is to find scholarly sources that answer your RQ. While the Web is a fabulous source of information, and you can find many of the same materials you will uncover using the methods I suggest, you need a certain degree of knowledge to use the Internet wisely for scholarly research. You cannot trust that every article posted on the Web is important or accurate. This is also not the time to search for facts or turn to encyclopedia-type sources. An encyclopedia can provide important basic information as you are starting your process, and it is fine for primary and secondary school reports, but report writing is behind you. So, just to be clear, no Wikipedia for your research paper. Never.[7] Now, you are to engage in the scholarly debate and process.

Back to our search of course materials. Use the tables of contents and indices to find the sources on your subject. Reread and take notes on (1) the key concerns, arguments, and issues involved with this concept and (2) the authors and sources (sometimes in the text and footnotes and usually at the end of the chapter in the "For Further Reading" section). The materials mentioned should be the next place to look for information, and if you find important substantive material in that chapter—for instance, definitions of the concepts and characterizations about the debate in the field—then you should make your first bibliographic entry—either the old way or using citation management software, taking care to note the source and other relevant information.

When Gabriela went back over her Introduction to American Politics syllabus and found the section on polarization (yes, it was there, but of course, she hadn't really noticed it the first time through), she saw an article that she vaguely remembered, Scott Stossel's "Subdivided We Fall."[8] She decided to reread the piece and then noticed that it was a book review of a work by Bill Bishop, *The Big Sort: Why the Clustering of Like-minded America Is Tearing Us Apart* (New York: Houghton Mifflin, 2008). Thus, Gabriela found two sources just from looking at her syllabus! If she went back through her textbook, she would find even more materials in the related section if she checked the reference list and suggested or further readings for that chapter. She will seek to obtain Bishop's book at her library.

How to find other books? Gabriela could browse, looking at books she can find on the shelf near Bishop's work, or browse electronically: after looking up *The Big Sort*, she could click on the subjects that come up in that record or on the call number. What happens when you begin your search and you don't have a work to start from? What should you do to find books? If you are a student at a research university—one that trains graduate students in our field and thus is likely to have an excellent scholarly book collection—you can search your own library catalog; if not, anyone can use the online Library of Congress

(LoC) catalog. Why search the LoC when you can't take out its books? Because it will help you find out what are the most important works in your field, which you then can check out from your own library or request through interlibrary loan. I can't stress enough how convenient and easy ILL is for obtaining excellent materials; the only issue is that receiving the books takes a little time. I have found, however, that the wait is relatively short, usually about one week, and that is typically plenty of time if you're starting your assignment on time. This search also helps you identify who the important authors are in your field. When you're looking at article databases (or even doing a Google search), you can zero in on works they have written, obtain them immediately, and know that they will be of high quality.

Gabriela went to the LoC site and typed in "polarization and American politics" as a keyword search. Box 3.2 contains some of what she saw.

BOX 3.2   Results from a Library of Congress Online Catalog Search

DATABASE: Library of Congress Online Catalog

YOU SEARCHED: Keyword (match all words) = polarization and American politics

●●●●●Baumer, Donald C., 1950- Parties, polarization, and democracy in the United States / Donald C. Baumer, Howard J. Gold. 2010

●●●●● Abramowitz, Alan. Disappearing center : engaged citizens, polarization, and American democracy / Alan I. Abramowitz. 2010

●●●●●McCarty, Nolan M. Polarized America : the dance of ideology and unequal riches / Nolan McCarty, Keith T. Poole, and Howard Rosenthal. 2006

Notice six things about these results. First, the dots in front of the author's name (if there is a name supplied) indicate how relevant the search results are likely to be given the terms used. In Gabriela's case, the results I've shown you are all highly relevant (receiving the top number possible). Second, if the book has authors (not editors), the first author's name appears first and again after the title. The book, then, is not an anthology, an edited volume that collects the works of many writers. If a book has multiple authors, do not change the order of the list (even if they are not in alphabetical order). The sequence is intentional and often reflects the level of contribution to the work. Third, the titles are hypertext, and you can click on them for more information. Fourth, the publication date is provided, and often when you're starting your search, you want to look at the most recent publications because they will give you the newest perspectives while also citing (and often summarizing) the arguments of the old. Thus, they help do some of your work. Fifth, while the information you will need for your bibliography is here in the citation (after you click the hypertext), please realize that depending on the format you are using, if you're not using a citation manager, you might have to change capitalization and the order of the information. The listing also may provide extraneous material that you don't need. So have your style guide near you when you are doing your work so that you can write your citation properly the first time. Sixth, Gabriela received a "Goldilocks" number of hits on her search—not too many, not too few (more than 10, but fewer than 50). Actually, Gabriela first searched for "polarization and politics" and got more than 100 hits. Then, she added the adjective *American* and obtained a more manageable and more relevant set of books given her research interests.

Remember that the search process takes careful thought, sometimes a little luck, and always perseverance. If your search terms are not leading you to other sources, you likely need to do a better job generating these terms. So go back to your course materials or those articles that aided the generation and refinement of your question. Search for those sources in the relevant database and see what subject terms are related to them. Also, ask yourself again, What are the key concepts at stake? Whom does my textbook identify as important? If you can locate new authors, titles, or search terms, use them to lead you to new ones. If you still haven't had success, consult a reference librarian for help. That person will be well versed in subject searching and will be able to identify new terms. The librarian, however, can only help you. You need to do the primary thinking about your question and what you're really interested in. The important points, however, are not to give up and to use the resources you have to your advantage. Also, finding sources takes time. Be sure to allot yourself enough.

Now let's return to Gabriela and her search for sources. She decided to click on the first two titles to find out more. Clicking on the hyperlinks not only will give her all the publication information she needs and the numbers she will need to find the books in the library but also will provide great information to help her assess the potential value of the books and will lead to more sources (see Box 3.3).

What's interesting here are the two publishers: Paradigm Publishers and Yale University Press. These are different kinds of publishing houses, both of which have value in Gabriela's search. Paradigm Publishers typically publishes specialty textbooks, to be used in upper division classes for undergraduates. Thus, this work will have lots of relevant information, citations, and arguments and will be presented in a style that is highly accessible to college students. This kind of book can offer a great start. Other similar presses are CQ Press, W. W. Norton, Rowman & Littlefield, Routledge, and Lynne Rienner, among others. The second book's publisher is Yale University Press. As Yale University is a

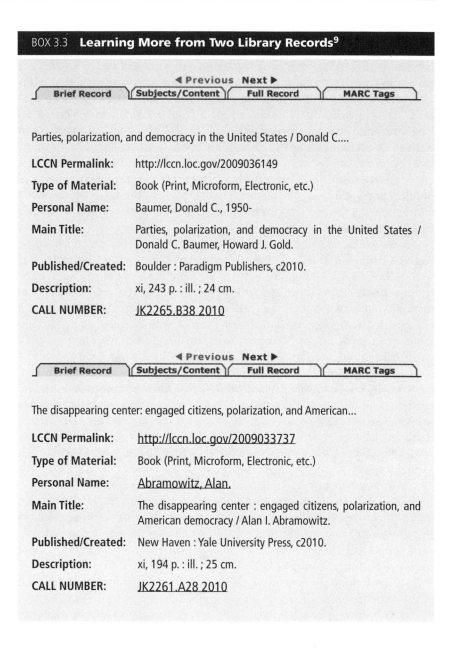

BOX 3.3 **Learning More from Two Library Records**[9]

◀ Previous Next ▶

| Brief Record | Subjects/Content | Full Record | MARC Tags |

Parties, polarization, and democracy in the United States / Donald C....

LCCN Permalink: http://lccn.loc.gov/2009036149

Type of Material: Book (Print, Microform, Electronic, etc.)

Personal Name: Baumer, Donald C., 1950-

Main Title: Parties, polarization, and democracy in the United States / Donald C. Baumer, Howard J. Gold.

Published/Created: Boulder : Paradigm Publishers, c2010.

Description: xi, 243 p. : ill. ; 24 cm.

CALL NUMBER: JK2265.B38 2010

◀ Previous Next ▶

| Brief Record | Subjects/Content | Full Record | MARC Tags |

The disappearing center: engaged citizens, polarization, and American...

LCCN Permalink: http://lccn.loc.gov/2009033737

Type of Material: Book (Print, Microform, Electronic, etc.)

Personal Name: Abramowitz, Alan.

Main Title: The disappearing center : engaged citizens, polarization, and American democracy / Alan I. Abramowitz.

Published/Created: New Haven : Yale University Press, c2010.

Description: xi, 194 p. : ill. ; 25 cm.

CALL NUMBER: JK2261.A28 2010

major research university, its press publishes what it considers to be the best of contemporary scholarship. This book (also called a *monograph*, a scholarly work on a relatively narrow topic) by Abramowitz, then, is an essential part of the debate you are likely to enter (unless you transform your question away from its concerns) and is a must for you to understand. Moreover, as a good scholar, Abramowitz has included a discussion of the scholarly disagreements in a conceptual, or literature review, chapter. This work will also help you identify the key issues, though from Abramowitz's perspective. Because you know you need to examine the debate, you must be sure that you don't allow the first work you read to sway your opinion too much. Realize that authors will portray their approaches in the best light and will be stressing the weaknesses of others. You, on the other hand, need to look to those others and see how they justify their positions.

The records also tell you where to find the books. If you were at a research library, you could use both the call numbers and the locations to physically retrieve the books. This information (as well as the titles and author names) also allows you to search for the books in your own college library; however, if your institution doesn't own them, don't fret, because you can get them through ILL. A week's wait isn't bad, but it shows that those of you at institutions without large libraries need to start searching earlier.

There's still more useful information to glean from the records. As I have mentioned many times before, one of the key values of sources is in helping you find additional ones. For this, not only will the physical text be helpful, but you can also use the records to find better searching terms and similar sources. If you click on the hypertext that follows "LCCN Permalink," you will find the records shown in Box 3.4.

Clearly, that additional click brings you valuable information. For the first source, you learn the chapter titles, providing you a greater sense of what the book concentrates on and how it proceeds. In the record for both this book and the scholarly monograph by Abramowitz, you see new search terms to try (under "Subjects") as well as links to books about those related subjects. In addition, you can find more works by the authors by clicking on the hypertext after their names. Thus, you are on your way to finding many useful works *and authors*—don't forget that searching for authors in catalogs and on databases is important too. Notice how much you have learned, and you've been looking at only two sources! You are well on your way to constructing your bibliography. If you are using citation management software, some library catalogs allow you to easily transport this information into their programs. In the old-fashioned method, you should be copying and pasting this information into your draft references document.

After you find some important books (important because they are relevant given your topic and they are either very recent or what everyone tells you are the classics, i.e., older and essential works in the field), it is time for you to turn to database searching to find useful articles. Scholars write both books and articles (actually, some tend to write books, some write articles, and some write both). They publish their books with scholarly, textbook, and some trade presses, and they publish their articles in multiple kinds of journals, too. For

---

BOX 3.4   Learning from the Permalink

Parties, polarization, and democracy in the United States / Donald C. . . .

LC Control No.:	2009036149
Type of Material:	Book (Print, Microform, Electronic, etc.)
Personal Name:	Baumer, Donald C., 1950- » More like this
Main Title:	Parties, polarization, and democracy in the United States / Donald C. Baumer, Howard J. Gold.
Published/Created:	Boulder : Paradigm Publishers, c2010.
Related Names:	Gold, Howard J., 1958- » More like this
Description:	xi, 243 p. : ill. ; 24 cm.
Contents: 1.	Political parties in the twenty-first century — 2. Parties and the electorate I : images of the parties — 3. Parties and the electorate II : the dynamics of party polarization — 4. The midterm elections of 1994 and 2006 — 5. Parties in power : Congress, presidents, partisanship, and gridlock — 6. Political parties in Anglo-America — 7. Looking backward and forward : the election of 2008 and the future of American politics.
Subjects:	Political parties—United States. » More like this Elections—United States. » More like this Polarization (Social sciences)—United States. » More like this United States—Politics and government—1989- » More like this
LC Classification:	JK2265.B38 2010

The disappearing center : engaged citizens, polarization, and American...

LC Control No.:	2009033737
Type of Material:	Book (Print, Microform, Electronic, etc.)
Personal Name:	Abramowitz, Alan. » More like this
Main Title:	The disappearing center : engaged citizens, polarization, and American democracy / Alan I. Abramowitz.
Published/Created:	New Haven : Yale University Press, c2010.
Description:	xi, 194 p. : ill. ; 25 cm.
Subjects:	Political parties—United States. » More like this Party affiliation—United States. » More like this Polarization (Social sciences) » More like this United States—Politics and government—2009-» More like this
LC Classification:	JK2261.A28 2010

the AB, you're trying to uncover the most important arguments or answers to your question, so you want to find scholarly journals. Sometimes the journals of opinion, news articles, and/or editorials that helped you formulate your question are also relevant, and you can summarize them, but remember these alone are not sufficient. Too often, students rely too heavily on newspaper or popular magazine (e.g., *U.S. News & World Report*, *Time*, *Newsweek*, *The Economist*) articles. In your database searching, use these author names as well as those of some of the people you found in your book search to find new and excellent scholarly sources. These are the academic giants on whose shoulders you will stand.

To find these, begin searching databases that index journals, or if your search through books has already helped you identify some key articles or authors who make competing arguments, use the databases to find them. We've already become acquainted with some of these library databases from our work developing the Research Question. I frequently suggest that my students start in Academic Search Premier and ProQuest (under "Research Libraries"). I like these because they index a number of scholarly journals, and they usually have very recent issues online. As mentioned before, other useful databases include Project MUSE and JSTOR, but be careful with JSTOR, because there is a delay in bringing materials online.

When you search, you will want to use all that you have learned before to help you find appropriate sources. Search using your key concept (from your question), the names of the authors you found (in your texts or from the LoC search), and the additional subject terms you turned up in your earlier efforts. Then, use those terms and similar techniques to return just the right number of good sources. What's nice about database searching is that you can also read an abstract of an article and get a sense of the argument and the article's utility before you read the whole work. You can also easily export these articles and citations into Zotero, Mendeley, or EndNote and get a copy of the citation, often in the correct form. Use the abstracts to help you choose the best articles (be very careful not to plagiarize here!). Once you have picked a manageable number of good sources, you will have to read them and write original summaries for the AB, summaries that help you understand not only what the authors are arguing but whom they are arguing against, whom they agree with, and how they came to their conclusions. Ultimately, these summaries will allow you to make groups of similar sources.

IDENTIFYING SIMILAR ARGUMENTS AND GROUPING YOUR SOURCES

When you are working on your AB, I recommend that you create a new document that will contain both the source information and the summary paragraphs and ultimately become your AB. In this document, you will play around with, in violation of the bibliographic conventions, your source list, grouping sources with other works that make similar arguments. (In the AB, sources are not arranged alphabetically, as they would be in a reference list, but conceptually.[10]) My logic here is to get you to see whether you actually have multiple, different answers to your RQ and to identify what the essentials of those answers are. If you know you have *three or more* answers, then you will be in a good position to write about the debate in your Literature Review. (You can't have a debate with just one argument with which all your authors agree!) Yes, some debates have only two positions, but generally, my students are too willing to stop searching when they have found a couple perspectives; thus, I'm trying to encourage you to obtain a broad and early overview of the field. Having an incomplete understanding of the scholarly debate hampers too many projects and puts students in an early hole, which they never seem to dig out of. And as early as possible, you need to put those answers to the question or positions in the debate in your own words. That way, you can identify the differences and similarities in the work of scholars. Don't just assume that two works are different or the same; read and think carefully about the theses and supporting arguments. Ultimately, if you can articulate what those answers have in common, then they are likely to be similar, and you are likely to have found what academics refer to as a school of thought, a similar approach to answering the question. Thus, your goal is to have about three or four scholarly approaches to your RQ, and in order to achieve that end point, you will need approximately ten to fifteen sources at the outset. One work does not make a school! So, don't be satisfied with the first materials you find. You may be lucky and they may be excellent, but particularly when you are new to an area of research or simply a novice researcher, you must spend a good deal of time understanding the field. Expect to put some time in learning and reading sources that you ultimately don't use. I wish there were a way for me to tell you how to be perfectly efficient, to find and read only those sources that will benefit you directly. Frankly, the more experience you have with research, the more efficient you will be, but even those of us who have been working in the field for decades always spend a little time on pieces that aren't really that helpful. It's all in your perspective; even negative findings (i.e., learning that an article isn't helpful) reveal that you are learning and understanding more about your work. In other words, you are still making progress.

So as you are working on the AB, consciously group your works. Now, if you've found an important scholarly work—like Abramowitz for Gabriela— you will also know how that author divides the field. You will want to be aware of her or his categories, but not necessarily committed to them. Maybe you'll like the author's labels, maybe the categories are the standard ones for everyone who studies polarization in the United States, or maybe you will think that her or his perspective is misguided. Keep in mind all of those possibilities. If you end up liking the author's approach, you can borrow the terms (giving proper credit in a citation, of course) and use that scheme (and the citations) to help you make sure you have the most important sources in your bibliography. If you don't like it, you can look for others that better match your ideas and needs or you can even make up your own set of labels. Remember, the research paper is your chance to put your stamp on the field, so feel free to be original.

The main points, however, are to be sure that (1) your sources respond to your question, (2) you focus on the answer to *your question* and not on recording what your sources are writing about, and (3) the answers you are finding are different. If you determine that your source isn't interested in your question at all, then you have to abandon that work. Now, there are times when an important piece might have a different main focus than yours but in addition has an answer to your question. Particularly when that work is by a famous political scientist or is a "big book" that "everyone" cites, you want to include it. In general, though, this is the time to zero in on answers to the Research Question. I also strongly recommend that you seek to state the response in a very short (one word, if possible) as well as a longer, more explanatory form. What factor(s) does the author see as important? If you look back to Table 3.1, in which I summarize our students' questions (in a short form) and hunches (if they had any), you'll notice that those answers are very short: "social media" (Kevin) and "gender" (Zoe). Of course, such a brief response is not sufficient for the AB, but what it does is ensure that you understand the core of the author's argument, which might be the essence of one school of thought. Just as with question writing, I have seen students get lost in the wonderful verbiage of a respected author. They are unable to state the basic point. Force yourself at this early stage to focus on your question, the author's question (if it is different), a short response (factor), and a longer answer (thesis). Ask yourself, does this argument sound familiar or very different from what I have read in my classes? If you jog your memory, you are likely to find additional good works for your AB from your previous courses. If you keep this focus on the answers, you will help yourself arrive at a well-balanced set of works that provide you a broad view of the field, with multiple contending perspectives. As you are writing up your summaries, if you find that all your sources agree, you need to go back and search for more works. Use the works you have to find out with whom these authors disagree. Writers always point out who they think is wrong and why, so you can use your sources to help you identify alternative schools. Again, realize that no matter how much advice I give you, neither your professor nor I can provide the magic formula for looking only at the works you will use in your research. If you use these techniques, you will minimize the time you perceive as unproductive; however, most of us need to go down a few blind alleys as we learn more about our questions and topics. Just try to be as directed as you can, and stay focused on your goal of finding the most important scholarly answers to your question, responses that should not all agree.

ONE LAST WORD OF ADVICE: GENERIC SCHOOLS OF THOUGHT

When you're in the midst of locating sources, finding only the most recent ones or the arguments with which you agree can be really tempting. You can also sometimes have a hard time thinking about what else might be relevant or how some previous readings (e.g., from other courses) might be helpful. That's when you should remember that in political science there are (arguably) four broad schools of thought.[11] For ease of remembering them, I refer to the group as IIIE, or "triple I E"—*i*nterests, *i*nstitutions, *i*deas, and *e*conomics. Thinking through these factors and their possible impact on your subject of interest can be very helpful, and I guarantee that you have all seen explanations that use these elements.

Interest-based approaches assert that actors make decisions that maximize their priorities. In American and comparative politics, these are often called rational-choice theories; in international politics, some refer to these as rational-actor approaches. From this viewpoint, agents take the steps that best serve their interests, whether the actors are voters deciding whether turning out to cast a ballot is worth the effort, protestors thinking about coming out for a demonstration when the threat of violent regime retaliation is looming, or a country determining whether an intervention will serve its power position. *Institutional* perspectives focus on the rules or structures of institutions and show that these established routines or patterns have an impact on outcomes. For instance, in studying elections, political scientists know that the type of electoral system—whether it is first past the post or some form of proportional representation scheme—affects how candidates and voters behave and the outcome of the contest.[12] The third I here—*ideas*—is actually a catchall term for ideas, identities, and cultures. These types of explanations contend that what actors think, who they are (or who they think they are), and what they value determine results. Some of the factors involved might be called psychological, whether these are the schemas and scripts that actors use to make sense of the world or one's orientation (e.g., positive and outgoing) toward society or sociological, that is, elements of an identity such as race, gender, ethnicity, or socioeconomic status. Culture could mean a particular world culture, as well as those sets of values and practices specific to an organization or group. Last, a final group of explanations stresses the role of *economic* (or sometimes socioeconomic) factors. Typical assertions of the primacy of economics include those that argue that recessions cause the party in power to lose in midterm elections and that wealth produces democracies around the world.[13]

This discussion about the generic schools, I hope, helps you focus on the driving forces in politics, reminds you of perspectives you have learned about in your classes, and links you to the debates in the field and even the broader culture. How do different people account for your phenomenon? The value of remembering these generic schools is that they can keep your mind open to multiple possible understandings as well as link you to other scholarship and perspectives. They also help you think in terms of that one-word answer to your question that I was encouraging above and again connect you to scholarship you already know (thus helping you place what you might see as an isolated argument into a "school"). Using these generic approaches to spin out possible explanations is a kind of mental exercise to help warm you up as you conduct your research to find the actual scholarly explanations out there; moreover, this activity helps you avoid missing an obvious answer. After you have a set of answers to your question, ask yourself, Have I covered IIIE? Which ones are missing? If one or more is lacking, does the absence make sense, or can I imagine an answer from that perspective? For instance, I find that students generally are drawn to interest- and identity-based answers but miss institutional and economic ones. Sometimes, those arguments are very important, and students have even been exposed to them in their classes, so reminding them, for instance, of modernization theory as an important explanation of why some regimes are able to become democratic and others aren't is very important. Thinking about IIIE should help you, too, to have the insight and stamina to keep looking for different approaches when you are seeking to understand your field as well as to provide some ideas for creatively linking your research to other strands of inquiry to which you have been exposed in your academic career.

WRITING THE ANNOTATED BIBLIOGRAPHY

As we have seen, your goal is to identify the scholars who have made the biggest contributions to answering your question and use them to help you move forward on your paper. Those great works enhance your own understandings and help build a solid theoretical foundation for your project. After you have located some excellent sources and begun summarizing them as suggested above, you can classify your answers and write your AB. I suggest that your AB contain five distinct and important elements, stated here in the order in which you should work on them. First is your Research Question. You want to be sure that you have a clear one and that ultimately your sources are answering it. You need to state the query in the AB not only for your benefit but also for your instructor's. This way you both will be able to evaluate whether your question and your sources are well suited to each other and whether you are finding alternative answers. Second is your sources, listed as bibliographic entries and written in a consistent form. This should be the easiest part of your AB. Third, you should work on finding the thesis and identifying the fundamental factor(s) upon which the author of your source is basing her or his argument. Fourth is to flesh out a paragraph discussion of the author's argument, and last is the job of grouping sources and trying to characterize the school of thought, stating what is essential to the argument, and perhaps even giving the approach a label. That fifth step is the most complex, and you will likely have to puzzle over your notes for a while until you are ready to handle it. In fact, I recommend that you concentrate initially on the first four steps as you begin this task.

Let's look at Gabriela's early efforts. At the outset, she read her assignment and noted that her professor wanted her paper written in American Political Science Association form. Gabriela began using the works from the journals of opinion she had consulted as she was mulling over her topic and trying to identify a question. Through interlibrary loan, she received the Abramowitz book first, which then led her immediately to the works of Morris Fiorina, an author Abramowitz was arguing against. She also noticed that the work excerpted earlier in this chapter to demonstrate plagiarism and paraphrasing, *The Parties versus the People*, would also be appropriate and obtained that from her own library. Here you can see her working through the early steps of the AB, using a table I recommend you use too (see Table 3.2).

What can Gabriela (and we) learn from this first exercise? First, that a book review, her first source, does a very nice job of summarizing a larger work. While Gabriela would be better off reading Bishop for herself, this review gives her a nice sense of the book. Second, that in their theses, authors often explain who and what they are arguing against, so that can help us look for other "big arguments" we need to find. In explaining Bishop, Stossel says that gerrymandering is less important (in other words, some other author must have blamed electoral districts and their redrawing), Abramowitz contends that elites aren't at fault (someone must be saying they are), and Edwards argues that the problem is not our Constitution (another author likely assigns it responsibility). And right after they identify what is *not* the source of the problem, they identify the "real" answer. In order, these are "the movement from below" (Bishop/Stossel), the ideologically extreme views of citizens and their increased activism (Abramowitz), and "the political party framework" (Edwards) or, as the authors have identified in their titles, "the big sort," "the disappearing center," and "parties."

The next job is to state the author's brief answers to your question and see how each argument (might) link to the generic schools. Gabriela could continue by adding two more columns on the earlier table, but for the purposes of presentation, look at Table 3.3 below.

This exercise allows Gabriela to see that she has some competing explanations here: are citizens, elites, or the party and electoral structure to blame for the polarization in American politics? It also shows her that while some scholars agree on a factor, such as "citizens," they might analyze the role of citizens differently. In other words, Gabriela should explore further the extent

Table 3.2   Beginning Your Annotated Bibliography: Gabriela's Basics

<u>Research Question:</u> Why is U.S. politics so polarized now, and what are the policy consequences of polarization?[14]

Author	Brief Title	Answer to Research Question or Thesis[a]
Stossel	"Subdivided We Fall" (book review of Bishop's *The Big Sort*) *NYT* book review	"Bishop argues that this clustering of like with like [i.e., 'the Big Sort'] accelerated in the tumult of the 1960s when, unmoored from the organizations and traditions that had guided their choices about how to live, Americans grew anxious and disoriented—and reflexively sought comfort in the familiar, cocooning themselves in communities of people like themselves."…"Gerrymandering—the redrawing of political districts by partisan legislation from above— partly accounts for increasing polarization. But the more significant force, Bishop argues, has been movement from below."…"Bishop cites research suggesting that, contrary to the standard goo-goo exhortations, the surer route to political comity may be less civic engagement, less passionate conviction. So let's hear it for the indifferent and unsure, whose passivity may provide the national glue we need." (no page, online source)
Abramowitz	*The Disappearing Center*	Among American citizens, the ideological center is disappearing, instead being replaced by extremes that are more active and influential in politics. A polarized majority, then, does not follow politicians but leads elected officials and candidates to more partisan and ideological positions. More citizens than ever are highly engaged in politics, as recent voter turnout, activism, and political contributions show.
Edwards	*The Parties Versus the People*	"The dysfunction that has almost paralyzed our federal government has its roots not in the people, not in any fundamental flaw in our constitutional processes, but in the political party framework through which our elected officials gain their offices and within which they govern" (p. xiii).
Fiorina with Abrams	*Disconnect: The Breakdown in Representation in American Politics*	The media and some academics are mischaracterizing contemporary American politics. Elites and not citizens are the ones who are polarized and highly ideological (pp. 11-20). Citizens are usually moderate and not very interested in politics, but elites and the media take extreme positions and leave citizens unsure and frustrated as they vote. Thus, the American system of representation has broken down (pp. 27-28).

a. A verbatim answer can be easiest; put it in quotation marks, and supply pages if available. When you are capable, seek to write in your own words.

Table 3.3 Identifying the Key Factors or Short Answers

<u>Research Question:</u> Why is U.S. politics so polarized now, and what are the policy consequences of polarization?

Author	Brief Title	Key Factor	Generic School (IIIE)?
Stossel on Bishop	"Divided We Fall" and *The Big Sort*	**Citizens moving** to live with, **listening** to, and **interacting** with only those like themselves	Identity/ideas?
Abramowitz	*The Disappearing Center*	**Americans** becoming increasingly **ideological** and **involved**	Identity/ideas?
Edwards	*The Parties Versus the People*	Political **party** and **election structure**	Institutions? Economics? (because money and elections are important)
Fiorina with Abrams	*Disconnect*	**Elected officials** and the **media** (system elites) are disconnected from ideas and priorities of ordinary people. The system of representation has broken down.	Interests? Institutions?

to which Bishop (and she'll really need his book here; the book review isn't enough) and Abramowitz agree. Are the factors motivating the moving Bishop sees the same as the ideological intensity and activism Abramowitz identifies? And as Fiorina focuses on elites, is it something about those elites (are they self-interested actors) or, digging deeper, is he making a more institutional argument, one like Edwards's, which focuses on the structure of the American party and electoral system? Moreover, Gabriela can see that there might be other explanations out there, ones that focus more explicitly on interests, culture, or economics to answer the question. Still, this targeted focus on theses, fundamental factors, and generic schools of thought puts Gabriela on a firm footing to proceed with identifying, reading, and understanding additional sources and, ultimately, writing her Annotated Bibliography.

Let's imagine that Gabriela has spent some more time looking for other sources, adding them to her tables, and then starting to write her Annotated Bibliography. She carefully locates the theses of her sources, paraphrases them, thinks deeply about the fundamental factors they were identifying, rethinks, and revises her work, and then begins writing up her entries. While she is not finished yet, I want to share her draft below. Notice that she was able to link her research to works she had read or learned about in her classes (see Putnam, Yglesias, and Robinson and Ellis, in addition to Stossel), and she still might decide to add something on wedge issues[15] to her elite school. She also still needs to get the Bishop book so she can carefully compare his argument with that of Abramowitz, as well as to find other adherents of each school, search for any additional perspectives, and look for some scholarly articles, but she is on her way to developing a good AB and a strong understanding of the scholarly debate around her Research Question.

Now, let's see what Gabriela has written for her AB so far. Look at her form here, and seek to mimic it yourself (while using the citation form your professor requires).

The Beginnings of Gabriela's AB

Research Question: Why is U.S. politics so polarized now, and what are the policy consequences of polarization?

School 1 – *Brief Name:* Elite Extremism School; *Basic Argument/Answer to Research Question:* Elites are highly polarized, and their vitriol alienates many citizens and leads to a breakdown in representation.

Fiorina, Morris P., with Samuel J. Abrams. 2009. *Disconnect: The Breakdown of Representation in American Politics.* Norman: University of Oklahoma Press.

Fiorina, Morris P., with Samuel J. Abrams and Jeremy C. Pope. 2006. *Culture War? The Myth of a Polarized America,* 3rd ed. New York: Pearson Longman.

Responding to both media characterizations and what they see as incorrect academic readings of the data, Morris P. Fiorina and colleagues contend that ordinary Americans tend to be comfortably situated in the middle of the ideological spectrum (2006, 11-12; 2009, 12-20). Elites, on the other hand, occupy the ideological extremes. Thus, the polarized debate in politics is simply a product of elite and media manipulations. Citizens are not always very well informed, because they don't pay close attention to politics, and when they are they do not necessarily have very strong likes or dislikes. They are often forced to make choices (especially at election time), but those selections do not capture accurately their political views, which are usually moderate (2006, 27-28). This risk of elite polarization is that citizens become further turned off by politics. Politicians, then, increasingly do not adequately represent the views of their constituents (2009, 24-48).

Robinson, Michael, and Susan Ellis. 2004. "Purple America: The Country Is Really an Even Mix of Blue and Red." *The Weekly Standard,* August 16, 27-29. http://ezproxy.sju.edu/login?url=http://search .proquest.com.ezproxy.sju.edu/docview/232985619?accountid =14071 (April 2, 2014).

Although they differ with Fiorina and his coauthors on the emphasis on elites' being disconnected from their constituents, Robinson and Ellis stress that there are no "blue" or "red" states. Instead, citizens from all states elect people from both parties (27). While the Pew Research study finds significant evidence of polarization, these authors claim that a closer look at the data shows something else. Citizens are, for the most part, in the middle, and "purple" reflects their partisanship more than blue or red (29).

School 2 – *Brief Name:* Party and Election System School; *Basic Argument/Answer to Research Question:* The American party and electoral system has created highly ideological parties and rewards extremism as the most partisan (citizens and leaders) control who win the nominations, how to draw districts, and the funding of campaigns.

Edwards, Mickey. 2012. *The Parties Versus the People: How to Turn Republicans and Democrats Into Americans.* New Haven, CT: Yale University Press.

Polarization in American politics is rooted in neither the ideology of elites and citizens nor citizen behavior. Instead it results from the nature of the contemporary and interrelated party and electoral systems (4). Ironically, the harmful elements of the institutions developed as a result of the efforts of reformers, beginning in the Progressive Era, to provide citizens with more of a say in elections and to take control away from back-room-dealing party bosses. The reforms put into place primary systems so that partisans could pick candidates and later led to more party influence over the drawing of districts (5-6). The reforms continued into the mid-20th century, as government was growing. With this expansion came more questions over government's role and more reasons to disagree over its use (30-32). Ultimately, these structures and the reach of government have caused the highly ideological nature of American politics and the end of across-the-aisle voting and fluid congressional voting coalitions. Instead, party-line votes tend to rule the day today. Not only has the Congress become highly partisan but so too has the presidency. Instead of focusing on problem solving, presidents tend to be looking for ideological advantage (146-48). Only when we institute structural reforms to the system to reduce the role of parties (36-38) and big, private money (70-73) in elections and force partisans to find ways of cooperating and thinking first about the country, and not party victories, will we effectively undermine polarization.

School 3 – *Brief Name:* Citizen Engagement School; *Basic Argument/Answer to Research Question:* Citizens are highly polarized; this polarization has positive and negative consequences.

Abramowitz, A. I. 2010. *The Disappearing Center: Engaged Citizens, Polarization, and American Democracy.* New Haven, CT: Yale University Press.

In direct opposition to Fiorina, Alan I. Abramowitz (2010) argues that most citizens are politically engaged, and they are taking increasingly polarized views. He concedes that a portion of Americans have little interest, but this portion is a minority and is shrinking. This polarized majority, then, does not follow politicians but leads elected officials and candidates to more partisan and ideological positions. More citizens than ever are highly engaged in politics, as recent voter turnout, activism, and political contributions show. These behaviors are positive because they reflect the democratic ideal, the rule of an informed and involved citizenry. In fact, American political parties are now approaching the once-longed-for goal: ideologically consistent, responsive, and responsible groupings of representatives (4-5). Engaged citizens have strong ideological views, and they tend to seek out people like themselves. Unlike in the past, people tend to live, go to school or work, and worship with people who share their own positions. Given the changes in the media, citizens can also block out sources of information that don't correspond to their views (Chapters 3-5). Thus, not everything about this polarized America is positive for politics, as U.S. institutions were not designed for ideologically consistent and responsive parties. Given U.S. institutions, as well as the almost even ideological split among the public, polarization means gridlock and the increasing frustration and alienation of the remaining part of the public, which is not as interested in politics (111-38).

Yglesias, Matthew. 2007. "The Great Divider." *The American Prospect* 18 (4): 47-49. http://search.proquest. com.ezproxy.sju.edu/docview/201159517?accountid=14071 (April 2, 2014).

Partisanship and ideology are increasingly aligning. Geography, religion, gender, and of course race are now more than ever correlated with citizens' political views (47). While events may drive popularity of presidents and enhance their ability to govern, this support can be fleeting, particularly among those who aren't strong partisans, when the relevance of a crisis fades (49).

Stossel, Scott. 2008. "Subdivided We Fall." *The New York Times*, May 18. http://www.nytimes .com/2008/05/18/books/review/Stossel-t.html?pagewanted=all&_r=0 (March 31, 2014).

Scott Stossel provides an excellent summary of Bill Bishop's book *The Big Sort*, in which Bishop argues that citizens are taking steps to close themselves off from people who think differently about political and social issues than they do. These actions include moving to certain areas of the country, state, city, or town to be with like-minded individuals, watching or listening to only certain programs that confirm their existing view of the world, and socializing with others of their ideological persuasion. Perhaps surprisingly, Bishop argues, according to Stossel, that the United States would be better off if fewer people cared so deeply or were involved in politics. This indifference would provide more places for compromise and a less polarized America.

School 4 – *Brief Name:* **Declining Social Capital School;** *Basic Argument/Answer to Research Question:* **Polarization is worse today because social capital is much lower. People have very little contact with those they don't agree with and have constructed dense social networks among the like-minded. The consequences, however, are negative for encouraging deliberation and considered choice.**

Mutz, Diana C. 2006. *Hearing the Other Side: Deliberative Versus Participatory Democracy.* New York: Cambridge University Press.

According to Diana C. Mutz (2006), dense social networks are great for creating an enthusiastic and engaged citizenry but not good for engendering a tolerant society (7-10). Characteristics we have tended to idealize in a citizen—informed, engaged, opinionated, and involved—are actually contrary to the flexible and open society our national narrative and our democratic theory praise (34-44). Polarization has come about because people who are actively engaged are increasingly inclined to shut themselves off from ideas that and others they neither like (perhaps seeing those others as "liberals," "rednecks," or "extremists") nor want to know. The consequences for democracy are significant. People are less exposed to opposing viewpoints and policies and less willing to consider seriously alternative perspectives. Mutz claims this loss threatens tolerance as well as the quality of the political process and political outcomes (Chapter 3). We may have a good deal of participation, but not enough deliberation—thoughtful and comprehensive consideration of issues. Both factors—participation and deliberation—are equally important and essential to the good health of the American polity; deliberation must be revived today without losing participation (128-35, 147-51).

Putnam, Robert, with Robert Leonardi and Raffaella Y. Nanetti. 1994. *Making Democracy Work: Civil Traditions in Modern Italy.* Princeton, NJ: Princeton University Press.
Putnam, Robert 1995. "Bowling Alone: America's Declining Social Capital." *Journal of Democracy* 6 (1): 65=78. http://muse.jhu.edu.ezproxy.sju.edu/journals/journal_of_democracy/v006/6.1putnam.html (April 3, 2014).

Mutz's argument builds on a line of reasoning most associated with Robert Putnam. In the first work here, *Making Democracy Work*, Putnam and his colleagues seek to understand whether regional variation in the quality of democracy in Italy has continued since the 1970s institutional reforms that put in place common structures throughout the country (8-13). In particular, they contrast the impact of socioeconomic modernity and civic community on institutional performance (their proxy for democracy) and find that civic community—how engaged citizens are in associations—is a far better predictor of the quality of democracy than is modernization (see Chapter 4, especially). In the second work, "Bowling Alone," Putnam changes the name of that key factor from civic community to social capital and contends that the decline in social capital—the links that citizens have with others, particularly others with whom they wouldn't ordinarily associate—in the United States has led to a decrease in social trust and has dangerous consequences for democracy.

As you can see, Gabriela has made great progress: She has four schools, multiple sources under each, important works in the form of books and articles (though she is heavy on books here), as well as articles from her courses. Like Gabriela, you should try as soon as you can (even when you haven't finished identifying all your key sources yet) to begin your AB. Better to know sooner rather than later whether you have different approaches, whether you understand the arguments, how to group and what to call the schools, and what you are lacking. And don't be surprised if you find that you have to jettison some of the early sources you have summarized because they actually stray from your ultimate focus. Also, expect to rearrange your groups. Here, perhaps Gabriela will decide that schools 2 and 4 should be combined into a single perspective. Students often refine their summaries (go back to the original sources) and think through their groupings for some time after completing their first pass through some of the literature. Moreover, Gabriela will have to decide whether she wants to focus on the causes of polarization or its consequences. As this AB stands now, Gabriela is more concerned with the sources, so she may want to eliminate the discussions of the results. If her goal, however, is to study the effects, then she needs to shift her emphasis to outcomes. Thus, Gabriela needs to think and write, as the way forward is to circle back while thinking ahead. This is a stage, then, to refine the Research Question, cull some sources while finding some new and more appropriate ones, sharpen understandings of the schools, and improve summaries. All those steps should help you arrive at an organized and excellent understanding of the existing scholarship on your RQ.

PRACTICAL SUMMARY

To succeed in writing your Annotated Bibliography, you must have access to an appropriate style guide, a well-formed Research Question, excellent academic sources that provide competing answers to that question, and an understanding of exactly how those scholarly responses are similar and in what ways they are different. Early in the process, you start by finding sources, and as we have seen here, identifying good works to use is not automatic. The job does not have to be hard, however, if you use the steps identified here of using works you already have, generating search terms from those existing sources or from brainstorming, and then methodically identifying sources and using them to lead you to more works. Absolutely follow the same steps Gabriela did (thinking about her course materials, turning to the LoC, interrogating the LoC results, and going to the databases).

The next phase includes summarizing the arguments of these works. Telling your reader what these sources are about will not get you far. You must explain how they answer your question and, in particular, what factors they focus on as the main response. Seek to write paragraph summaries of the works, as well as to characterize the answer with one word or a phrase. Also be sure that you are keeping track of your sources with citation management software or in the appropriate bibliographic form and that you know the precise page numbers for your specific information. Take this opportunity to reread Box 3.1 on plagiarism and vow that you will never make that kind of mistake.

The more works you read and summarize, the easier it will be for you to understand the arguments being made and the small distinctions between them. So, even after you think you are done with your summaries, you will want to take some time and rethink your characterizations and groupings. You may need to reread sources, rewrite summaries, and even refine your RQ. While at times frustrating, proceeding through this iterative spiral will ultimately bring you the most success and the highest quality paper, because this kind of precision and care translates into a better understanding of the phenomenon and what you will be studying. And again, the foundation of the project is so important for its proper construction and your ultimate follow through.

RECIPE 2: ANNOTATED BIBLIOGRAPHY
INGREDIENTS

- Research Question
- Access to the reference guide for the citation style you will use
- Syllabi and materials from previous, related courses
- Resources for the AB (online materials), which are Tables 3.1, 3.2, and 3.3 as blanks
- Access to Gabriela's various efforts at writing the AB

INSTRUCTIONS

1. Open the resources for the AB and start filling in the first chart (Table 3.1) for yourself. Take special care to write your question and your hunch(es) as clearly as possible.

2. Using the various methods spelled out in this chapter, identify sources, search terms, and authors who respond to your Research Question. Whenever you find one that appears good, use it to find more, by locating both authors your source agrees with and those with whom it disagrees. Begin filling out the second chart of the resources for the AB (Table 3.2), which will require you to write the summaries of your sources' arguments, focusing on the way they answer your RQ.

3. Record your sources so that you will be easily able to cite them and access them later.

4. After you have think you have found a "good" number and variety of sources—when you read new ones, you're not learning about new arguments, and you seem to have an array of answers to your question—start identifying the fundamental factors and generic schools for your sources. Turn to the last table in Resources for AB (Table 3.3).

5. Most likely, you lack the variety of sources you had hoped for. Go back and find some additional ones that make different arguments. Find them by looking more carefully at your existing sources and seeing whom your authors are arguing against. Summarize and categorize these new sources in your table.

6. Move rows of your chart around so that you are grouping sources with similar fundamental factors and arguments.

7. Begin to write the AB, using Gabriela's as a model. Your RQ should be at the top, to keep you focused. Group your sources into schools with brief names as well as longer answers to your question. Include the bibliographic information and a summary (in your own words, but with page numbers included for relevant information) of the author's answer to your RQ.

8. Rethink and revise your classification. Refine your question if necessary.

9. When you have a set of sources, arranged into three or more schools (with typically several scholarly sources in each category), for which you can identify a common approach to answering your RQ, then you can be satisfied. Remember, your professor will be the ultimate judge of "doneness" on all your efforts, and most of the time, you can always do more refining (there's that iterative spiral again). Still, following these guidelines will give you a great start.

EXERCISES

1. Pick one of our other students, Kevin, Max, or Zoe. Search for a few excellent books using the LoC catalog or your own institution's research library. Then perform a search for articles in one of the online databases available at your institution. Find what you think are the four best works. Explain why they are best (e.g., most cited? prestigious authors, presses, or journals? most controversial? a literature review?). Using your searching work, identify some search terms for this student.

2. Using the citation form your professor has specified, take the sources listed in Gabriela's example AB and create an appropriate reference list for a paper that relied on all of them.

NOTES

1. While the fundamental ideas of this quotation are typically attributed to Sir Isaac Newton, many believe the original source is John of Salisbury and his work *Metalogicon* of 1159. This quotation reflects his precise words. For discussion, see http://www.phrases.org.uk/meanings/268025.html.

2. This book (in its footnotes and its bibliography) uses Chicago style, and I am using its term here (and will continue to do so throughout) for the list of works consulted in a project. The Modern Language Association calls this the "Works Cited," and the American Political Science Association and American Psychological Association use "References." In all styles, the works are listed in alphabetical order by author last name. They are not numbered. Each approach treats the entries slightly differently, so consult a manual for the precise format.

3. For more information on which program is right for you, please consult Penn State Libraries, "Choosing a Citation Manager," http://www.libraries.psu.edu/psul/lls/choose_citation_mgr.html.

4. See Diana Hacker, *A Pocket Manual of Style*, 4th ed. (Boston: Bedford/St. Martin's, 2004), 115–26, 157–64, 185–92.

5. Sometimes, you can find an article that is solely a literature review. This will be very helpful in understanding the different approaches to your research question. Still, you should not copy or reiterate all of that author's analysis. You must think through the literature on your own. A great place for finding articles that summarize a field of inquiry is Ira Katznelson and Helen V. Milner, eds., *Political Science: State of the Discipline*, centennial ed. (New York: Norton, 2005). More recent compilations are Robert E. Goodin, ed., *The Oxford Handbook of Political Science* (New York: Oxford University Press, 2011); R.A.W. Rhodes, Sarah A. Binder, and Bert A. Rockman, eds., *The Oxford Handbook of Political Institutions* (New York: Oxford University Press, 2008); Carles Boix and Susan C. Stokes, eds., *Oxford Handbook of Comparative Politics* (New York: Oxford University Press, 2009); and Christopher Reus-Smit and Duncan Snidal, eds., *Oxford Handbook of International Relations* (New York: Oxford University Press, 2010).

6. In the supplemental Web Resources, I have made a list of some of the "big concepts" for each of the subfields. If you are absolutely stuck regarding the central point of your question, read over my list and use that to help stimulate ideas. In addition, carefully reviewing the list might also help if you are still struggling over a topic and question.

7. Do I dare say this? These resources can help you identify important works and authors and so can be useful at the bibliography-building stage or when you are looking for data. But absolutely go to the original source; do not use and cite the encyclopedia, online or otherwise, itself.

8. *New York Times Book Review* (May 18, 2008), http://www.nytimes.com/2008/05/18/books/review/Stossel-t.html?pagewanted=all&_r=0.

9. I have excluded information I have deemed extraneous, but you can go to the LoC and see the full record.

10. You may also do some of this in your citation management program. How you work here is up to you.

11. Not all political scientists are satisfied with this division of the field. Some prefer a focus on levels of analysis, and others would say that the subfields are too different for commonalities. I remain committed, however, to seeing the overlap within the discipline and encouraging students to think in terms of causal or key factors as they search for answers to their questions, and thus I think that this scheme works well.

12. Note, of course, that institutionalist explanations can also be rational-choice perspectives, as the rules within institutions establish the incentives and guidelines for gains-seeking behavior.

13. Students of global politics will know these perspectives by different names. IIIE maps onto realism, liberalism, constructivism, and Marxism, too, although not all explanations that focus on economics are Marxist in international politics or other fields.

14. Notice that Gabriela actually has two questions here. At this stage, I typically allow students to proceed with two questions because they are still learning and trying to understand what they want to study. Other faculty might have a different opinion, and students themselves should acknowledge that asking multiple questions typically means more complexity and work.

15. See Daniel A. Smith and Caroline J. Tolbert, *Educated by Initiative: The Effects of Direct Democracy on Citizens and Political Organizations in the American States* (Ann Arbor: University of Michigan Press, 2004); Peter Shrag, *Paradise Lost: California's Experience, America's Future* (New York: New Press, 1998).

Making Sense of the Scholarly Answers to Your Research Question

Writing the Literature Review

The next phase of the project is when you start writing actual parts of the paper. The work you have done so far is extremely important for laying the proper foundation, and now is the time to begin the aboveground construction. I can't stress enough the importance of a high-quality framework—a good question, excellent sources, detailed summaries of the arguments, and schools of thought. If you don't have this foundation, please spend more time and/or get some help from your instructor or a reference librarian *now*. If you do not, you will be frustrated trying to complete the Literature Review (LR), and you'll have trouble on all future parts of the paper.

The LR is typically the first section of the paper after the Introduction. It explains to the reader how scholars have answered your Research Question (RQ), in both its generic and specific forms. In laying out the scholarly responses, the LR groups the answers into schools of thought (replies that share common elements) and labels each group. In other words, the work you have done on your Annotated Bibliography (AB) serves as your notes and even a rough draft for the Literature Review. In addition, however, the LR assesses the strengths and weaknesses of each school, examining the quality of the logic and how well each approach accounts for cases other than the ones being addressed directly in the paper. Sometimes, the LR concludes by choosing one approach as the most compelling. Later, you will use that preferred perspective to develop a thesis for your paper. As you write the LR (and all the other sections), you should strive to make it a coherent essay that could stand on its own, although it also is linked to the rest of the paper and performs precise functions for your project. Each part of your paper, then, should have an interesting and appropriate heading that captures its argument and purpose. Great headings communicate a contention and justify your writing goals. In addition, longer paper sections (like the LR) will also have their own introductory and concluding paragraphs, as any proper essay should. So in this chapter, you will also be learning a bit about some fundamentals for structuring an essay—coming up with a good title and writing appropriate Introductions and Conclusions.

PREPARING FOR AND UNDERSTANDING THE LITERATURE REVIEW

In your AB, you have done much of the heavy lifting for the LR. However, after you have turned in your AB, you likely will hear from your professor that you need to adjust or narrow your question in some way and/or that there were some important authors you forgot to include or some arguments you didn't understand precisely. You may even want to rethink the names of your schools of thought. Don't be discouraged by these comments. They are normal at this stage because starting a new research project is difficult, and precision comes only with time and familiarity. Thus, cheerfully (well, at least not dejectedly) refine your question, find additional sources, capture their arguments, and rethink how to characterize and label the schools. Taking the work of the AB a step further, the LR is a coherent essay that identifies, explains, names, and assesses the answers to your Research Question in an interesting way.

The first time you heard the term *literature review*, you may have been somewhat confused. You may be used to thinking of literature as fiction, works that you read for pleasure or in an English or foreign-language class. Academics, however, use the term *literature* to refer to a scholarly body of work. In your search so far, you have been identifying the literature—essential books and articles I have been calling "sources"—for answering your question. No empirical research paper goes forward without this section, as you must literally demonstrate that your work "sit[s] on the shoulders of giants." In fact, as you read literature reviews (embedded in your sources), you will often notice that scholars explain the literature or scholarship on their research questions, linking their writing to classic works as well as the books and articles everyone seems to be talking about at a particular moment in (intellectual) history. You should try to do that too.[1] If you haven't spent sufficient time in the preparation of your AB mulling over your relevant introductory textbooks (for Gabriela and Zoe, their American government textbooks; for Kevin, an introduction to comparative politics; and for Max, global politics), as well as any specialized courses (for Gabriela and Zoe, again, any number of classes related to parties, campaigns, and elections; for Kevin, any class on revolutions, social movements, the media and politics, or politics in the Middle East; and for Max, a course on international security, Russian politics, foreign policy, or theories of international politics), do it now. In these classes, you likely learned about fundamental debates and schools of thought that can help you both interpret and organize the relevant literature.

There is no magic formula for answering your question and dividing the field. In the last chapter, I asked you to find the fundamental factor and the brief explanation, and I told you about "IIIE"—interests, institutions, ideas, and economics—which are often key factors in explanations. What is essential for writing the LR is finding good works that answer *your* question. These authors, who are concerned with the same issues that you are, will lay out the debate for you, particularly in their own literature reviews and their characterizations of their own contentions and those of the scholars against whom they are arguing. Thus, working hard to find excellent sources is essential, and thinking carefully about how participants in the debate about your question frame their answers is crucially important.

Our student examples here can be instructive. In answering the question "Why is U.S. politics so polarized now, and what are the consequences of polarization?" Gabriela found four answers: first, scholars arguing that elites were to blame and that their behavior imperiled representation; second, a group that moves the blame from the agents to the structures, faulting the American party and electoral system; third, observers who argue that citizens have become more engaged and partisan and that these developments are good for democracy; and last, those who agree that people are involved but worry that a new kind of intolerance is pervading politics, which reflects the decline in social capital and undermines careful deliberation. While Gabriela found some of the schools easily after going back to Stossel, looking at Edwards, and reading Abramowitz (and his points sounded familiar, given what she had read in her American government text), more digging led her to her last school. Then, she had to sit and think for a while about how to capture the essence of all these arguments (the answers to her questions) in coming up with labels. She succeeded, and now she is ready to write her LR.

THE FUNDAMENTALS OF THE LITERATURE REVIEW

In this first substantive section of the research paper, your goal is to write a coherent essay that typically answers these four fundamental sets of questions:

1. What is the literature on your main concept or what are the different schools of thought that have developed in response to your RQ, in both its general and its specific (if possible) forms? Who are the most important authors identified with each school, and how have they influenced subsequent scholarship?

2. How would each school answer your question? (The label for the school should be associated with the essence of its response.)

3. What are the strengths and weaknesses of the answers of each school?

4. Which school's argument is the best for your purposes and why, or which school would you like to continue to pursue and why?

Let's take some time to understand each of these questions better. The first one assumes that you will communicate your RQ in your section. It acknowledges that you have found schools that provide relatively coherent answers to your question. While you need to identify the authors who are central to each school, you typically don't organize the LR around them, as in "Smith argues X, but Johnson states Y, and Brown says Z matters." You need to find a group that coheres around an argument, an answer to your Research Question. This is why I ask you to spend so much time thinking about your sources when you are writing the AB. If you have a good classification scheme, labels (highlighting the fundamental factors) for the schools, and summaries already, writing the LR is easy.

Please note, also, that question 1 recognizes that you need to consider what scholars say about the general concept at stake in your question as well as some of the details of the specific instances you are interested in studying. For instance, you may remember that Kevin posed a question about the 2011 uprisings in the Middle East and North Africa (MENA). Well, while this tumult is still rather recent, there is a huge body of work on revolutions and the subset of color revolutions (i.e., nonviolent attempts at system overthrow). Kevin's work will not be complete unless he taps into the classics from the older conceptual literature, in addition to examining what has been written about 2011.

As you lay out your different schools of thought, you should also provide their answers to your RQ. Stay focused on characterizing the answers and using the replies to group your sources. Being able to state the basic answer and see how scholars differ in replying is key here. Sometimes, students think that if they just keep reading more on their topics, they will be OK. As you can see from the AB experience, you must be more focused now. You want answers to your question, and if you haven't found any (or if they all seem to agree), then you have a problem. Predicting exactly what is wrong is difficult, but typically the lack of a variety of answers means you need to find other (perhaps more or wholly different) sources and maybe adjust your question. It could also indicate that you need to read more carefully and that you need some help understanding the materials. Still, you should not ignore your inability to find answers and group them into schools. Don't assume it will somehow get better. Take some action now. Any combination of the strategies of spending more time (using the various methods suggested in chapter 3) and getting assistance from your professor or reference librarian will help. Please, however, do not assume that others will do the work for you. Faculty and librarians will guide you, but it is neither their jobs nor their goal to tell you what to do. They want to give you tools to enable you to move forward. Thus, before you seek help, you must have questions, and you must have put in significant effort.

Returning to our set of objectives for the LR, the third one is to evaluate the quality of each of these answers. This one is tricky because students often make up their minds about an approach too early and try to skew their discussion of it when they first introduce it. My goal is for you to introduce and explain the school with as little bias as possible. In fact, when you present a school, you should have no words of judgment in your discussion, and you should explain it *as one of its adherents would.* Try to get inside the heads of those scholars and see why this group of very smart people finds this perspective compelling. After you have approached each school with an open mind and given its adherents their chance to convince you, you must take on the task of evaluating the schools. Does each response make sense logically? If not, explain why. Also, does an answer seem to be empirically correct, at least when applied to some cases? (This is not the place for evaluating how well your argument fits the specific reality you are interested in, although if an approach is clearly not applicable to your favored situation, you should note its inadequacy.)

Last, one of the goals of the LR is to have criteria for limiting what you will study. Remember our quotation about giants? Well, if each school is analogous to a behemoth, you need to pick only one to sit on. Typically, you don't have the capacity to work in multiple, different theoretical traditions (just as you physically can't straddle between two giants), so you have to choose. Sometimes, this choice will be relatively easy. You will likely perceive one school to be best, given the analysis that you did in response to the third question.[2] Other times, however, you won't be sure that one answer is superior, yet you will still need to make a choice. Then, you have to state the criteria you are using for pursuing one approach and not the others. One way of choosing is deciding that one approach is new and understudied; another reason for selecting may be that a certain argument is currently getting the most attention in the popular media or from policy makers, and you would like to subject it to scholarly attention. Whatever your reasons, you need to explain them and use them to help you choose. Typically, though, authors proceed by concluding that one school is logically and empirically best.

In the end, remember that this type of essay—one that evaluates conceptual or theoretical approaches—is probably familiar to you. You have likely taken essay exams in which you were asked to explain the different answers to a question or different interpretations of a key concept, assess them, and make a final judgment, on the basis of logic and evidence, in which you state which one you prefer. Thus, you have already had practice in this type of writing and thinking.

WRITING THE LITERATURE REVIEW

As was already mentioned, when you write this section (and any other), you are trying to write some text that could serve as a stand-alone essay—with a purpose all its own—but that also performs an essential part of the greater whole: to communicate the conceptual basis of your research. Because this is the first section you are writing for the paper, we will discuss not only what is specific to this section (the previous examination and explanation of the four key questions above) but also what is common to any essay: the LR needs its own title, introduction, and conclusion. While you will find an extended discussion of how to write each of these important parts of the whole paper in chapter 9, consider this an important preview.

When writing longer papers, you use headings to set off sections (making the work easier to write, read, and understand), communicate the structure of the essay, and keep your focus. What is a good title for an LR? You may think, "'Literature Review,' that's perfect." Well, as you were reading the scholarly works, did you see many published authors who used that title in their papers? Typically, authors use more informative headings, just like you would use a more specific title than simply "Essay 1" for the first essay that you wrote for one of your classes. Good titles (just like good research papers) do not simply describe the contents; they communicate the purpose and usually the argument. The objective of the LR is to lay out and explain the scholarly answers to your RQ, assess their quality, and come to some conclusion about which one you will pursue further. Because of the emphasis here on understanding the literature, classifying it, and explaining the multiple arguments, I suggest that LR headings revolve around the various approaches to your question and not your conclusion or favorite school.

Gabriela, the student whose draft AB we've read, could offer the following titles for the LR section: "Polarization and Its Effects: Four Views" and "Why American Politics Is Polarized and What It Means for Politics." Both of these headings are far better than the purely descriptive "Polarization in America and Its Effects." Can you see why? This third title does not capture what the section is really about. This part of the paper is looking at explanations for polarization and assessing its implications; it is not simply describing each. Something to notice from Gabriela's exercise in title writing is that she doesn't have just one Research Question but two—why polarization occurs and what its effects are. Gabriela wants to think before she proceeds further: does she want to have two questions, and can she handle both? These are questions about her desired focus (is she interested in both questions, or should she simply concentrate on one?) and the scope of the paper (how much time does she have, and how long should the paper be?). She may be able to choose herself, or perhaps when her professor assesses her RQ and her AB, the feedback will steer Gabriela in one direction. Typically, in writing their LRs, students must choose what exactly their question(s) will be and whether they will answer more than one.

After the title, you need to provide an introduction, which serves as an overview to this section. For the LR, then, the introduction explains that (1) there is a scholarly debate on your RQ, and there are roughly X number of schools; (2) each school offers a specific answer to your question (and be sure to convey precisely what that response is); (3) the approaches have various strengths and weaknesses (with some brief specifics); but (4) one school seems to be the best one or is the most compelling to investigate for these reasons. Notice how closely the introduction mirrors what your purpose is. Of course, the introduction expresses these points in brief. You develop them further in the rest of the section, and the last element is the main focus as you conclude your LR, although your conclusion also reminds the reader a bit of what the section's goals were. Also important to realize is that your introduction contains the *thesis for this section*, and for all students the basic argument in the LR is just about the same. It is "the scholarship on my question can be divided into X schools." (That part of the thesis you can include as your opening sentence or near the beginning of the first paragraph. The final part of the thesis belongs at the end of the LR introductory paragraph and it is "School Y is the preferred school because" (fill in your reasons). Of course, you can include these ideas in a more elegant way, but this basic information must be in that first paragraph of the LR so that both you and the reader have an understanding of the field and know briefly, at the outset, where you stand on the literature and why.

As you move beyond the introduction, you may think that all you need to do is string together the summaries of the works in your bibliography. A more sophisticated approach is to focus on explaining each *school*, using the sources to illustrate different elements of that intellectual approach. Remember, a school of thought is an answer to your Research Question that many authors hold, so you need to explain the answer and show why these scholars agree. This section also assesses the logical strengths and weaknesses of the answers and then ultimately settles on (concludes with) one approach that the author finds particularly compelling. And don't simply assert that one is better or preferred; my students often make this mistake until I correct them. You need to explain and justify why your chosen approach should be pursued further.

There are several ways of organizing the LR. One is to present the approaches in chronological order, as a means of showing the historical development of an area of inquiry. Another is to mention and discuss the schools from the least to the most preferred. If your instructor has not identified a way to proceed, choose the order that best works to highlight the debate and makes your tasks (of introducing the schools, the various arguments, their strengths and weaknesses, and your preferred position) easiest for you.

As I noted earlier, when you are first setting out a perspective, you should discuss a school in its most favorable light. To give each school a fair chance, I recommend that you present all of them before you begin the evaluation. Moreover, as I noted above, you should try to think like a member of each school. Thereafter, when you have examined the strengths of each approach, you can assess them critically, particularly with respect to their logic and explanatory power (for cases other than the ones you want to study). If you wait, you will reduce the risk of mixing the analysis with the exposition, in other words the explanation of the school's argument. In addition, if you try very hard to respect each perspective, I am hoping that you will move beyond your initial intellectual prejudices.[3]

In addition to knowing what it should contain, the best way to understand how to write the LR is to look at good examples and model your work on them. In preparing your AB, you have surely found sources that have literature review sections (for articles) or chapters (in monographs) that are organized as I have suggested and accomplish the goals I have laid out for you. Because matching a scholarly example might seem intimidating, I offer you here two student examples. First, let's look at the introduction to Gabriela's LR, which gives you excellent insight into her whole section.

Understanding Polarization in Contemporary America: Four Perspectives

Scholars advance four explanations to account for the division and incivility in contemporary U.S. politics, three of which focus on agents and their ideology and behavior, while a fourth highlights the role of structures. The first two schools claim that citizens have become more ideological and intolerant, and they drive contemporary polarization. To adherents of the Citizen Engagement School, Americans are taking direct steps to be involved in politics, particularly at the extremes, by volunteering or donating money to various causes and are walling themselves off from others with different ideas (Abramowitz 2010; Stossel 2008; Yglesias 2007). A related approach looks more to the effects of this isolation on society as a whole. Building on Robert Putnam's ideas, the Social Capital School argues that the decrease in interaction among different types of individuals undermines the ability of citizens to trust one another and seek what is best for the community (Putnam 1995; Putnam with Leonardi and Nanetti 1994; Mutz 2006). The third, the Elite School, argues that citizens are simply responding to politicians, pollsters, and media commentators who have been using increasingly inflammatory and nasty speech and have raised the stakes on every issue to serve their own interests and undermine the potential for compromise (Fiorina with Abrams 2009; Fiorina with Abrams and Pope 2006). Americans here are viewed as middle of the road and well mixed throughout the land, with some authors, such as Robinson and Ellis (2004), claiming that America is neither blue nor red but mostly purple. Finally, the last school points not to agents—people, whether they are citizens or elites—as the source of increased polarization but to American party and electoral institutions, which set the rules for granting political power and create a system to which elites and citizens respond (Edwards 2012). While each of these perspectives makes compelling arguments, this last, the Party and

Electoral Systems School, is most convincing because recent experience seems to confirm that party hardliners and big money bring out the extremists, who then refuse to compromise and drive polarization.[4]

Clearly, Gabriela has taken my basic advice well. She has an appropriate section heading that focuses on her central concept and the scholarly debate around it. Then, we see the paragraph structured as suggested, with a first sentence that establishes the concept and the number of schools and a final one that provides us with her decision about which one she will pursue and why. In other words, Gabriela briefly and effectively communicates her question for this section: How have scholars studied polarization in American politics, which answer is best, and why? In between her first and last sentences, she names her schools and provides a brief summary of their arguments, as well as citations of the major works. Of course, she will tell us more about each of these approaches, but in the introduction, she is establishing her classification system and briefly explaining each school. Sometimes students think that the introduction should be enough of a Literature Review, but they are mistaken. A research paper requires a more thorough discussion of both the school and its strengths and weaknesses. The introduction provides a useful preview, for both the reader and you, because it requires you to state concisely the basics of each school and your judgments. Last, I want you to notice that Gabriela has changed the order of her schools here from what she had in her AB. In her AB, she hadn't yet figured out which one she preferred, while here, she has decided to save her favorite for last and group the two citizen-centric schools together. The order of the schools that Gabriela establishes in the introduction will follow her throughout the section.

Because understanding the structure and purpose of the LR (and their interrelationship) is so important for not only writing your own but also reading others' research, I want to share another example. With Gabriela, you have seen her AB, and you can easily see how this introductory paragraph emerged. Now, I want to show you Kevin's introductory paragraph as well as the exposition of one of his schools. By examining this example, you can see what is common to all LR introductions, while also getting a "taste" for reading research with which you might not be wholly familiar. I am hoping that both examples will lead you to a better understanding of the LR and provide you with useful models for writing your own complete section. Again, what I am providing here are excerpts; your LR will be longer, with a section heading, an introduction, expositions (discussions of each school), analyses of the strengths and weaknesses of the schools, and a conclusion.

Remember that Kevin wanted to explore why the uprisings of 2011 occurred, and he was particularly interested in the effects of social media. After writing his AB and thinking carefully about the literature, this is how he decided to start his LR:

The Power behind the People: Six Scholarly Explanations of the Arab Spring

Although the world watched with surprise as the Arab Spring erupted in 2011, students of revolution and mobilization have long sought to understand why and under what conditions citizens gather and work together to overthrow their repressive leaders. As Jack Goldstone (2001, 140) explains in his comprehensive review of the literature, until the 1980s, most scholars pointed to structural factors such as the distribution of power in the international system (Skocpol 1979) or socioeconomic conditions (Moore 1967; Huntington 1997; Ross 2001) as the most important causes of uprisings and political change. For the past 30 years, however, the focus has shifted to emphasize the role of individuals. More recently, academics have attributed sudden political upheavals to the work of agents, whether they are social movement leaders (O'Donnell and Schmitter 1986; Karl 2005; Bunce and Wolchik 2006) or more ordinary citizen activists responding to their own sense of justice and power (Havel 1978; Kuran 1991). In the case of the Middle East and North African (MENA) countries, while some contemporary analysts stress the role of domestic political structures, in other words, the nature of the authoritarian leaderships in each country and the ways in which they are connected to key constituencies in society (Anderson 2011; Gause 2011; Geddes 2004), others believe that, in conjunction with the people power that earlier scholars mentioned, technological changes—including satellite TV, cell phones, and social media—helped democratize information, giving citizens access to interpretations of current events that varied from official propaganda and made organizing and mobilizing in 2011 different (Lynch 2012). Thus, the media revolution is the essential factor in enabling people to challenge and sometimes topple long-standing, authoritarian MENA regimes.

Kevin has approached his Literature Review in a slightly different way from Gabriela; he hasn't taken my advice as literally, although this excerpt certainly has what I would expect from an LR. Perhaps most surprising is that in his introductory paragraph, he doesn't name each school here, but he can (and must) do that in his expositions. Part of the reason for the different form was that Kevin found a great literature review by the highly influential revolution scholar Jack Goldstone,[5] which told him that there were many possible schools but that the field was generally divided in two big ways (structure- vs. agent-based arguments) and that these approaches had been dominant at different times. But Kevin does give you an idea of six schools in his opening—see his heading and note that his text claims two structural schools, two agent-centered approaches, and then two approaches (one structure, one combining agents and new technologies/structures) that emerge from the literature specific to 2011. Because Kevin has provided such clear understandings of the basics of each approach, I am sure you can offer labels for his schools—International Structure, Socioeconomic Structure, Elite, People Power, Domestic Structure, and Media Empower Activists—and will be able to follow him in the rest of the essay. Last, he finished the paragraph by communicating his preferred approach (and you can infer it from the order). Thus, Kevin has found another, effective way to proceed.

Now let's see how Kevin explained one of his schools of thought. We'll jump to his exposition of the fifth school.

Like scholars of revolution in general, those studying 2011 see the importance of both structures and agents. According to adherents of a fifth, Domestic Structures, school, the internal politics and institutional arrangements in MENA countries account for why and how these states experienced revolution and which ones were more vulnerable to political unrest. Highlighting the political diversity among authoritarians, Barbara Geddes's work helps explain that they collapsed in different ways, and, in fact, she argues (prior to the Arab Spring) that military regimes are far more susceptible to a peaceful democratic transition than are either personalist (those in which an individual and his family dominated) or single-party-dominated regimes. Geddes notes that the military as an institution had interests distinct from the leader and would often abandon the ruler if it believed that the armed forces had a better political future in the new regime without the dictator. In the other two types of authoritarianism, the structures—links between ruler, the elite, and ruled—were different. In personalist dictatorships, the ties between the ruler and the elite were those of blood, and they could not abandon their connections and expect to remain in power (or even alive) if the head were removed, because those not directly connected to the regime were typically severely repressed by and resentful of the system. In single-party regimes, party members were usually more tied to the system than were military officials, but less identified with it than family members in the personalist arrangement. Thus, military-based systems would be more likely to experience revolutions that proceeded with the help of the professional military, while in personalist dictatorships, the members of the elite would put up the bloodiest of fights to remain in power.

Arguing in a manner consistent with Geddes, MENA experts Lisa Anderson (2011) and Gregory Gause (2011) contend that domestic

(Continued)

(Continued)

structures affected what happened in Tunisia, Egypt, and Libya, all countries that were in turmoil when they were writing. They both underplay the role of economic challenges and social media for explaining what happened and stress the importance of the differences in the regimes. For Anderson, the institutional differences account for the uprisings and how they unfolded. While both Tunisia and Libya were personalist regimes with enormous corruption, Tunisia had an excellent educational system and a well-functioning bureaucracy, as opposed to the highly diverse society, geographically dispersed population centers, and deficient state institutions of Libya. As the challenge emerged in Tunisia, ordinary people and low-ranking members of the regime were united in the opposition to the ruling family, while in Libya, Qaddafi's formula for rule was much more clearly based on patronage through blood ties, and the diversity and division came to the fore with the challenge to his dominance, opening civil war in Libya. In Egypt, on the other hand, the military ultimately supported the protesters against the regime and Mubarak's thugs, including the police. Thus, the military, along with the protesters and the Muslim Brotherhood, emerged as important actors in the postrevolutionary era (Anderson 2011). Gause (2011) notes the importance of the military in both Tunisia and Egypt and sees the fact that it sided with the protesters as being very important in toppling the dictators. In addition, Gause also stresses the role of ethnic and religious homogeneity in Tunisia and Egypt, other elements of the domestic structure, which helped maintain the army's loyalty to the nation as opposed to the ruler or their particular ethnic group or clan. As Gause explains,

> In divided societies, where the regime represents an ethnic, sectarian, or regional minority and has built an officer corps dominated by that overrepresented minority, the armies have thus far backed their regimes.

Thus, Tunisian and Egyptian protesters could count on the sympathy of their national armies, while those in countries with ethnic, religious, and clan divisions—like Jordan, Bahrain, and Saudi Arabia, respectively—could not. In sum, for both Anderson and Gause, domestic structures, specifically the nature of the links between powerful constituents and the leadership, explain why uprisings occurred and why some were more successful than others.

What should we note about this continuation of Kevin's LR? Importantly, Kevin has a transition that links the discussion of his new school with what came before. He also has signal words to tell the reader that this is the fifth school (I know I lose track when there are more than three), and he names the approach. Then he explains the relevant argument for answering the question. Notice how nicely Kevin provides some intellectual history here by including Geddes and mentions both the similarities and the different emphases of Anderson and Gause. Perhaps you winced when you saw the Gause quotation in this text, but while writing in your own words is preferred (and Kevin has done that throughout most of the essay), he must have decided that this piece of information was too critical and that he couldn't rewrite it without plagiarizing. So he included it verbatim, which is fine because Kevin has not relied on too many other quotations. Last, Kevin ends the exposition on a strong note by reminding us what the crucial elements of this fifth school are.

To finish our analysis of the LR, let's look at Kevin's conclusion. At this point, we can assume that he has named and explained all six of his schools. He has even assessed their strengths and weaknesses, and now he is summing up and helping the reader and himself transition to the next phase of his work, where he has a preferred answer to his RQ and will pursue that school and its argument closely in the rest of the paper.

Thus, while the agent-structure debate characterizes the literature on revolution, the most useful approach for thinking about the 2011 uprisings in MENA seems to be the final, Media Empower Activists, school. Structural conditions—like the balance of power, economic conditions, or even domestic structures—seem to account only for so much. All countries in the world face the same global structural conditions, with American power eroding and democratic values sporadically ebbing and flowing, but for some reason, other regions did not erupt in demands for change. Similarly, poverty and demographic challenge face countries throughout sub-Saharan Africa, South Asia, and Central Asia in addition to the Arab states, but they remained stable. Activists, too, have been seeking to promote democratic change in various parts of the world, with varying degrees of success, but they didn't succeed in MENA until there was a great confluence of technological developments. While domestic structures appear important in understanding why revolutions turn out as they do, they seem less to be able to predict when and why uprisings emerge, even in the case of 2011. As Lynch (2012) explains, the rise of satellite TV and the unity that emerged as result of the new Palestinian intifada and the Iraq War that these stations broadcast helped citizens of MENA believe they were interconnected. They also provided alternative sources of information from state propaganda. In addition, social media also undermined the official stories, helped citizens see that they were not alone in their dissatisfaction, and, perhaps most important, gave activists and ordinary people an organizing tool. Together, the media and the people were most essential for challenging these regimes and account for the Arab Spring.

In this last paragraph, Kevin reminds the reader of his RQ and the answers he found. He briefly explains the weaknesses in the schools he is leaving behind and restates why he prefers the sixth school. Kevin finishes strongly, leaving no doubt in the reader's or his mind as to where he is heading. I want to emphasize, however, that I have seen students write equally convinced first drafts of the LR, only to rethink their conclusions as they work on the next stage and keep reading. Changing your mind and rewriting the conclusion of your LR is fine at this point. Once you design the study (on the basis of this preferred argument), however, you are committed to that approach. So, just be aware that you have a little time to spiral back and rethink, but at a certain point, the possibility of changing your argument will be closed. And that is precisely as you want it! To finish, you have to pursue one thesis. Notice here that I am not telling you that your argument has to be right, just that you have to have reasons for preferring it. More on that difference in future chapters.

PRACTICAL SUMMARY

Here, you have learned how to write an LR. This task is highly dependent on the work you have done so far, designing a good Research Question, finding appropriate literature, and summarizing the answers to this question. If you haven't had success in the previous stages, then you will have difficulties in the process of writing the LR as well as in putting forth a good one. Look at how much Gabriela's and Kevin's essays depend on the quality of their work so far. If you have doubts about your question, your literature, or your summaries, determine your weaknesses and then address them, either on your own or with help. Speak to your professor and/or a reference librarian early in the process, and keep in mind that refining the question, finding literature, and understanding it is an ongoing process. Ignoring any deficiencies will only hold you back and create snowballing (yes, unfortunately, it's true!) difficulties for you.

Central to writing the LR is finding excellent (i.e., appropriate and important) works, identifying the most important scholars involved in the debate, understanding the different answers to your RQ these authors posit, and placing these scholars into schools of thought by determining the key factors or underlying points that unite and divide them. You now know how and where to find academic authors and how to make sense of debates. In addition, the chapter gave you the four objectives you need to satisfy (and the questions that will help you accomplish that goal), showed how Gabriela's AB work would prepare her for writing the introduction to her LR, and included multiple excerpts of Kevin's LR. You also learned that all sections will have substantive headings (not simply named after the function of the part, such as "Literature Review") and that longer ones will also have their own introductions and conclusions, and we gave special attention to the writing of these fundamentals here. The steps to follow when you write the LR are laid out in the four questions above (and are included in the recipe below).

RECIPE 3: LITERATURE REVIEW

INGREDIENTS

- Your Research Question
- Your Annotated Bibliography
- Access to Gabriela's and Kevin's excerpts of the LR
- Access to online examples of the LR

INSTRUCTIONS

1. Looking carefully at your AB, think again about how many schools of thought you have, what they should be called, and how they should be arranged. You might choose to combine some, divide others, change the order so that you can more effectively explain them and lead yourself and your readers to the desired conclusion. Remember: you will make some adjustments and revisions in the process of writing, but do your best to start strong by doing your work steadily and seriously from the outset.

2. Remember that your focus on the LR is to explain the scholarly debate around your RQ and to arrive at an approach you want to pursue. Create your section outline on the basis of the RQ and AB, which will include four basic parts:

   a. Introduction

   b. Expositions (the longest subsection)

   c. Analysis of the schools

   d. Conclusion

Note that I prefer the analysis to be separate from the expositions, so that you will be as unbiased as possible when you explain the schools and to give you more time to think through the strengths and weaknesses of the different approaches. You or your professor might prefer to integrate the assessments into the exposition. There is no "right" way, and you should proceed as instructed or as works best for your question. Also realize that your introduction contains embedded within it this outline. Don't forget that you also need a substantive title to communicate the Research Question and debate.

3. If you feel comfortable with your overview of the whole section, write your introduction and heading first. If not, skip this stage and come back later. Use the recommendations—the basic formula for the first and last sentences— as well as Gabriela's and Kevin's examples to help you. It is fine to mimic them; that's why I include them. Just as when you begin cooking, you follow a recipe (like these examples) exactly. As you become a more accomplished cook and writer, you can stray from the guides.

4. If you are still not understanding or "seeing" the interconnections within the literature, start writing the expositions. Begin with the school with which you feel most comfortable, then write the others. The goal is to increase your understanding as you write. You will likely find that you have to go back to some sources to improve your knowledge of a school. Believe me, you want to do that now and be confident of what you write in the LR. I can't tell you how many times a research paper goes astray because a student never bothered to understand the literature well. As you write the expositions, keep thinking about whether your labels for the schools are appropriate (I'm guessing you'll refine them as your understanding of the approaches becomes more sophisticated) and consider the order that is best for presenting your schools. I recommend proceeding from least preferred to most, but you may have a different logic for organizing yours. Use Kevin's example to help you, but remember, I have included his exposition of only one school. He had to do this six times, and Gabriela had to write four.

5. If you now realize that you lack a diversity of scholarly answers, go back and find some additional ones that make different arguments. Find them by looking more carefully at your existing sources and seeing whom your authors are arguing against. You don't need to write these up as formal entries in your AB, but you need to use the techniques offered in chapter 3 for summarizing the sources and keeping track of their information to incorporate it in your LR. Remember, you need at least three schools of thought that provide different answers to your Research Question.

6. Write your assessment of the strengths and weaknesses of the schools. Use Kevin's brief discussion to help you see the kinds of points you should be making. Thinking about your schools, if one is clearly stronger (you can't just assert that it is), then you have found your preferred approach. If not, you need to think of another criterion for making a choice. Perhaps you will choose the one that is currently most talked about or the one that is the newest argument. Ultimately, you must have an explicit reason for proceeding as you do.

7. If you haven't written your introduction, do so now, using the examples of LR introductions and reflecting on what you have learned from writing and assessing.

8. Write your conclusion using Kevin's as a model. Feel free to mimic it.

9. Read the pieces of your LR as a whole and compare them with the models you have. Do you have all the parts of the LR, as well as a substantive title? Have you accomplished what you should in each of the distinct elements of the outline (introduction, exposition, analyses, and conclusion)?

10. Make revisions to improve the logic and argument of the section and edit for good style.

11. When your section reads like an essay that lists the three or more most important scholarly answers to your Research Question, describes what each school asserts, and states which one you prefer, you are done. Remember that you will likely return to revise and refine your ideas and expressions at a later date, but if you have this basic structure down, you are well on your way to having a good Literature Review.

EXERCISES

1. To the best of your ability, write the introduction to the Literature Review for Max's or Zoe's project. Also develop a heading for this section.

2. Thinking back to your Introduction to Global Politics class and using realism, liberalism, and constructivism as your schools, write the introduction to a Literature Review that answers the question "Why or under what conditions do states cooperate?" What would be a good heading for this section?

3. Using your own AB, write the introduction and the exposition of one school of thought for your Literature Review. Develop a heading for your LR section.

NOTES

1. Notice that Gabriela does this by bringing Putnam's works into her Annotated Bibliography and showing how Mutz's book derives from Putnam's research.
2. Under some conditions, faculty may not want you to combine two or more schools. Be clear about whether your instructor expects you to pick one alone or would be satisfied with some integrated approach.
3. Certainly, this is not an easy task. Social psychologists tell us that our first impressions are hard to move beyond. Still, the best you can do is to proceed with respect and give each approach its best chance to make its case. You may want to imagine that you are the attorney for each school, its advocate, laying out its explanation. Thereafter, you can serve as jury when all the evidence is available. Be mindful, however, that juries are supposed to leave their biases behind them and make their decisions on the basis of the information presented.
4. Choosing a preferred school took Gabriela a good while, so she originally struggled with the order of presentation. She realizes that she might change her mind as she works on the model and keeps thinking about her thesis—party and electoral systems cause polarization. If she does make a new choice, Gabriela will have to change the order and rewrite the final sentence. Neither will be hard, but she must keep track of how her decisions affect the overall paper.
5. Jack A. Goldstone, "Toward a Fourth Generation of Revolutionary Theory," *Annual Review of Political Science 4 1* (2001): 139-87.

Effectively Distilling Your Argument

The Thesis, Model, and Hypothesis

As we proceed in this paper-writing marathon, finishing the Literature Review (LR) is like running the first eight miles. You've completed a little less than a third of the race, and you can see a long, slightly upward sloping stretch in front of you. But you are well trained and ready for this challenge. You will persevere by proceeding steadily and remembering that the parts of the paper are interrelated in ways that help you move from one phase to the next. The conclusion of the LR leads the writer to a bottom line: one answer to the Research Question (RQ) appears best to pursue. In effect, that conclusion is the fundamental *argument* or *thesis* you will be sustaining, evaluating, or testing in your research paper.[1] Stating this conclusion in the LR is often sufficient for guiding experienced writers through the rest of the process. For less tested authors or for particularly complex arguments, the Model and Hypothesis (M&H) section is brief but important. It forces the author to state precisely what she or he expects to find. In an empirical paper, that statement will come in two forms—in a picture or flow diagram (*model*) and in words (*hypothesis*).

THE THESIS

Almost all of the writing (except creative writing, i.e., fiction) you do in college will have a *thesis* or an *argument*, two terms used interchangeably in this book.[2] A thesis is a contentious statement, that is, a declaration or description with which reasonable people could disagree. A thesis can be either a normative claim or an empirically verifiable contention. For our purposes, a hypothesis is a special type of thesis that explores the connections between the key factors that it names. If you are investigating a hypothesis, you will try to determine whether these elements are correlated or causally connected.

You are used to reading works with theses, as you are exposed to them in the essays you read for classes. Op-ed pieces in newspapers, journals of opinion, and journals, particularly ones that minimize footnotes, may lack bibliographies and are written for more general audiences (such as *Social Policy, Foreign Affairs, Current History,* and *Foreign Policy*).[3] Political scientists, too, develop these types of arguments; however, we will see that to be published in the most prestigious journals, typically, authors in American, comparative, and global politics must assert hypotheses.

When writing your research paper, your thesis is both (1) your preferred answer to the RQ and, ultimately, (2) your assessment of whether the data show that it holds.[4] You have examined potential replies in the Literature Review and concluded that one is most compelling. You made that judgment on the basis of your assessment of the quality of the argument's logic and its ability to account for similar occurrences of the phenomenon in question. Because there is debate about what is the best response, you know that this thesis is contentious. As we saw in chapter 4, Gabriela is arguing that party and electoral structures explain the polarization in contemporary U.S. politics, and Kevin is maintaining that social media enabled activists to topple governments in the Middle East and North Africa (MENA) in 2011. Their Literature Reviews tell us that not all scholars agree with these claims. Gabriela found three competing arguments, and Kevin five. The goal now for these students is to state their hypotheses clearly so that each will be able to design an appropriate test for determining whether the available information supports her or his contention. Thus, only through the evaluation of data will the students be able to assert the second part of their full theses, which will appear in the Introductions of their papers.

THE MODEL

While *thesis* or *argument* is the broad term for the contention that you are investigating throughout your research, I will use another set of terms for work that is explicitly and self-consciously empirical. Theory-advancing research and public policy research explore correlations (the simultaneous varying of factors) and causations (when changes in one phenomenon lead to variations in another) and seek to chart carefully the relationships between variables. Frequently, scholars use the language of science when engaging in their research and explaining it to others. In chapter 2, we noted that your research should seek to explain a particular phenomenon or solve some puzzle. In its most basic form, an empirical argument can be reduced to relationships between *variables*, where a variable is anything that can vary or change in value. What you are trying to explain is the effect or the *dependent variable*. This effect depends on some other factors (the causes), and it is a variable because if the value of the causes change, so too will the effect. The cause is referred to as the *independent variable*.[5]

Upon first consideration, thinking of concepts in political science as variables with values can be quite strange for students. Probably, you are used to conceiving of variables as something that you find only in math class—x or y—and values bring up the idea of numbers. Most political science majors are attracted to this subject because they believe, among other things, that this discipline will be about words, not manipulating equations with numbers. But concepts in political science can be variables and take on values. In saying that they can be variables I am simply noting that they can change. Take, for instance, the concept of party identification. In the United States, there is more than one party, and people identify with different ones or have no attachment to parties at all. Thus, the values that the variable party identification in the United States can be are Republican, Democratic, Independent, other, and none. While a large number of variables in political science cannot be measured in numbers, there are also many that can be quantified. Voter turnout, presidential popularity, educational outcomes, Supreme Court voting patterns, election results, and budget deficits are just a few examples. Other important concepts can vary by degree, for instance, partisanship (strong to weak) or level of violence (high to low). Given a particular time and place, these variables may take on different values.

In empirical research, literature reviews often divide the field into schools that identify one or more independent variables (key or causal factors) as more important than others. Moreover, the RQ asks about the dependent variable (effect). Thus, as a result of your Literature Review, you should be able to generate a number of independent variables that potentially have an impact on the phenomenon (a single dependent variable) in which you are interested. In effect, by performing a review of the literature, you have identified the information you need to develop a number of competing models. A model is the pictorial representation of your argument or thesis, reducing it to its bare bones.

You may wonder why you must develop a model if it follows so nicely from the LR. Well, in one sense, the model is a check on your work; it makes sure that you have done a good job on your Literature Review. Unfortunately, students sometimes use the LR to discuss in very abstract terms the ways different schools of thought conceive of politics, instead of focusing on how each perspective answers the RQ at hand. If you have done your LR correctly (by following the advice of looking for fundamental factors and stating clear answers to the question), and your question is seeking to explore the relationship between concepts, coming up with the variables will be easy. If you have improperly written this section, developing models will be very difficult. So if you're stuck on the model, then you know that you need to go back and redo your LR before proceeding with your research.

Let's think back to Gabriela and use her interests to look at the relationship between the Literature Review, variable identification, and models. Gabriela asserts that party and electoral institutions affect polarization, and she can generate the following model:

Type of Party Institutions

Type of Electoral Institutions → Level of Polarization in the United States

Please notice that in formulating the model, Gabriela transformed the factors into variables, things that can change. Thus, in the model section, she added the words *type* and *level of*. While some models investigate correlations, this one asserts that causation flows in a particular direction. To find that the arrow is reversed would not substantiate this model and would compel Gabriela to make a different argument.[6]

Moving to another student, Kevin concludes his LR with "Together, the media and the people were most essential for challenging these regimes and account for the Arab Spring." Like Gabriela, Kevin asserts two causal factors to explain uprisings in different states. His model would be as follows:

Level of Traditional and Social Media Influence

Level of Citizen Activism → Strength of the Uprising in 2011

As Kevin writes his model, he begins to realize that he has some questions to consider. Does he want to explain the uprising and its size, or does he want to understand the success of the revolution itself, whether the regime was toppled? As he proceeds, he will have to refine that dependent variable and consider what impact any of his changes have for his LR. If necessary, he will have to make adjustments in that section.

Both of our students here have two independent variables, and you certainly do not need to advance two causes. In fact, for the ease of performing the research, I encourage students to be as simple or *parsimonious* as possible. The more variables you insist are important, the more you have to analyze. Particularly in qualitative studies, obtaining information on many concepts is very difficult, so that is one reason I tell my students to assert no more than two causal factors. Also, both students have one dependent variable, and this *is* typical for research, as scholars are interested in understanding one phenomenon at a time.

Before we move on, let's remember our other two students from chapter 2, whose research we haven't followed as closely, but who have continued refining their ideas. Max is investigating contemporary Russian foreign policy and why that country intervenes when it does, while Zoe wants to understand whether American female legislators are more likely to support legislation on women's issues than are men. Those of you familiar with the global politics literature will find Max's argument and model familiar. In doing his literature search, Max found schools of thought consistent with the realist (focusing on material power position), liberal/domestic politics (looking at Vladimir Putin's links to powerful constituencies in Russia), and constructivist (emphasizing the role of national identity and preferred global norms) paradigms.[7] Convinced by the realists, Max asserted that the Russian power position determines whether it intervenes. When the balance of power favors Russia, it is likely to intervene. If not, it won't intervene. His model then is as follows:

Imbalance of Russia's Power Relative to Regional and Global Rivals $\rightarrow$ Likelihood of Intervention

Zoe's research was fundamentally concerned with whether electing women serves women's interests. Beginning with insights from Hanna Pitkin's (1967) classic work *The Concept of Representation* and working through the literature on minority representation, Zoe found two competing perspectives on what difference female legislators might make. The critical mass school asserted that underrepresented groups would have an influence on policy when their numbers reached a certain threshold in the legislature. An alternative approach, the critical action perspective, claimed that the "right type" of female representative was essential. Seconding that insight, Sarah Childs and Mona Lena Krook, and Kathleen A. Bratton, also found that just having a certain number of women was not enough, and the literature also suggested that ideologically sympathetic men could be advocates for women, too.[8] Zoe, realizing that she would likely have to look at both contentions in order to convince anyone of her findings, offered two models, the first for critical mass and the second for critical action:

Critical Mass

Relative Size of Female Group within the Legislative Body $\rightarrow$ Number of Bills Offered That Improve Women's Lot (Women's Issues Bills)

Critical Action

Gender of Legislator $\rightarrow$ Number of Bills Offered That Improve Women's Lot (Women's Issues Bills)

Going back to our students, we discern a range of models, some with two independent variables, others with a single causal factor. We can also see how closely the cause is related to the name of the school (and that name should help us identify the factor), and the effect is the issue or phenomenon that inspired the research and question. The models, however, might seem incomplete to you because they do not provide explicit information about the direction or the extent of the independent variable's effect on the dependent variable. Gabriela's model on its own doesn't explain which party and electoral institutions affect polarization and how. The same is true for the other student models, and that is why I ask you to communicate the nature of the relationship and the range of values the variables can take on in the hypothesis.

THE HYPOTHESIS

As noted before, the hypothesis is a particular type of thesis, one that asserts that a particular cause (or causes) either is correlated with or leads to certain effects. As a thesis, the hypothesis also provides an answer to the Research Question on the basis of what you learned in your Literature Review.

The easiest type of hypothesis[9] to understand is often stated in the following terms:

> **For positive relationships:** The more of X (the independent variable), the more of Y (the dependent variable).

> **For negative relationships:** The more of X (the independent variable), the less of Y (the dependent variable).

Kevin's and Max's models assert these types of positive relationships between the independent and dependent variables. Their hypotheses follow below:

> The greater the level of access to traditional and social media and the greater the people power (popular presence on the streets), the stronger will be the uprising against the government.

> The greater the imbalance of power in favor of Russia, the more likely Russia will intervene in post-Soviet states.

Writing his hypothesis made Kevin think, Am I really saying that the level of media access and the citizen effects occur simultaneously, or do I want to change my argument to assert that the media affect citizen activism, which *then* influences how strong the uprising is? The model for that alternative line of reasoning would be as follows:

| Level of Citizen Access to Traditional and Social Media | → | Level of Citizen Activism | → | Strength of the Uprising in 2011 |

Kevin has restated his model to include not only independent and dependent variables, but also an intervening one (level of citizen activism). As Kevin pondered his assertions, he began to wonder if level of citizen activism was distinguishable from the strength of the uprising and decided that he was really interested in whether the regime fell or not. Thus, he inserted two changes here, to eliminate the intervening variable after all and to conceive of his dependent variable slightly differently:

| Level of Citizen Access to Traditional & Social Media | → | Likelihood of Toppling the Regime |

Now, Kevin may tinker some more with both concepts, but his rethinking shows you why you need to take this stage seriously. It also reinforces the importance of spiraling through your work (thinking, writing, rethinking, and rewriting), in order to be absolutely clear about your ideas.

In sum, this first look at models and hypotheses shows that the Literature Review defines the variables and helps you put forth a model, indicating how variables influence one another. You are not plucking these linkages from thin air, as you have uncovered them in your previous research. Still, explicitly writing this relationship out helps you think precisely about your argument and, again, allows you to verify that your LR accomplishes what it should as well as forces you to clarifying precisely what you want to explain. Like Kevin, you may play with your model, make sure that your concepts are really distinct, and rethink your hypothesis, working between them to arrive at a clear statement of your argument. This consideration can take some time and can even occur as you move into the next stage of the process, but don't be afraid to refine. Also important to recognize is that Kevin and Max assert positive relationships between variables. Note that in making these contentions, each student is also asserting the converse: decreases in media access decrease the likelihood that the regime will fall, and a balance of power that is not in Russia's favor would make its intervention much less likely.[10]

For both of these hypotheses, we can think of all the values that the concepts can be—levels of citizen access to media, imbalance of power, and likelihoods—as occurring on a continuum, and thus we call these *continuous* (or *interval*) *variables*.[11] There are values for each that span a continuous spectrum and include all the gradations in between. But not all variables can be measured in this way; instead, some reflect *categories* in which we might be interested, and if you were wondering why we skipped the hypotheses from the other two students initially, the reason is that they use *category* or *discrete variables*.[12] For Gabriela's research, there are types of party and electoral systems (even within the U.S. context). From Edwards's work, what Gabriela learned is most important is the role party elites play in choosing candidates, funding elections, drawing districts, and disciplining members who stray from the party line. In essence, Edwards is saying that in the "old style," elites had more of a role in choosing candidates and were less important in funding, establishing districts, and disciplining. This system allowed politicians more freedom to act according to their conscience and provided more opportunity for compromise which resulted in less polarization (Edwards 2012). The new framework is the opposite, and the modern way leads to more polarization. So here, the hypothesis Gabriela would assert is that the contemporary party and election system lead to high levels of polarization, whereas the older system (which started breaking down in the Progressive era and continued to erode through the 1990s) causes less polarization. We would expect intermediate levels of polarization in that period of the transformation of the two systems during the twentieth century. As categories, Gabriela is saying that her independent variable (party and electoral system) can be new, old, or transitioning, and levels of polarization could take on the corresponding values of high, low, and intermediate. Note here that Gabriela is not looking for continuous, precise values for polarization but relative, category assessments of how badly divided U.S. politics is.

With Zoe, we see a model that links category concepts to continuous ones. Her competing independent variables—relative size of female legislative group and gender of legislator—are discrete variables. Depending on how fine a gradation Zoe wants, she can set the relative size in different ways. A simple way to begin is to think in terms of critical/noncritical (since that was the initial insight from the school, that there is a critical mass that matters), or she could choose high, medium, and low if she realizes that no one knows what the magic threshold is, so that she might be better off not trying to define it. For her second hypothesis, the insight is that certain types of women matter. There are a couple points here—that women make a difference and that some characteristic about them has an influence too. Thus, Zoe uses the term *gender*, not *sex*, here because for her, the issue is not just women or men but women identifying strongly with a feminist agenda. Here gender could have a range, distinguishing feminist and nonfeminist women and perhaps leaving men together in a single category. Zoe might have to explore that insight further and consider whether and where feminist men belong in her classification. Zoe, then, is investigating two hypotheses: if the number of women in the legislature is high, then the number of women's issues bills is high, while if the number of women is medium, then the number of women's issues bills is either high or very low (depending on whether this "medium" is enough to reach the critical mass), and if the number of women in the legislature is low, then the number of women's issues bills is very low. Again, with this argument, capturing the idea that there is a certain threshold that needs to be reached for anything to be achieved is important. That's why the drop-off as Zoe moves through the categories is not continuous but sudden. Regarding the critical issues, the hypothesis is that feminist women are more likely than other women and men to advance women's issue bills, so large numbers of feminist women will mean relatively many bills that improve the lot of girls and women. Notice that, here again, Zoe is reformulating the dependent variable in the second model because the case is different, not the size of the women's legislative group, but the representative herself or himself, and that requires the new focus on the probability of introducing legislation.

Note one last and interesting point about hypotheses: when you state one, you always give a hint as to which values of the independent variable are associated with which particular values of the dependent variables. So that you can think about variables, values, and how the value of the independent variable affects the dependent variable (which is the assertion in the hypothesis), I have summarized our students' efforts in Table 5.1.

Each paper, then, will make a contentious statement. If that argument is a causal or correlational one, the student should also (1) posit a model that isolates the variables (or key factors) and (2) state a hypothesis that explains the nature of the relationship between them.

Table 5.1   Models and Variable Values

Model	Possible Independent Variable Values	Corresponding Dependent Variable Values
Level of Citizen Access to Nonofficial Traditional and Social Media → Likelihood Regime Will Fall	If access is high	Expect high likelihood of collapse
	If access is low	Expect low likelihood of collapse
Level of Imbalance of Power → Likelihood of Russian Intervention	If high imbalance in Russia's favor	Expect high likelihood of intervention
	If power is about balanced or in favor of the target	Expect low likelihood of intervention
Type of Party and Electoral Institutions → Level of Polarization	If type is modern	Expect high polarization
	If type is old	Expect low polarization
	If type is transitioning	Expect moderate polarization
Relative Size of Female Group in Legislature → Number of Women's Interest Bills	If size reaches critical mass	Expect relatively many women's interest bills
	If size doesn't reach critical mass	Expect relatively few women's interest bills
Gender of Legislator → Propensity to Introduce a Women's Interest Bill	Feminist Women	Expect greater propensity
	Nonfeminist Women and Men	Expect lesser propensity

APPLYING THESE INSIGHTS

As a result of your work in this chapter, you should be able to develop a thesis or M&H section of your paper. The conclusion of your Literature Review should contain the kernel of your thesis, and with a little work for an empirical paper, it can be developed into an M&H section. Why should this information already be in the conclusion of your LR? Because in that section, you put forth a preferred response to your RQ. Thus, in asserting that a specific answer is best (for some reasons), you are making a contentious statement with which others can disagree. Notice that you do not have to tell the reader explicitly, "The thesis is . . . ." By concluding that one answer appears best and defending that choice, you have effectively communicated that you have a thesis.

But what if you need to put forth a model and a hypothesis because you are investigating a correlation or causation? In that case, you have a little extra work to do and need an additional section to express these ideas. As with the Literature Review, you should develop a specific title that fits your purposes and your paper. Because this part is short, however, you do not need introductory and concluding sections. Still, you want to include an appropriate transition sentence to link the section with what came before. Similarly, write a strong concluding sentence at the end to wrap up this section. Here is how Kevin, excerpts of whose LR we read at the end of chapter 4, wrote his M&H section (after he revised the LR to reflect his decision to use one independent variable):

The Impact of Media Access on Activism and Their Effects on the Success of the Uprising

Nonofficial satellite television and social media helped revolutionize the atmosphere in the Middle East and North Africa by 2011. With the regimes no longer controlling the airwaves and citizens having ways of communicating with one another outside of the state's control, activists could more explicitly state their grievances, galvanize support, and organize opposition to the regime. The effects of the media, then, were to free more citizens to more intensely challenge the regime, and enormous demonstrations ultimately led to the toppling of the longtime leaders. Without the media and the people in the streets, the authoritarians would not have given up. In simple terms, this argument can be understood as:

Level of Citizen Access to Nonfficial Traditional and Social Media	→	Likelihood the Regime Will Fall

In other words, *the greater citizens' access to nonofficial traditional and social media, then the greater the likelihood the regime will fall*. The MENA revolutions show that the truth sets people free under authoritarian conditions, and tools to spread the truth, organize people, and bring them out on the streets in large numbers convince the repressive regime that it has no hope of holding on.

Kevin has provided a great example of the M&H section, which demonstrates that it is short and easy to write once you have thought through your model and hypothesis. Again notice that even this brief section has a heading, and this title puts the emphasis on the variables that Kevin is exploring. Because this section follows right after the LR, the first sentence moves Kevin forward in the job of identifying the model and the hypothesis. Notice that Kevin includes in the text both his flow diagram and his hypothesis (and I recommend that you, like him, italicize the hypothesis so that it is easy for you and your reader to spot). Also look at how Kevin actually positions his model on the page. He does not type his variables as if they were in a paragraph, but instead stacks up the concept names so that the model flows visually in an X → Y form. He also puts the model in boldface type and gives it blank space all around (above, below, and on the sides); all these actions help make the model noticeable.

Although the M&H section may be brief, do not shortchange the amount of thinking that is required to write a good one and the importance of paying close attention to the details. You have to be able to perform that step, as Kevin did, to identify the underlying factors. You are asking yourself, What do all those words in the Literature Review really mean is fundamentally at stake? What are authors signifying as crucial for explaining the phenomenon—the political issue or policy—I am interested in? The phenomenon is the dependent variable, and the key factor(s) is (are) the independent one(s). You also need to make your model look good on the page and use the proper terminology, including a value kind of term as well as the actual variables.

As you read this section and the LR excerpt, you may think that Kevin has repeated himself a bit. That may be true, but some repetition—of the main points—is good. While you never want to duplicate your words precisely, you will see that in this paper, you are often previewing what is to come or reminding readers of what you've done. In a longer paper that is concerned with complex issues, both you and the reader need a certain amount of reiteration to grasp all your ideas and understand their relation to the whole project.

PRACTICAL SUMMARY

Before proceeding with the rest of the paper, you need to be able to state your argument precisely. That succinct formulation of your argument is the thesis; it is a contentious statement that can be upheld on the basis of normative or logical principles and verified by data. If you are performing empirical causal or correlational research, your thesis will identify variables, and you will be interested in showing exactly why and how these factors are related. Thus, you will need a separate section in your paper that provides both your model (isolating the variables you will investigate and showing the direction in which causality operates) and your hypothesis (indicating the ways in which variables are related). If you are not making a causal or correlational argument, you still want to be sure to refine your thesis so that it is extremely clear. You will state that thesis at the end of your Literature Review if you do not need an M&H section. No matter which kind of research you are pursuing, however, you will also include your thesis or hypothesis in your paper's Introduction, which we learn about in chapter 9. Also please remember, the model is a diagram and the hypothesis is a statement, but the M&H section is a paragraph that includes both. Do not simply insert the model and hypothesis on their own in your text without providing the context. Kevin's example demonstrates what you are seeking and the challenges you will face. I suggest that you practice asserting basic models and hypotheses to prepare for the development of your own and for writing this section. Use the M&H handout available in the online resources for that precise purpose.

One last word of advice. My presentation of the students' efforts to state their models and hypotheses might make the tasks seem rather effortless. In the space of a few paragraphs, they move from ideas in their LRs to their flow diagrams and guiding arguments. These tasks, however, were neither easy nor automatic, and the students took a good deal of time to think about and refine their ideas. You get a small sense of that effort from Kevin's and Zoe's adjustments. Remember to give yourself that time to think. The writing of the section will be easy once you know what you want to express.

RECIPE 4: MODEL AND HYPOTHESIS SECTION

INGREDIENTS

- Your LR, with special emphasis on its conclusion
- Access to the examples of models and hypotheses in this chapter
- Access to Table 5.1 to help you think more about values
- Access to Kevin's M&H section

INSTRUCTIONS

1. Return to the conclusion of your Literature Review, and look carefully at which school of thought you believed was the most important. By choosing one approach, you are asserting a thesis.

2. If you are working on empirical research, you would be well served to create an additional section to state the underlying argument of this approach—which factors affect the phenomenon at stake? Here you'll want to pay special attention to the exposition of your favorite school in the LR. Your discussion should explain which factors lead to what outcomes, why, and how. If these causes and the effect are not apparent after working on your LR, then you need to go back to it and rework that section so that it focuses on the factors that explain (possible independent variables) the development you are interested in studying (dependent variable). If you cannot, then you need help from your instructor.

3. You will present your argument in both its bare-bones (model) and its relational (hypothesis) forms. The model should appear on the page in a prominent way, with the independent variable(s) on the left and the dependent on the right, separated by an arrow. (See how all the student examples look in this chapter.) Be sure to use a value word—*level, type, strength,* and so forth—that is linked to the actual factor, for example, "level of citizen activism," "type of party and electoral system systems," "strength of uprising," and "likelihood of intervention." If you are having trouble, consult the M&H handout available in the online resources for extra practice.

4. Be sure that you know which kind of values (continuous or discrete) your variables will take on if you are performing empirical research. This information will help you more precisely state your hypothesis and might lead you to refine your concepts as you consider—what am I really trying to get at?

5. When you write your hypothesis, use the precise words from your model to express the hypothesis. If these terms don't capture what you wanted in your hypothesis, then you know you have a problem and need to rework one, either the model or the hypothesis. Look carefully at how both Kevin and Zoe rethought and refined their work. Also remember, your hypothesis should give you an idea of how relative values (for continuous variables) or actual values (for discrete variables) will be linked. If you are not sure, go back to your LR and look carefully at what the adherents of that approach argue. Also remember the basic formulas for the different kinds of values. For continuous variables, your hypothesis will typically be, "The more of X, the more of Y" (for positive relationships). For discrete variables, the hypothesis will be in the form "When X takes on one value, Y takes on another value." (Table 5.1 helps here.)

6. Use a heading to separate the M&H section from the previous one. Try to pick a title that puts the focus on your variables. Then, try to create a section like Kevin's; mimic his example, even seeking to mirror what he does in each sentence. Remember, the overall section is short and consists of

    a. a transitional sentence to link this discussion with the Literature Review;

    b. some additional text to remind the reader of the thesis;

    c. the actual model;

    d. some text to explain the relationship you expect between the independent and the dependent variables—here, you are also reminding the reader of what you learned in the Literature Review; and

    e. the actual hypothesis, stated in basic form.

7. If your work on your Model and Hypothesis section caused you to restate your ideas, you must make the appropriate changes in your Literature Review so that your sections will be consistent.

8. Congratulate yourself for your accomplishment when you have written an M&H section that looks like Kevin's and accomplishes what his does. If your M&H section doesn't resemble the example above—for instance, it has no heading, is one sentence or two pages long, and has a model that is not arranged nicely on the page—then you have more work to do.

EXERCISES

1. Read the op-eds in a recent *New York Times*, *Washington Post*, or *Wall Street Journal*. Identify the thesis of at least one of the authors. Can you also develop a corresponding hypothesis and model for that argument? Why or why not?

2. Imagine that you wrote a Literature Review that contained these sentences in its conclusion:

> The "Money Talks" approach appears to be the best one for explaining why congressional representatives in competitive districts vote the way they do. Lobbyists who and businesses that give enormous amounts of money receive access and sympathetic action on issues important to them from elected officials who are worried about staying in office. Constituent concerns, on the other hand, have less of an impact on these representatives when it is time to vote on legislation.

Develop a model and a hypothesis for this argument. What would you call the M&H section of this paper?

3. On the basis of the literature to which you have been exposed in this book, develop an alternative Model and Hypothesis for Gabriela.

4. Write a Model and Hypothesis section for Gabriela using either the Model and Hypothesis developed in the book or the pair you created in exercise 3. What would you call this section?

NOTES

1. This thesis will also appear prominently in your Introduction, as you will see in chapter 8, but as we saw, your LR has its own thesis, which is essential for writing a good section and which is located, like the paper's thesis, at the outset of the section.
2. Two exceptions to the universal claim at the opening of this sentence include some types of journals and journalism.
3. Please note that textbooks frequently do not have theses, instead describing the state of a field without taking a position that one approach is best. Of course, some texts do have embedded theses. Most famously, Hans Morgenthau and Kenneth Thompson's (1985) *Politics among Nations* is a text in international politics that puts forth a realist view of the field.
4. Janet Buttolph Johnson and Richard A. Joslyn, *Political Science Research Methods*, 3rd ed. (Washington, DC: CQ Press, 1995), 53–54.
5. Certainly, there can be multiple causes or several independent variables. For simplicity's sake, I will be talking about a single cause here. Also, technically, when first stated these are concepts, and through operationalization they become variables. See chapter 6 for more about operationalization.
6. Theodore J. Lowi made a mark early in his career by reversing the causal arrow and claiming that "policies cause politics," not the other way around. That politics caused policy had been the conventional wisdom before Lowi came along. See his "American Business, Public Policy, Case Studies and Political Theory," *World Politics* 16 (1964): 677–715 and *The End of Liberalism: The Second Republic of the United States*, 2nd ed. (New York: Norton, 1979).
7. In the case of Russia, Andrei Tsygankov (2014) does an excellent job of explaining these schools for accounting for Russian foreign policy. The important works in the field of international relations, in general, come from Kenneth Waltz (1979) and John Mearsheimer (1990) in the realist field, Michael Doyle (1986) in this brand of liberalism (and George Kennan [1947] for the Soviet/Russia case), and Alexander Wendt (1995) for constructivism.
8. For the critical mass school, see Rosabeth Moss Kanter, *Men and Women of the Corporation* (New York: Basic Books, 1977) and Drude Dahlerup, "The Story of the Theory of Critical Mass," *Politics & Gender* 2, no. 4 (2006). The most important proponents of critical action for Zoe were M. Tremblay and R. Pelletier, "More Feminists or More Women?" *International Political Science Review* 21, no. 4 (October 2000): 381–405; Sarah Childs and Mona Lena Krook, "Critical Mass

Theory and Women's Political Representation," *Political Studies* 56, no. 3 (2008): 725–36; Kathleen A. Bratton, "Critical Mass Theory Revisited: The Behavior and Success of Token Women in State Legislatures," *Politics & Gender* 1, no. 1 (2005): 97–125; and Karin L. Tamerius, "Sex, Gender and Leadership in the Representation of Women," in *Gender Power, Leadership, and Governance*, eds. Georgia Duerst Lahti and Rita Mae Kelley (Ann Arbor: University of Michigan Press, 1995).

9. This form applies to variables that take on continuous or interval values. The generic statement for hypotheses for data that are expressed as categories (nominal or ordinal data) will be discussed later in this chapter as well as in chapter 8, regarding performing the Analysis and Assessment of the thesis.

10. We could, however, generate a hypotheses that has the same meaning but posits a negative relationship. For instance, Max could say that the greater the imbalance of power in favor of Russia's target of intervention, the less likely Russia is to intervene.

11. Please see W. Phillips Shively, *The Craft of Political Research*, 5th ed. (Upper Saddle River, NJ: Prentice Hall, 2002), 61–62, for a discussion of continuous and discrete variables and the way these are linked to types of data—nominal, ordinal, and interval.

12. As Gabriela and Zoe are using them, type of party and electoral system and gender are ranked or ordinal variables because there is an underlying understanding that certain party and electoral system combinations and gender identities have more of a certain quality that affects the dependent variable. For Gabriela, the issue is the extent to which the institutions promote extremism—the newer system promotes more extremism than the older one. For Zoe, the underlying ranking is about ideology—how feminist is a legislator. Discrete variables can also be unranked or nominal (such as party affiliation), so that the issue is simply in what category a respondent belongs. In addition to continuous and discrete variables, researchers also identify dichotomous variables—variables that can take on only one of two variables, such as yes or no and on or off. In social science, we typically call these *dummy variables*, and they measure the presence or absence of a characteristic. For instance, we might be looking at female or not (i.e., male), Caucasian or not, or Catholic or not.

Revising and Editing Your Work

The Writing-Thinking Spiral

As I have tried to emphasize, although I discuss writing paper sections in a particular order, the research process is not linear; instead, it spirals, with authors moving forward for a while and then considering how their new intellectual advances affect previous decisions. We have already seen three of our students (Gabriela, Kevin, and Zoe) refining and rethinking their work, and those efforts will continue until they hand in final drafts. Thus, rather than a straight line, picture a spiral or spring to capture your efforts. Yes, you are making forward motion, but you also need time to reconsider your earlier decisions. The tricky part is to achieve the "right" mix of rethinking and forward motion; otherwise, you can become trapped in efforts to create an unachievable, perfect early draft. I'm going to provide you with some advice here for striking a balance: write a few sections, revise and edit them along with what came before (usually your work on the new sections will give you insight into ways to improve the old), hand in your work for comments (if possible) or pass it along to a trusted reader, and then write some more new material.[1] At the end—when you have a completed draft—you can give the whole text another dose of significant attention so that you are very pleased with what you turn in.

In addition to stressing iteration and the writing-thinking connection, another important purpose of this chapter (and book) is to banish some misconceptions about writing. Many students believe that the world is divided into good writers and not-so-good writers: some people are born knowing how to craft great arguments, sentences, paragraphs, and essays, and the rest of us are condemned to poor prose for eternity. This idea is nonsense! Writing, just like any talent—from sports to the arts, from cooking to calculus—is part inspiration but primarily skill. And you need to practice and hone skills to improve them. Thus, you should see your draft (whether you have completed your first two sections or the whole paper) as a huge accomplishment, because you have put your ideas on paper. In subsequent iterations, as you work through more of the elements of the research, as your understanding of the issues involved increases, and as your writing abilities improve, your work will take on its polished shape. The vast majority of authors write numerous drafts, and scholars produce many versions of their work before the pieces actually land in a journal or with a publishing house. All authors, then, revise and edit before handing in a final draft.

What makes a "good" final draft? In general, a successful paper follows from attention to two sets of factors: structure and style. Structure or organization is the foundation of the paper, or the "macro level." In this book, I am teaching you about a new organizational convention, the one for a research paper, but you have been writing essays for years, and the structure has always been one key to your success. The thesis statement of your paper is central to your structure, as is the need to identify and substantiate key concepts and to provide evidence in support of what you argue. Obviously, these concerns with argument (hypothesis), concepts (or theories), and evidence are essential in your research paper, too, and I hope that the more progress you make on your research paper, the more you will see how your efforts this semester can translate into good writing in many different kinds of assignments, not just research papers. The second element operates on the micro level and consists of well-constructed paragraphs and sentences, good transitions, and appropriate word choice. Style involves writing in a clear and concise fashion, not seeking to impress with jargon or many words, but developing your ideas in ways that flow nicely and are easy to understand. In response to some of the typical problems in student papers and in an effort to help you with some of these foundational principles of good writing, I have created an online resource called "10 Rules (and Then Some) to Write By." You should use this handout when you are working on your research paper, as well as other college essays.

This handout maps into thinking about revising and editing, two distinct though interrelated tasks. *Revising* entails making the macro-level changes to your text, any significant modifications to the structure or the main ideas of your paper. *Editing* refers to the micro-level corrections. When you edit, you make sure that paragraphs are well formed; sentences flow well and are grammatically correct; your language isn't repetitive, odd, or ineffective; and all your citations are provided and typed in the proper form, according to your professor's specifications. You also ensure that you have followed the proper formatting and other presentation instructions. Did your instructor insist on a certain font, a particular size for margins, or a minimum word count? Did she or he say that you must turn in two hard copies and that no electronic copies would be accepted? Pay attention to the details!

A polished paper is carefully revised and edited, and it conforms to all the various requirements. While you may view revising and editing as tedious, think again about the metaphor of a race for your paper. Imagine if athletes could rerun their events to correct for mental and physical mistakes made or mishaps incurred. Revising and editing give you a chance to fix any of the problems that remain so that you can submit the best possible paper (or, meta-phorically, run that great race). What a fantastic opportunity! In addition, you can think of the presentation—conforming to the instructions—as a great chance to make a good impression. Just as you shouldn't and wouldn't arrive in shorts and flip-flops for your interview for a summer job as a paralegal at a large corporate law firm in the city, make sure your paper looks right—as your professor and the style manual you are using define this—when you turn it in.

To revise effectively, you need to do several things. First, if you have previously handed in drafts, be sure to respond to all of your reader's suggestions. If you don't understand them, go talk to your instructor. If you disagree with them, also discuss your objections. If you are unable to have this conversation with your professor, explain your reasoning for rejecting the advice in a foot-note or a text comment the next time you turn in a draft. That way your reader can see that you took her or his words seriously. The worst mistake you can make is to ignore the suggestions of someone who has read your work carefully (and who is going to grade it).

Second, go back to the provided student examples, Practical Summaries, and Recipes at the ends of this book's chapters, as a way of ensuring that each section looks at and accomplishes what it should. Third, look again at how the pieces of your paper fit together. In other words, see that the transitions between sections work well, that introductions properly introduce and conclu-sions effectively conclude. Fourth, you will likely have new ideas about the significance of some information or concepts you have developed during the writing process. You want to integrate these new thoughts throughout the rel-evant parts of your paper. In other words, ensure that there is consistency throughout your work. You shouldn't feel disappointed about either adjusting or reconsidering what you have written before. Imagine that a friend is visiting you for the first time in five years. If you failed to update your directions, or if Google or Siri didn't have the newest digital maps available, your friend might become lost, as exits on highways get renumbered (as do highways them-selves), streets are renamed, and landmarks change or are eliminated. Think of the conceptual modifications you have made over the course of writing your draft as infrastructure improvements to your paper.

In general, when you revise you will be changing, deleting, or adding major sections to your text. While the first draft is an excellent beginning, do not be afraid to throw away or significantly modify parts of the paper that no longer work, that is, that do not help you achieve your goals or make your precise argument. When you are in this taking-apart stage, I recommend that you keep an electronic file of the original draft under a separate name. You never know when some text you thought was expendable will turn out to be useful in another part of the paper or even where it was originally placed. For anyone, but especially for first-time authors, the idea of cutting or altering big sections of text can be very painful. You feel that all the work you have done must show in explicit ways. Here again, remember the marathoner. We can see neither all of the six- and ten-mile runs nor the weightlifting, yet this person would not be the runner she or he is without having trained in this manner. All we see is the runner's race on the day of the marathon. A pared-down paper—with irrelevant words, sentences, paragraphs, and even sections cut—will demonstrate the quality you desire. An experienced reader knows that a well-crafted text reflects a great understanding of the research process, the question, and the findings. So do not be afraid to make changes and lose some of the work you did before. You would not have arrived at your (higher) level of understanding of the problem if you had not written these now extraneous sections. Cut them, recognizing that this information was valuable to the process but is not needed for your paper anymore.

In addition to making sure that the structure and logic of the paper are coherent and that every sentence and paragraph is essential to your overall argument, you want to pay close attention to micro-level issues. In many ways, editing is about presentation. So at the outset, you should consult your syllabus and any special instructions your professor has given you about this paper. Be sure that your final product conforms to all of the specifications. Second, *run the spelling and grammar check program that is standard on your word processor.* As I am sure you know, these programs cannot find all problems—they sometimes identify specialized terms as misspellings, or they may cause you some problems by identifying sentence fragments when you are trying to summarize qualitative information in a chart—but on balance, these tools are enormously useful, and I am amazed that more students haven't made a habit of using them. The spelling and grammar check will allow you to avoid silly errors, for instance, checking subject-verb and pronoun-antecedent agreement—singular subjects take singular verbs, and singular pronouns replace singular nouns. This computer function may even teach you a bit about grammar, helping you identify mistakes you tend to make so that you can correct them in future writing, without the help of the program.

Third, you should take great care with your word choice, and there are four dimensions involved here. One goal throughout your paper is to express your ideas succinctly and accurately. While a great vocabulary is impressive, you embarrass yourself and undermine your argument when you use language imprecisely and incorrectly. So don't worry about including enough big words. Instead, seek precision. Also, make sure that you vary your language sufficiently throughout your paper. You might have found a great adjective, but if you use it five times in one paragraph, it becomes far less interesting and effective. Find another term—use a thesaurus. Other problems with word choice come when, because of the topic or concept you are researching, you need to mention a particular event or term many times. Here again, you need to come up with new ways of expressing this fundamentally important issue, occurrence, or idea, and you should consult a thesaurus. Again, convincing students to care about overusing words is difficult, but varying language makes enormous improvements in your paper and makes your writing seem more sophisticated; so look for those synonyms! Speaking of word choice, use pronouns with great care. Not only should you limit their use, but you must make sure that the antecedent for any pronoun is clear and matches your term in number and gender. In addition, remember that *this*, *these*, and *that* are indefinite pronouns you can use to refer to complicated ideas or developments, but these words are called "indefinite" for a reason. Instead of using them, find synonymous phrases for concepts or events; if you do use them, be sure their antecedents are clear.

As you edit your paper, you also want to pay close attention to your citations and any quotations or paraphrases you have used. Make sure that your in-text citations or footnotes are complete and accurate. If you say that an idea appeared on page 117, or the journal volume number was 36, you had better be right. Be certain that you have cited where you should, and check that your source list is in good shape. Is every referenced work also in the bibliography? If you're using footnotes, use the short form where appropriate. When looking at quotations, make sure that they are accurate and that the quotation marks are properly placed (unless you're using a long, indented quote, which does not require this form of punctuation). In American English, commas and periods belong within the quotation marks, even if they are not the original author's. For paraphrases, go back and double-check that the material is significantly different from the original text. Be certain you have not plagiarized. Also, whether paraphrasing or quoting, verify that you have included the correct page number or other identifying information for books, articles, and sources from databases and Web sites so that an interested person could find your source if she or he wanted. In addition, confirm that your headings and your overall title accurately convey the meanings and purposes of the sections and the paper as a whole.

To be truly happy with your paper and its flow, you would be well served to get someone you respect and trust to read the paper too. You should not expect your instructor to give you a preread before the assignment is due! Still, having another pair of eyes and another brain thinking about your text is a great idea, as that person might see things you miss because you are, by now, so close to the text. If you do not have a friend you would like as a reader, consider taking your paper to your institution's writing center to get the perspective of a fresh pair of trained eyes and some advice. Getting into the habit of sharing your work is an excellent one that will serve you throughout your college career and beyond. You should also read your paper aloud. That recommendation might seem funny and sound painful—oh no, I have to listen to my own words! To listen carefully to the sound is precisely the point—you want to rely on your ears now to help you find any problems your eyes may have overlooked. Your ears will tell you what sounds funny, and you should make the necessary adjustments on the basis of what the text sounds like.

You may think that your ears are unreliable, and perhaps you are right. Please realize, however, that you can improve your use of language (maybe not today, but over the next few months and years) if you pay attention to it. To improve your ability to identify good usage, I suggest that you read as much as you can—fiction or nonfiction books, newspapers, magazines, and anything else you find interesting. Make a habit of reading for pleasure every day, even if only for fifteen minutes. Surely you can find that time! And when you read, *listen* closely to the language; don't just zoom across the page. You might even consider reading some things aloud so that you can hear what good, clear writing sounds like. Then, start to be aware of how you talk and consider how you can communicate verbally in a clearer and more effective manner. You will be amazed at how much you can change your mode of expression if you put your mind to it.

Before handing in your paper, you may also want to consult one of the many pocket style manuals to help you with problems you may have with punctuation or *homonym confusion*.[2] If you learn the rules of punctuation, or become familiar with any words that are giving you trouble, you should be able to cure this difficulty for the future. Also, you should try to transform *passive constructions*—places in the text where the subject is not performing the action of the verb—into active ones. Again, a good style manual can help you both identify and change these. Generally, English speakers consider active constructions to be clearer and better style than passive ones.

One last piece of micro-level advice—avoid using *colloquialisms* and personal pronouns, especially the second-person (either plural or singular) pronoun *you*, in formal writing. I know that I have violated this rule throughout this book; I have purposely written it in a conversational style. You should write your research paper in a formal style, like a journal article or a scholarly book. Thus, you want neither to use colloquialisms (unless you are quoting an important source directly) nor to have a conversation with the reader.

Obviously, if you want to benefit from any comments you receive, you have to finish with enough time for someone to read the essay and for you to react to any remarks. Thus, plan ahead! You are wise to finish a draft of any work at least twenty-four hours before the due date, with the idea that you will take a little break from the essay and then return to it for final polishing. When I have students writing a yearlong thesis, I suggest that they finish a draft with about a month to go before the final due date. Often, for such an involved paper, the writer needs the time to consider the whole. For a semester-long research paper, my goal for students is to have a completed draft done about three days (a week is actually ideal) prior to the final deadline. Having some time away provides you with a bit of necessary distance that enables you to be a better critic of your own work.

After you have performed that last set of revisions and edits, you are almost ready to print the relevant sections of your paper or send the essay off to your professor electronically, but you still have a few more steps to perform. First, for those still working with hard copies, make sure you have black ink in your printer! (Actually, check that the day before, and get any supplies you need then.) While that advice may sound silly, I can't tell you how many times I have read (with displeasure) a blue or red paper. (And you don't want to put your reader in a bad mood when she starts grading your work.) Second, run the spelling and grammar check again. Third, read over the text one last time (you probably have made additional changes; even after the machine has confirmed that the section is fine, sometimes in making small corrections you can introduce some silly errors.) Fourth, confirm that you have included page numbers in your text. Fifth, view each printed page on your screen. If you need to, change the page breaks so that any chart, graph, or table fits fully on one page (unless it is too long) and headings are not left "widowed" or "orphaned" from their sections. (In other words, you want to be sure that a section heading or one line from a table is not found on one page while the rest is on another.) Why do all this seemingly additional work? You are making sure that your presentation is as good as possible; again think of the interview analogy: you want to look just right. Now you are finally ready to print or, if your professor has asked for the work electronically, to send your paper. If you are printing, look at what comes out of the printer to verify that the pages are in the proper order, and staple (some professors prefer clips) your paper at the top left corner. (You have double-checked all the relevant instructions, so you know how to present this work to please your professor.) Great! You are finished with this stage of your project.

I want to stress here that you should be proud of finishing each phase and also realize that you will be circling back to consider what you have done when you add new sections. Again, the iterative process of revising and editing does not take away from having made progress and shows that you are a sophisticated and careful writer.

PRACTICAL SUMMARY

After you have finished your draft—whether we are talking about a part of the paper or the whole text—you are still not done. You need to revise and edit. Accomplishing these tasks requires your close attention and is an effort at creating an excellent work at the macro and micro levels. For revising, your focus is on the overall organization, argument, and quality and fit of your ideas. In some ways, editing is nitpicking, but in the best of ways! A good writer-editor pays attention to all the details that make a paper great— flow, proper spelling and grammar, good style, and appropriate presentation. These efforts best position you to earn an enthusiastic response from your professor.

Remember, you will use these revising and editing tips throughout the paper-writing process, and you should come back to this recipe repeatedly, but especially before the final draft is due. As a surfer-writer might say, "Spiral on, dude!"

RECIPE 5: REVISING AND EDITING

INGREDIENTS

- Time away from the work
- Your draft, preferably complete with comments from an outside reader to reflect on
- Access to the assignment instructions and rubric or checklist
- Access to a dictionary and/or thesaurus
- Access to a style guide
- Access to the advice in this chapter
- Access to the online resource "10 Rules (and Then Some) to Write By"
- Good concentration during the revising and editing process

INSTRUCTIONS

In General

Put your completed draft to the side for a time, and, ideally, get feedback from a trusted reader. Then turn to the paper for the purpose of revising and editing. You will be most effective when you are in the appropriate frame of mind for careful concentration and attention to detail. You will work on revising first (although certainly the two processes are intertwined, and you can make editorial fixes as your revise), and then when you are satisfied with the overall structure and argument of the draft and the coherence of its sections, you can turn to editing. Of course, sometimes we mismanage a deadline and time isn't sufficient; in that case, never, ever fail to run the spell and grammar check before submitting a work.

To Revise

1. Read and think about the comments on your paper, realizing that outsiders tend to make three different types of recommendations: global ones that ask you to think about the overall structure or argument of your paper, local recommendations that call for clarification or rethinking of a point or paragraph, and editorial comments that require you to fix spots or typical mistakes. Work from the most complicated comments to the least (global to editorial). If you don't understand or you disagree with some of them, discuss your questions with the reader or your instructor. (You are wise to clarify comments from your instructor as soon as you get them. Don't wait until you're writing the next draft to ask, because spiraling back will help you make the forward motion instead of slowing you down. In the global comments, your instructor is trying to focus your attention on any problems that will inhibit future progress, so they need immediate attention.)

2. Before addressing the issues your reader raised, reread the Practical Summary from the relevant chapter in this book to determine what the goals were for that section, and use the Recipes and online checklists to guide you in making global or local improvements to your paper. Then go to the text, and consult examples or sources so you can address any weaknesses in your organization and argument, as well as any problem paragraphs. Always ask yourself, Have I accomplished what I should for this section (according to all the advice)? Have I effectively communicated my line of thinking? Pay special attention to the student examples. Ask, does my section look and read like the ones in this textbook? What can I do to mimic those examples?

3. For local problems, such as a paragraph or sentence that might not be as well written as you would like, imagine yourself explaining these points out loud, and then use that conversation to help you write clearly. Eliminate jargon and confusing words or constructions.

4. When you are satisfied with the quality of the sections, turn to the transitions between them, making sure that the parts logically flow into each other, headings are adequate, and introductory and concluding paragraphs do their jobs well. Again, use the examples provided here to guide you.

5. Verify that any new ideas that you developed as you proceeded with your paper are effectively integrated in earlier sections and do not contradict your previous points. Make any necessary changes for consistency.

6. For most of us, we can imagine adding or rewriting text as a natural part of revising, but do not hesitate to make deletions! Often, the first time through, we use more words or are redundant when we explain our ideas. Seek to be "lean" while still being clear in your discussions. Again, use the student examples to show you what is precise and sufficiently clear.

To Edit

1. Run the spelling and grammar check function in your word processor. Make the changes recommended if they make sense to you. Remember that the program is usually right, but it can also find problems that might not actually be mistakes, such as special terms it identifies as misspellings or sentence fragments that are purposely included in your text. So be a critical and thinking user of this tool.

2. Pay close attention to word choice. Access a dictionary and thesaurus whenever necessary; don't hesitate! Make sure that your language is precise (e.g., get rid of big words you cannot define), avoid using the same word or term over and over again, watch out for overuse of pronouns, and try to eliminate indefinite pronouns. (You can even search your text for "It is" or "It was" passive constructions so that you can find and fix them. In the same fashion,

you can identify and change any instances of *this, these,* and *those* that are acting as the main nouns, as well as *you,* to prevent your text from having an inappropriately conversational tone.)

3. Make sure your citations (both within the text and at the end of the paper) are complete and accurate. Take great care that any quotations or paraphrases are accurately included. Check a style guide to be sure.

4. Double-check your syllabus and any assignment sheets to make sure that you have abided by any special formatting instructions your professor has given you.

5. Check the overall quality of your paper by consulting an outside reader (again) and/or by reading it aloud. Listen carefully, and change the text wherever it doesn't sound good.

6. Fix other grammar or usage mistakes, such as misused punctuation, homonym confusion, passive constructions, colloquialisms, and the use of second-person pronouns. Do not just ignore this step. Look for these issues (particularly if your professor or reader has mentioned to you that you tend to make a certain mistake), and change them. (As you start paying more attention to your "typical mistakes," they will soon go away, as you will change them before you complete a first draft, and you will break these less desirable grammar and usage habits.)

7. Run the spelling and grammar check again, because people often introduce new errors even when fixing problems. Make the necessary changes.

8. Read the draft again, because spelling and grammar checks can't find all the silly mistakes you made in the revising and editing process. Correct any remaining errors.

9. Before printing, make sure that you have included a number on each page. Look also at how the printed pages will appear, and adjust page breaks to keep key parts of the text together on the same page. Make sure your layout looks good, without big gaps or with breaks to separate sections and tables. Learn how to use the page-break function to force material to appear on a new page, as opposed to relying on embedding returns in the text.

10. Depending on what is required, submit your paper electronically or print and staple or paper-clip it (depending on your professor's instructions), being sure that the pages are in the proper order.

11. You are done with this stage. Celebrate and feel proud of having a polished draft!

EXERCISES

1. Before handing in your assignments, exchange them electronically with a peer in your class. Use the guide in chapter 6 to help you offer advice about editing (pay special attention to homonym confusion, word choice, passive voice, spelling, and grammar). With respect to revising advice, think about whether your peer has done what she or he needs to do given the recipe for each section and where ideas need to be clarified or communicated more effectively.

2. After letting your draft sit for a day, go back to revise and edit your own work (preferably after a peer has had a chance to evaluate it). Use the advice in chapter 6 to guide you.

NOTES

1. You would likely benefit from rereading this chapter after you finish every two or so sections of your paper and certainly when you have completed a full rough draft.
2. One of my favorites is Diana Hacker, *A Pocket Style Manual*, 5th ed. (Boston: Bedford/St. Martin's, 2009).

Making Your Plan and Protecting Yourself from Criticism

The Research Design

With the conceptual framework of your paper completed, you have one more step to undertake before proceeding with your analysis: the Research Design (RD). By now you're at mile 12 in the paper-writing marathon.[1] You're almost halfway done, but you're starting to hurt. How are you going to make it? This is a difficult point, but if you can just keep going, the excitement and adrenaline rush that will come from being ever closer to the end will propel you on. Just hang in there and keep working.

Depending on the expectations of your faculty member, your RD could become quite sophisticated, and you could be asked to consult methodology textbooks and take a whole course on this issue alone.[2] For others of you, this chapter will suffice in summarizing the basic logic for testing a hypothesis and for explaining the writing goals involved. In the RD section, you are communicating your plan for evaluating whether your thesis can be sustained, and you will explicitly defend the choices you make regarding which instances of the phenomenon you are studying, how to translate your concepts into knowable entities, and which types of sources or actual information you will use to determine their values. In addition, you explain exactly how you will perform your analysis. In effect, the RD is a first line of defense against criticism of your conduct of the project: you present the logic for your decisions so that readers can see that you have made the best choices about how to proceed, given the limitations that face social scientists (i.e., not rocket scientists!)[3] regarding concept formation and translation, case selection, data availability, and general design issues.

Typically, the Research Design section completes four and sometimes five tasks. While I am presenting them in a certain order, you will later see that often you need to consider several factors simultaneously. Your to-do list includes the following:

1. select cases for study;

2. define the key concepts and establish a strategy for knowing their values (recognizing that values do not have to be quantitative);

3. identify sources of information for your analysis;

4. if necessary, write instruments, such as surveys or interview questionnaires, for generating information; and

5. discuss methodology, explaining exactly what you will do and how.

Try to work through each step and then move on to the next; however, recognize that sometimes you may need to reconsider an earlier decision. In addition to setting out your plan here, you also justify your choices and strategies as the best for evaluating your thesis given the constraints (including resources and time) under which you are operating.

RESEARCH DESIGN: THE MEDICAL SCIENCE ANALOGY

While these five steps might be clear enough, why and for what purpose you undertake them might be fuzzy. So let's turn to research that is, I hope, familiar so that you can see an analogy to your tasks. If you watch, listen to, or read the news on a regular basis, you will hear reports about the latest medical or drug tests. One of the first things to notice about these results is that physicians are often finding that what they thought earlier is now wrong or at least open to question. Going back in history, we may remember that doctors once used leeches to bleed patients in the hope that this would eliminate all the bad elements and speed recovery. While medicine has come a long way from bloodletting, remember that negative findings (that the hypothesis is not upheld) are just as important as positive ones (that the information seems to sustain the argument). A researcher is proud of following the appropriate process and doing a good job in the evaluation, not of being right, that is, confirming a hypothesis.

Second, our medical analogy reminds us that evaluating a claim involves determining whether what we think is important really is. The medical community may know, for instance, that being physically active is essential for maintaining cardiovascular health, especially for those who are likely (because of family history or other behaviors, such as smoking, for instance) to have heart attacks. I might want to know, however, whether vigorous exercise three times a week is more useful than moderate exercise every day in combating heart attacks among those at risk for them. If I pursue this research, I am investigating a model:

Type of Exercise	→	Likelihood of a Heart Attack for Those at Risk

Its corresponding hypothesis is "Vigorous exercise three times a week is more likely to reduce the risk for heart attack than is daily moderate exercise, although both are better than being primarily sedentary."[4] Here, I have a discrete variable (type of exercise) for my independent variable and a continuous one for my dependent variable (likelihood of heart attack). I am asserting that exercise—of a certain form and regularity—matters for cardiovascular health in those at risk. Is my supposed value—vigorous exercise three times a week— really better? Will it keep vulnerable people from having heart attacks?

This medical hypothesis highlights nicely the ideas of cause and effect and the contingency of the claim. Here, I am saying that vigorous but less frequent exercise will have clearer positive outcomes (avoiding heart attacks) than will moderate daily exercise. Similarly, back in chapter 5, Kevin was asserting that more access to independent old and social media would increase citizen activism and increase the likelihood of a regime's fall, while Gabriela claimed that the contemporary party and electoral system result in more polarization today. In each case, does the factor posited—vigorous exercise almost every other day, more media access, and these new political and electoral arrangements—actually lead to the posited outcome—fewer heart attacks among people at risk, higher probability of regime collapse, and more polarization?

To answer that question, we must design a study that determines whether our factor is what is really responsible for the difference. That simple statement has many important points packed into it. Returning to the medical example alone, to figure out whether vigorous three-times-a-week exercise is the better form of activity, we have to also be sure that

1. we can isolate a group of people who are at risk for a heart attack;

2. we hold that level of risk relatively constant throughout the group by being sure that all or even some of the people aren't by their genes and family histories or their behavior—such as smoking (which would increase) or becoming vegetarians (which would decrease)—at different levels of risk for recurrent heart attacks;

3. we know what the approximate risk level is for this group; and

4. we can put these people into subgroups, one that exercises vigorously three times a week, one that exercises moderately every day, and a last that is sedentary, in order to monitor the effects of our key factor.

In thinking about what needs to be done to evaluate our hypothesis about exercise and heart attacks, we gain insight into political science research. Each of the points above (1 through 4) corresponds to the following methodological considerations in our research project:

1. We can identify a group of common incidents or cases. For medical research, a case is often a person and her or his health outcome. But in political science, a relevant instance can be many things. If we wondered, as Zoe does, whether a critical mass of female legislators can affect the amount of gender-sensitive legislation, a case would be a particular congressional session. In her alternative hypothesis, Zoe wants to explore whether the gender of a legislator influences the types of bills that person introduces. Here, a case would be a single elected official. For Max, the interest is in explaining post-Soviet Russian intervention policy; thus, he must look at temporal and geographic instances when Russia intervened or didn't (for instance, Ukraine in 2014 or Estonia in 1993). When we consider cases or specific instances, we also need to ask ourselves, to do a good job on our research, must we study all the cases (the *universe*), or can we evaluate a *sample* (a subset) of them? Medical research rarely looks at the universe; it is virtually impossible to control the behavior of all people who are at risk for something doctors are trying to understand. However, when we sample, we must choose very carefully.

2. As we seek to assemble a good sample, we need to know the factors others think affect the phenomenon in which we're interested, and we must try to minimize their impact. Do we know the alternative explanations? Yes, because the Literature Review (LR) acquainted us with the scholarship. Now you can see that your conceptual research was not simply an exercise in intellectual history. The LR is enormously useful to us for identifying the other potential factors that could exert influence on the outcome. In our study, we must try to isolate the importance of our preferred cause. The literature told us that smoking increases the risk for heart attacks, while being a vegetarian reduces it. Even though our goal is dampening the risk, we don't want our patients to stop eating meat. Why? If they become vegetarians while taking part in our research, then we can't tell which factor—exercise or diet—affects their heart attack risk. So in the medical study, everyone would be prevented from smoking and from becoming a vegetarian (or doing any other things we know affect the risk for a heart attack) so that we could be sure that exercise is responsible for the medical outcomes we see.

3. Embedded in the third point about risk level are a few insights. When selecting incidents to study, each case must be similar on the most important issues. (For the medical example, that means all participants are at risk for heart attacks and, as we saw in point 2, that they are behaving similarly to manage their conditions.) In addition, we need to know what heart attack risk we would expect from this group. Thus, when we put our cases into a group, we would have some knowledge

that all people with these characteristics exhibit the risk for having a heart attack and more precisely, for instance, that 25 percent of people with their characteristics will have another incident within three years. That "25 percent in three years" gives us a benchmark against which to measure the effects of different forms of exercise. In our experiment, we would divide the participants into three: a first group doing nothing (the *control*), a second exercising moderately every day, and a third exercising vigorously three times a week. This dispersal allows us to know whether (1) exercise makes a difference at all and (2) vigorous exercise (less often) is better.

4. Finally, in this example, we make people do something, or we create the change in the value of the independent variable that we think will have an impact on the dependent variable. In addition to stressing that we are looking here to see exactly what different values of our key factor do to our outcome, the last point highlights a key difference between medical and political science research. People choose to be involved in medical trials, and they then typically do what doctors ask of them.[5] In political science, a true experiment—wherein the researcher can affect how much of the cause the experimental group receives—is rarer. Perhaps most commonly, we see focus groups around election time in which a group of citizens are brought together to watch a debate. Before and after, they are asked about their political attitudes in general as well as with respect to these candidates. In so doing, those holding the focus group are conducting an experiment. They are seeking to learn what effects the debate had on the attitudes of the focus group members. But usually, political scientists can't influence variable values and then watch how the experiment unfolds.

Thus, this familiar scientific process—that of medical trials—highlights what you seek in evaluating your thesis. Your job is not to find out that you are right. You choose the universe or a set of cases that are appropriately similar and try to isolate the factor in which you're interested. In particular, you want to keep other potential causes, those that other scholars have said are important, from having an impact. You also need to see what different values of your key factor lead to. Do they result in changes in the value of the dependent variable as hypothesized? For Kevin, then, do higher levels of media access lead to more citizen activism and more governments falling? For Gabriela, has the party-election system really changed and caused the increase in polarization? Now that we have a better understanding of the overall idea here—that we're trying to figure out whether our preferred factors are really most important in affecting outcomes—let us leave the medical analogy behind and turn to the challenge of designing a project in political science.

WRITING THE RESEARCH DESIGN

When you approach the Research Design, your starting points are your model and your hypothesis. You can't make any progress without them, and at this point, you are focusing on them with laserlike intensity. As you move through the RD, you use the Model and Hypothesis (M&H) section to determine your test. The model identifies beyond a doubt what the concepts are, and the hypothesis tells you what the relationships between those parts are. Does your idea represent what we observe? That's what your research is trying to uncover and study. In planning your study, you have multiple tasks to accomplish in the RD, but the actual text will be relatively short because you are not actually enacting your plan here, just laying it out and defending it. The thinking and the time involved, however, are significant. So be sure that you devote the effort required and handle this section in its parts and in sequence. A poorly designed study can lead to worthless results. An appropriate analogy to the medical example is that if you allow some people to smoke, or you're not sure that all participants are exercising as they should, then you cannot tell whether vigorous exercise is better or not.

CHOOSING CASES

For some students, the Research Question itself identifies cases, and these instances are likely related to a person's enthusiasm for the project as well as to the puzzling nature of the query. Such questions might include the following:

- Why is U.S. politics apparently so much more polarized now than it was in the early 1980s, when similar big questions about the budget, the role of government, and foreign policy were at stake and government was also divided?

- Why was Congress able to pass immigration legislation in 2008 but not 2014, when in both cases control of the body was also divided between the two parties, the president was weakened, and an upcoming election was going to be hard fought?

- Why did Egypt have a strong uprising that toppled the government in 2011, but Algeria (which had experienced much upheaval in the 1990s) appeared unusually (relative to other states in the Middle East and North Africa [MENA]) immune to the turmoil?

- Why did Russia intervene in Ukraine in 2014 but not in 2004?

Each of these questions includes its respective cases: in the first two instances, the cases are periods of time—the early 1980s versus now and 2008 versus 2014—and in the second two they include countries or places and periods of time—Egypt and Algeria in 2011 and Russia and Ukraine in 2014 as opposed to 2004. These questions were inspired by puzzles the researchers instinctively saw. Remember that puzzles here mean cases that don't turn out as we would expect given our knowledge or, in these instances, cases that seem similar in many ways yet have surprisingly different outcomes. Instinct (and some knowledge about relevant history) told students that these were puzzling cases to study together, but in the case selection section, you want to make sure that you really have picked instances that will make a good test for your hypothesis, not just two cases you know about or two cases everyone seems to discuss. So what criteria help you confirm that your puzzling pair is a good sample (subset) of the possible instances? The watchwords are *variation* and *control*. I start with the concept of variation because students typically have an easier time understanding it. Variation means that there is some difference in your cases; you do not want to pick instances that turn out the same. Instead you want to evaluate different levels or types (depending on whether you have continuous or discrete variables) of outcomes. In the student questions and the proposed cases above, we can see that variation, with the focus in these questions on the dependent variable as shown in Table 7.1.

Table 7.1   Understanding Variation by Looking at Questions with Built-in Puzzles

Question/*Hypothesis*	Variable (from Model)	Varied Values (Presumed in Question)
Why is U.S. politics apparently so much more polarized now than it was in the early 1980s, when similar big questions about the budget, the role of government, and foreign policy were at stake and government was also divided? *Certain party and electoral institutions are linked to higher levels of polarization.*	Level of polarization	Higher today Lower in the 1980s
Why was the uprising in Egypt able to topple its government in 2011, but Algeria (which had experienced much upheaval in the 1990s) was relatively immune to the turmoil? *Greater access to free media made the toppling of governments more likely.*	Likelihood of toppling the regime	Very likely in Egypt Very unlikely in Algeria
Why did Russia intervene in Ukraine in 2014 but not in 2004? *The more the balance of power favors Russia, the more likely Russia is to intervene in former Soviet states.*	Russian intervention in Ukraine	Intervention occurred 2014 No intervention in 2004

Now any paper writer can determine whether the variable values are actually different across the cases, and this exercise also encourages writers to think again about both how they have stated their variables and whether they are appropriately continuous or discrete variables. Notice that with the last question, Max has moved to thinking not in terms of likelihood (as he did in his Model and Hypothesis section), which is continuous, but now is thinking about a category variable—intervention versus no intervention. Perhaps better still for Max might be intensity or type of intervention, as a quick look into the cases would tell him that yes, Russia was trying to exert influence in Ukraine in 2004, but not to the extent that it did in 2014. Again, we can see how our forward movement often causes refinement and improvements, and thus we move forward while also spiraling back.

In addition to verifying that you have actual instances of variation, you must also be sure that comparing these cases makes sense; in other words (thinking back to our medical case), you're not comparing vegetarians, smokers, and those who have little risk for heart attacks in the same sample. Your sample, then, must exhibit control, whereby you are doing your best to minimize the effects of other factors *scholars have told you could also be important* (but you think are not as essential as your key concept). How do you know what to control for? Your Literature Review tells you, because it identified the alternative explanations. So, the goal in controlling is to try to keep those other possible causes as constant as you can, so that one of those experts who prefers a different explanation can't say, "Well, my factor is really what is important, not yours!" Think of it this way: if in the medical example, all of your moderate exercisers also became vegetarians, how could you tell whether exercise or diet caused the outcome you saw? You can't be sure, so doctors try to control diet (and anything else that might matter) but vary exercise. Similarly, your goal in selecting your cases is to do the best you can to control other factors.

Table 7.2 then allows us to verify that our puzzling questions provide us with some control or certainty that we are comparing instances that are actually similar and will give us useful information about the effects of our independent variable. Here you see the value of the Literature Review: you know what other authors have said is important and how they might criticize your research if you're not careful. For Gabriela, she'll earn disdain if she hasn't kept constant across her cases the levels of citizen engagement, social capital, and elite polarization. Kevin has even more competing factors to think about, and Max needs to think about two alternatives. Our authors don't simply say in their heads, yes, I've got control; when they write up this section, they will defend their case selection by explaining why and how their samples (the cases they have chosen) help minimize the effects of other possible causes, while allowing them to look at variation.

Above, I simply told you that you want your cases to vary, but I didn't defend or explain that criterion. The reason is that in social science, we want you to explore not only similar instances (for Gabriela, high levels of

Table 7.2 Understanding "Good" Samples by Considering Variation and Control (in Two Steps)

Dependent Variable	Varied Value	Step 1 to Control: Remember What the Alternative Independent Variables Are	Step 2 to Control: Find Two Cases That Vary Also on the Independent Variable but Hold the Value of the Alternative Factor Almost Constant across the Cases
Level of polarization	Higher today Lower in the 1980s	Citizen engagement Social capital Elite polarization	With these cases (today and the 1980s), do you apparently have *different party and electoral systems* but similar levels of citizen engagement, social capital, and elite polarization?
Likelihood of topping the regime	Very likely in Egypt Very unlikely in Algeria	Distribution of power in the international system Domestic social structure/ socioeconomic conditions Effective society and political elites who negotiate pacts Activist citizens Domestic structures	With these cases (countries), do you apparently have *different levels of media access and activism* but similar levels in Egypt and Algeria of each of the other factors?
Intensity of Russian intervention in Ukraine	Very intense (violated sovereignty) in 2014 Less intense (economic and diplomatic pressure) in 2004	Russian domestic politics/ institutions (liberalism) Russia identity/main foreign policy ideas (constructivism)	With these cases (2014 and 2004), do you apparently have *differences in the balance of power* but similar domestic political institutions and identity and ideas in Russia?

polarization; for Kevin, strong uprisings; and for Max, times of intervention) but also the opposite or a very different level or intensity of your outcome. The idea is that your explanation should account for the various extremes or at different values of the dependent variable, and the hope is that being able to cover these differences means that you have better reflected the set of instances and truly understood how your concept in question works. So, Kevin would not have a good sample if he chose Egypt and Tunisia, because they both had uprisings; neither would a comparison between Egypt and Saudi Arabia be good, because even though one had a strong uprising and the other didn't, the socio-economic structure of Saudi Arabia is so different from that of Egypt that those who focus on socioeconomics would not be convinced by Kevin's research. Kevin wants to disarm the skeptics before they have a chance to disagree with him, so he will pick cases keeping the alternative factors as constant across them as he can. We can see Gabriela struggling with finding the appropriate variation and control, too. When the institutions were most different, so too were the alternative factors. She believes that she can defend her choice to compare the 1980s and the 2010s because the changes in the competing variables were relatively small, but polarization certainly increased, as did the nature of party and election systems. You might find that your first attempt to pick cases is difficult, because you just don't know enough about your phenomenon. That's why this case selection phase takes time, reading some basic history, identifying key information, and making some choices. This is the time when your data search is very targeted and focused on finding the "facts" (or, in other words, the "values" of the competing independent variable for your case). You may also use Google searches or even an encyclopedia to find basic information. As always, be sure that your source is a reliable one; for instance, you may use public opinion data from the Gallup organization or national gross domestic product (GDP) per capita according to the World Bank. And for that basic historical or case-based information, realize that you may not rely on or cite the encyclopedia later on.

As we have also seen, not all questions have built-in cases, and if you have chosen such a question, you then need to take special care either to decide to examine the universe or to choose your sample so that you are including both variation and control. Regardless of whether your contentious statements are causal, correlational, or assertions of fact, you need to plan your project carefully. Going back to our students' original insights, including Zoe's interest in gender and representation, we can find some highly general questions that are great ones, but that require thought for case selection:

- Why is U.S. politics apparently so much more polarized today than in previous periods?
- Why did the Arab spring occur where and how it did in 2011?
- Why does postcommunist Russia intervene when and where it does?
- Why do legislators vote on women's issues as they do?

The first option is to consider whether you should study the universe of cases, in other words, all the relevant instances of your subject. To make this decision, you need to identify the universe (figure out exactly what all the cases would be), consider your resources (do you have the time to perform the analysis on all the cases, and will you have access to sufficient information?), and determine whether this is the type of research you want to do. In many instances, the universe is very large, and so studying every case means that you will be converting the relevant data into numerical information and performing a statistical study. For many students, using their math skills in political science seems fun, and they enjoy this challenge. Others, for various reasons, are more attracted to writing case studies and performing qualitative analysis. While the ultimate decision of precisely how you will perform the analysis can come a little later, this is a situation in which you can see what I meant above about how the different choices you make in the Research Design are interrelated and aren't made linearly. For instance, if you want to do quantitative analysis, now you must pick a large set of cases or the universe.

One advantage to examining the universe is that no one can criticize you for improper sampling, because you aren't choosing—you're looking at everything. They may fault you, however, if you miss an instance, so you want to be very careful to have the complete set. For our general questions above, identifying (and examining) the universe is easiest for Kevin's general question, as he can find an agreed-upon set of MENA countries. For the others, might Gabriela want to examine every presidential election year? Every even-numbered year? Every year? Max will have the difficulty of not only finding the times when Russia intervened intensely, but when it applied subtle pressure or even chose not to intervene at all. Finding the times when the "dog didn't bark" (and Russia didn't intervene, though the situation was potentially ripe) is very hard and very controversial. Then there's Zoe, whom we haven't discussed in a while, who is interested in women's legislation and needs to choose cases too. For at least the past hundred years, Congress has been considering women's issues bills. Does she want to look at all the legislation in every Congress over decades? Not likely, and thus Zoe, like Gabriela and Max, will sample. When you face this decision, please consider examining the universe and then make a very careful decision about your sample. As you can see, when you sample, you often change the question slightly to make it more specific (e.g., not why the United States is more polarized now than ever before, but why the 2010s are more polarized than the 1980s). The general question will still have inspired you, but you will focus on a set of cases that provides you with variation and control, as we saw above.

Before we leave the issue of sampling, I want to stress the importance of being careful if you decide to choose a subset rather than to examine the universe. The goal in case selection is to find cases that adequately reflect the whole population (variation) and introduce as little sampling bias as possible (control). In other words, we do not want to pick cases we know will confirm our hypothesis and/or discredit challengers. We need a fair evaluation of the contention. A simple example from polling may help illuminate the bias problem in case selection and why we must be careful to avoid it.

Imagine that you were a strong Republican and you were unhappy with some of the polling data reported in the news in late October 2012. You decided to investigate on your own who was likely to win the upcoming presidential election. To figure that out, you went to your home state, Oklahoma, and traveled around asking the following question of registered voters: "For whom are you going to vote on election day, Mitt Romney, Barack Obama, or someone else?" You would have concluded from your research that Mitt Romney would win the election in a landslide, and your research would have been terribly flawed. Why? You made a major sampling error. By questioning people in a state that is strongly Republican, you skewed your results. Your Literature Review that examined American voting behavior should have made you aware that geography, region, and party affiliation are important predictors of votes. Thus, your sample needed to include cases (voters) in the proportion in which you would expect to find them in the likely voting population as a whole. To survey only Oklahomans would have a poor effect on your findings, because they are far more Republican than the national average. If you were interested, on the other hand, in understanding who was going to win that state's electoral votes in November 2012, your sample would have been a decent one.[6]

This scenario underlines a point we saw in the medical example: the Literature Review (with both your conclusion and the arguments you left behind) explicitly assists you in deciding which are good cases. Through your analysis of the scholarly answers to your question, you know which other items could affect the outcome. You think they are wrong, but you want to be sure (as in the exercise–heart attack example) that these other factors don't exert too much influence on your results. Therefore, you try to isolate the effect of your preferred cause—your independent variable—and limit or preferably eliminate the impacts of the others (e.g., smoking or a dietary change in our medical example). To do that, you typically need to *control* for other factors. When you control, you are holding these other elements constant or reducing their impact on the outcome as much as possible.

In addition, this idea of control means that you should not seek cases that are "good" only for "proving" your hypothesis. In fact, expunge the words *proof* and *prove* from your vocabulary for the duration of the research project. That's so important (and students ignore it so often) that I'm going to repeat it: *the point of any investigation is not to prove but to learn.* Would we be well served if medical researchers always found that their insights were correct? No. We want to know under which conditions their proposed solutions, be they exercise, drugs, or other procedures, appear to work; when they are ineffective or are harmful; and when the researchers aren't sure. The goal of your work, like that of medical researchers, is to design a reasonable test of your argument and to report accurately what you find. Your initial ideas do not have to be right; your job here is to evaluate and investigate fairly. In this way, you learn more about the phenomenon in which you're interested.

So in the preceding example about voting behavior, you can see that you have not controlled for party affiliation, region, race, and ethnicity. To do so, you would need to talk to a *representative sample* of likely voters: in other words, a subset that accurately reflects the universe of cases. Professional pollsters take great pains to define their samples and have found ways to choose only about 3,000 American voters and arrive at a good estimate of voting behavior. Note, however, that even those professionals typically identify a sampling error of plus or minus 3 percent. With a sample, it is impossible to predict perfectly, but with care you can get very close.

For other kinds of questions, you might need to control for some larger background factor that reflects changes occurring over historical periods. For instance, in examining many different kinds of questions in American politics, comparing pre- and post-1932 doesn't make sense, because the size and role of the federal government expanded after the New Deal. Similarly, in investigating questions of foreign policy or world politics, you might not find cases that occurred during the cold war to be comparable with those between 1990 and 2001, or after September 11, 2001. Those historical periods reflect major differences in the structure of the international system, and you might want to keep that factor—the structure—out of your study by holding it constant, that is, picking all your cases from only one of those three periods (the cold war, 1990 to 2001, or post-9/11).

Some kinds of questions lead to the examination of a great many cases, or what political scientists like to call "large-N" (for number of cases) studies. Large-N studies are conducive to performing statistical analyses of the data. If you have easy access to data in numerical form, using many cases helps improve accuracy. (As pollsters' work shows, you do not need to use the universe to obtain useful results, but you need to sample appropriately.) Other questions, however, particularly ones that involve examining particular historical phenomena, will not be evaluated in the same way. Usually those researchers choose a small number of cases, but not just one, to evaluate their hypotheses.[7]

In sum, when selecting cases for your study, keep in mind the following issues. First consider the universe and the feasibility of defining it and investigating it fully. If the full study appears to be too much, seek at least two comparative cases. When you select instances, you are not trying to *prove* your thesis. In fact, you need to eliminate that word from your vocabulary. You are seeking to give your thesis a fair evaluation, so you want to be careful not to introduce bias into your sampling procedure. When we sample fairly, we need to be aware of (and take into consideration) the alternative explanations. Our goal is to pick cases that hold the values of those competing factors constant (provide control) while varying the value of our preferred cause or outcome. We are trying to determine whether our favorite explanation accounts for the results.

In the real world, we find that sometimes our understanding of the literature isn't as clear as it should be when we initially make our case selection decisions. Then, at the analysis and assessment stage, we go out, gather data, start thinking about it, and realize, "Oh no! From the perspective of evaluating my thesis, I have not proceeded as I should have. I have not, for instance, controlled adequately for a competing factor or captured enough variation in my variables." If this happens to you, realize that you are not alone. Frequently, case selections are imperfect; then, however, you have to decide (here, often, in consultation with your instructor) how to proceed. If you still have the time to redo data collection, you may have to rethink the case selection and go back to the beginning in finding your information. For semester-long projects, however, students usually don't have this kind of time. If there is no justification or no time for fixing, then you have to admit the mistakes and consider their implications in the Conclusion. Thus, be very careful with your case selection and listen to the advice of your instructor. If she or he is skeptical of a pairing or sample you have chosen, hear out those criticisms and adjust accordingly. You should remember, however, that selecting cases perfectly is typically impossible. So do the best you can to have variation and control, and recognize explicitly the limits and problems with your cases. Then, move on to your next task, returning to think about these weaknesses when you write the Conclusion.

CONCEPT DELINEATION AND MEASUREMENT: OPERATIONAL DEFINITIONS AND OPERATIONALIZATION

The second job in the Research Design is creating operational definitions for the concepts and then determining a plan for translating them into identifiable entities and specifying their values, that is, *operationalizing* them. In political science, some values are easily knowable, such as per capita GDP, voter participation rates, or the percentage of women elected to a legislature, but others, like the level of polarization, the likelihood that a regime will fall, or the intensity of foreign intervention, require a good deal of thought.

All researchers use great care with concept definition and the translation of factors into actual variables. When we set out our models in chapter 5, we were technically identifying the major ideas we believed were related to each other. To make them true variables, we transform the theoretical concepts into actual measures. Where does any researcher—whether assessing a thesis or a model—find guides to specifying and measuring concepts? One of the best sources is other authors who have investigated similar questions or concepts; you may use their definitions and measurement strategies as long as you give them credit. The advice here is *not* to take their data or to replicate exactly their studies. I am suggesting that you *base your approach* on other works. To find these *strategies*, go back to the authors you identified in your Literature Review and look at what they did—What choices did they make when conceiving of their variables? What kinds of methods did they employ to measure them? Pick from among the approaches, and explicitly defend all of the choices that you make by explaining them in your text.

There is often a problem, however, with using existing work as your sole guide to specifying and operationalizing your concepts: established scholars may have access to far more resources (e.g., time, money, research assistance, information) than you do. One of my favorite scholarly (as opposed to student) examples to use is Robert Putnam's *Making Democracy Work*. Putnam's study, however, took about two decades, involved many research assistants, and required a number of large grants to complete. Thus, he was able to develop measures for variables that used multiple indicators (building blocks for determining his final value for the concept), required interviews of legions of local officials in Italy, and consisted of many statistical sources. If you were interested in probing the importance of culture versus economic development in explaining the efficacy of democracy in different regions of the United States, you might take Putnam's work as an inspiration, but you certainly could not strictly apply his approaches to measuring variables.[8] You would have to modify the strategies to make them doable, yet logically sustainable, given your time and research constraints.

Sometimes, if you have consulted purely theoretical articles in your Literature Review to help you answer your general question, you will be able to write an excellent section on the theoretical debate, but these articles will be a poor guide at the Research Design stage. In this case, you might look for more applied studies to help. Compare the ways others have defined and measured concepts, and pick one out of the new set that you find best, while being sure to credit your source. Or if you feel confident that translating the concepts into knowable entities is relatively straightforward, you can advance a plan based on your own logic.

When Kevin got to this stage in his research paper, he was struggling with both his question and his favorite school of thought again. Did he want to focus on the puzzle of Egypt versus Algeria, or did he want a global look at why uprisings succeeded or not in the MENA countries in 2011? Some of this change of heart resulted from his attraction to performing statistical analysis and having an independent variable that would be much more manageable to operationalize. His experience with case selection made him think about how important socioeconomic factors might have been in determining where the stronger uprisings were, and he was thinking, "If I were only exploring the relationship between general quality of life and the success of revolution." He knew from previous classes that the Human Development Index is a good measure of quality of life, he thought he could plan a strategy for operationalizing the likelihood of a revolution's succeeding, and he thought it might be fun to explore the whole region at once. So, he had a dilemma. Should he go back and redo the earlier sections and move forward on this socioeconomic school, or should he power forward with his original model and hypothesis and the case-study approach? As I told him, the choice was his, as I didn't think that the changes necessary to pursue this different school would require that much effort. The key questions were, what did he really want to study, and what kind of investigation did he want to perform? Research is about both satisfying your instructor's guidelines and your passion, and you should pursue what seems most appropriately intriguing in order to have a successful experience. If you are faced with a similar dilemma, you should also consult your faculty member about whether you should change your direction.

Let's give Kevin some time to think and look at examples of operationalizing concepts from another empirical paper. I'd like to examine one model-and-hypothesis pair from Zoe, who was wondering whether a critical mass of female legislators better accounts for female-enabling legislation or if a certain type of legislator (willing to engage in critical action) was a better predictor of woman-sensitive bills.

Critical Mass of Legislators

| Relative Size of Female Group within the Legislative Body | → | Number of Bills Offered That Improve Women's Lot (Women's Issues Bills) |

When a certain, critical mass of female legislators is reached within the body, the number of women's issues bills will increase greatly. Without that critical mass, the number of women's issues bills will be low or nonexistent.

In this model-and-hypothesis pair, we can easily identify two key concepts whose values Zoe needs to know: the relative size of the female group in the legislature and the number of women's bills. Now, how to determine them? Of course, your case selection affects this question, and earlier, Zoe decided to focus on the Senate because she had found an excellent existing study of a similar question by Michele Swers, *The Difference Women Make*. Because Swers focused on the House of Representatives, Zoe thought she could borrow from Swers's method, but look at Senate cases in order to do her own, original investigation. Zoe also chose to examine more cases (five Senate sessions) than Swers (still manageable, because the Senate is smaller), and all were from the recent past, with one from the period prior to "The Year of the Woman" in 1992. Since 1992, more women have been elected, and Zoe would examine four such contemporary cases, with the percentage of women ranging from 2 percent at the beginning to 17 percent at the end.[9] Thus, the proportion of women in the legislature served as the value of her independent variable. Her operationalization scheme then was to find the number of women in the Senate during that Congress and divide by the total (100 senators). For the dependent variable, she had to determine the number of women's issues bills offered, and she decided for the sake of proportionality to calculate the percentage of these relative to all bills. That sounds easy, but perhaps tedious, right? But wait—do you think there's some organization or clearinghouse that decides "this is a women's issue bill?" No, Zoe had to define which bills were relevant to her (so finding potential cases was not a simple matter). In this excerpt, she provides her operational definition:

For my data, the best definition is one that Childs and Krook (2008) propose. Under their parameters, women's issue bills "capture a broader range of issues affecting women's everyday lives" (p. 133). It is important to keep a part of the original definition because women are still closely connected to children and their families. Bills focused on child or family issues would certainly have an effect on the lives of women. Most obviously, bills that affect women's work or home environments directly also would be included.

She continued by explaining that not all health insurance bills would be tagged "women's issues," even though the public generally thinks of health care as a women's issue. To maintain her focus and the accuracy of her measure, Zoe includes all bills with "direct consequences for the well-being of women and children." Now this definition helps her know what she will include, but it doesn't explain how she will determine them. Here, again, she must explain. Ultimately, she went through the *Congressional Record* and evaluated every bill introduced for a particular session and determined whether the bill had "direct consequences." As you can see here, Zoe would be well served to establish some criteria that would help her easily categorize bills (and defend her from charges of bias).

Turning back to Kevin, he realizes that this is decision time. He must make a choice about which model-hypothesis pair he wants to pursue, the one he recently started to consider—the wealthier the MENA country, the less strong would be the uprising—or his original one—the greater the media influence, the more likely the regime will fall. Ultimately, he decided to pursue his first idea, because the media were what inspired his work. Now, Kevin recognizes that he has to find operational definitions and strategies for knowing the values of his variables: level of media influence and the likelihood that the regime will fall. This pair contains one relatively easy concept to operationalize (level of media influence) and another that is more difficult (likelihood). For media access, memories of poking around on the Freedom House Web site for his Introduction to Comparative Politics course made him think that he could find some information there on media freedom, and a Google search helped him find some statistics on social media use in MENA countries. Thus, Kevin realized that he would use at least two indicators to capture the level of media access, because he was interested in old and new media. But would this be enough to find the value of media access? The outcome presented more of a challenge: how was he going to determine likelihoods? That had been a nice concept, but nowhere were there agreed-upon probability estimates. Thus, after some thinking, Kevin realized that he would have to make an assertion and use a proxy (or stand-in) variable for this concept. Recalling his earlier line of reasoning, he remembered that for him, activism seemed to account for revolution—where there were a lot of people out in the streets and their commitment was intense, uprisings succeeded. As he thought more, part of what he was claiming was that the opposition becomes very broad based and strong, so that even members of the regime, like the military for instance, turn against the leadership. Thus, Kevin would operationalize the likelihood of toppling the government by evaluating the number of activists, their intensity, and their overall societal support, assuming that as these were all greater, the pressure would mount and the regime would fold. Thus, the likelihood would be higher.

As you can plainly see, operationalizing involves important decisions for the variables, which can have a huge impact on the study. When translating concepts into variables, be very careful that the measures are both *valid* and *reliable*. Validity means that the strategy for knowing measures' values provides accurate representations of the concepts (or at least as accurate as possible). Zoe worked very hard to capture the true meaning of "women's issues bills," so as to include only those bills that truly affect women and children (as women are still more likely to have primary responsibilities for children). Similarly, Kevin has to think about what will best represent his concepts, particularly the likelihood of the toppling a regime. For him, this will ultimately be a three-part measure that he will combine to estimate likelihood.

There's a second issue involved in knowing your value, called *reliability*, or the ability to repeatedly achieve the same measure—regardless of who is doing the evaluating. When you're choosing from a list of data, as with determining the percentage of women in the Senate at any one time, all you need to do is find the number and do the division. Unless your eye skips incorrectly across the column, the reliability of your value is very high because you have captured the proportion of female senators. However, when your measure entails judgment, it might be more subject to problems. Zoe doesn't know what proportion of female legislators is the "critical mass," and she is going forward thinking that she might discover that magic number. Kevin will be taking data from various sources and then coming up with a composite judgment about whether the various values of cable television access, media openness, and social media penetration are "high," for instance. To convince readers that his strategy is reliable, he needs to be transparent about how he will make his judgment. The goal in defining your strategy is to make it easy for others to perform the same task and get the same value.

If we think of operationalizing as a game of darts, a measure that is both valid and reliable consistently hits the bull's-eye. A measure that is valid but unreliable will scatter around the bull's-eye unpredictably, while a measure that is reliable but invalid will always land in the same vicinity but never hit the center. Validity means the aim is on target, and reliability means the throws are consistent. The best players (and strategies) are both valid and reliable, helping the research consistently capture the true value of a concept.

IDENTIFYING DATA SOURCES

The third part of the Research Design is to identify which information you are going to use to know the values of your variables and exactly where you are going to get that information. The focus is on finding the data that you need to evaluate your hypothesis. Here is where you seek primary sources, bits of unprocessed information, on which you will rely to know the values of the variable. We have already seen that when operationalizing, our students have had to be aware of data sources. Why? Because a strategy for knowing your values is worthless if the data you hope for don't exist.

When you are identifying your sources, you should not simply take information from any place you can find it. You want to be sure that you have the best source, given your constraints. While Internet searches for data are useful, be a critical consumer. In general, reference librarians will tell you that when you come across a source, you need to interrogate it along five dimensions: authority, accuracy, coverage, currency, and objectivity.[10] For the first, you want to ask yourself, Who is providing this information? Is it someone or some organization you have a reason to believe is credible and respectable? Here, look not only at the individual's name but at her or his title and institutional affiliation to determine whether this person has authority. Second is accuracy. When considering that factor, you must take the motives of the source into consideration. For instance, during the cold war, the Soviets provided false statistics about their economy, and students of the USSR used instead Central Intelligence Agency (CIA) estimates of that country's economic activity. While the CIA might have had some propaganda motives for underestimating the Soviet economy, it also was charged with gathering information so that the United States would be prepared for threats. Thus, most scholars thought its data were more valid than those released by the Soviet government. If you have some doubts about your source's accuracy, note them and explain why you still think that this source is the best.

Coverage refers to how broad in scope is the information or the site. Is the scope right for your purposes? If you need information from a particular time period, group of states, or candidates, your sources must have the coverage you require. Currency refers to how recent the information is. For historical projects, currency will often not matter. Gabriela, Kevin, and Max all need very current information, and you might too, so be sure to check how recently updated the site or publication is. Finally, you want to consider objectivity. Many organizations have explicit political agendas. Try to avoid taking data from these groups, but rather look for arguably more objective sources such as government or international agencies or nonpartisan organizations. For instance, you would not want to take all your data about the dangers of smoking from cigarette makers or information about the relevance of class size to student performance from the American Federation of Teachers unless, of course, you were trying to investigate what manufacturers argue about the ill effects of smoking or what union positions are on class size.

You may think that consulting your data sources now, when you are only making your plan for your research, is premature, but it is a crucial step in creating the Research Design section. By looking for data at this point, you make sure that what you hoped you could get—as you defined in your first two subsections—is available for the cases you want to study. In effect, then, specifying your data sources here and checking that they actually have what you need ensures that your wonderful plans for evaluating your argument are actually possible. If you can't get access to the information you require, you might need to modify your earlier strategy, and it's better to know that now rather than later.

We have already seen Kevin struggle with data, as he recognized that nowhere would he find a measure for "likelihood of uprising success," and instead he is introducing a *proxy* variable, which is actually the size and intensity of the opposition. Ultimately, he'll have to defend this as a measure for likelihood and consider any possible weaknesses. What does he lose by focusing on opposition? If you find that an approximation for your preferred factor is not strong enough, you may decide to go back and change the thesis under investigation (in Kevin's case, access to media → size and intensity of opposition), noting, "The data made me do it!" As long as you explain what you are doing and why (and these points are logical and accurate), you are safe from criticisms on methodological grounds.

STRATEGIES FOR UNCOVERING AND, AT TIMES, CREATING DATA

After you have operationalized your variables, picked your cases, and found your sources, there may be an additional step. There are times when the operationalization of your concepts means that you have to come up with ways for uncovering and, in a sense, generating data. I hesitate to use the word *create* because I do not want any reader to think that you should just make up your information to suit your purposes, but there are times when the information is available, but you have to do more to find it. Perhaps Gabriela decided that she wanted to explore polarization among students on her campus and see whether any of the purported claims about why polarization occurs and whether her peers really were polarized were true. To perform this study, Gabriela will need to design a survey to uncover these data. Similarly, imagine that Zoe wanted to explore a slightly different thesis that was inspired by her earlier reading. She wanted to examine the critical mass versus critical action at the state level in contemporary politics, but in addition, because her university was in the state capital and had a special state politics program, she wanted to interview legislators to understand their perceptions of the relative importance of mass and action in getting things done. While she knew that perceptions were not the same as reality, she thought that uncovering perceptions might help her understand better what legislators thought really mattered for accomplishing their goals and might give her insight into refining her ideas about representation.

In those cases, the students need to develop surveys or interview questionnaires that will help them amass the relevant information. These are time-consuming but highly rewarding tasks, for many reasons, but one that is particularly appealing to most students is that they are uncovering new information, and therefore, data creation provides an additional sense of excitement and accomplishment. Remember, any time you plan to perform research on human subjects, you need to go through a training program (typically, this is easily accomplished through an online module), submit your Research Design and instrument (survey or questionnaire) to your professor and the institution's research review board, and receive permission. This process takes time, so you want to begin early. And writing a good instrument is very important and requires attention to detail. You want to keep your instrument short (so that your respondents don't get bored or stop taking the questions seriously) and targeted to uncover the information you need. You also must write your questions very carefully, so as not to confuse, mislead, or suggest an answer to any of the participants in the study. Here you must pay close attention to reliability (meaning that neither you nor whoever is administering the instrument is *eliciting* particular answers) as well as validity (the questions you are using to generate information are good translations of the variables in your model). Consult an excellent methodology book and look for examples of similar survey or interview research as you design your instrument.[11]

In sum, whenever you need to develop a method for generating information, you must explain exactly what you are doing and how you are doing it. In addition, you must set out the logic behind your approach, justifying every decision you made as the best one for accomplishing the task at hand given the resource constraints under which you are operating.

METHODOLOGY

As a last part of the planning process, you should include an explicit discussion of how you plan to put all these pieces together, a discussion of what we might call your methodology. What you actually do is very much dependent on the earlier steps. If you have chosen a large-N study with quantitative data, you likely will perform a statistical analysis. At this point, you should inform your reader that you will be performing a particular kind of test, for instance, a chi-squared test or a simple linear regression. Both you and your reader should understand what that means (at least you will by the end of chapter 8).

Alternatively, you could perform a comparative case study, as Kevin (or even Max) will ultimately do. Despite using some numerical information, Kevin is not doing a statistical study to understand why Egypt's regime fell and Algeria's didn't. He will compare what happened to the values of his variables— access to media and likelihood of revolt success (on the basis of his proxy)— leading up to Hosni Mubarak's ouster in February 2011 and the relative quiet in Algeria throughout the period of turmoil.

Finally, you might have a thesis that lends itself to discourse analysis, which asks you to trace the meanings of concepts in the writings or words of key political actors and which behaviors then follow. Had Max decided to pursue an identity- or ideas-based explanation for Russian foreign policy, he might have found discourse analysis a useful tool for understanding why Russia intervened intensely in 2014, but not in 2004. How might this work? As Roxanne Lynn Doty explained in her study of U.S. intervention in the newly sovereign Philippines, the words used produce results. In this case, Americans' views of themselves as noble, well-intentioned protectors; of Filipinos as childlike, gullible decision makers; and of the Soviets as evildoing imperialists compelled the United States to disregard its earlier commitment to the Philippines' independence to intervene. Doty's method was to analyze primary sources, this time U.S. foreign policy documents, to see exactly which language American decision makers used to portray themselves, Filipinos, and the Soviets to come to her findings. Words and terms were her data, and she searched for the linguistic themes, contending that these words then compelled action. Before performing her analysis, Doty set out the types of phrases she would be looking for and what they would mean for her thesis. Then, she went through the government documents and literally counted the incidence of these themes and was able to show which ones were more prevalent. While she did not perform a statistical test, Doty summarized her findings in a table and was able to show where the preponderance of the evidence lay. That allowed her to support her claim that because American policy makers saw their motives as altruistic and protective, had very patronizing views of the Filipinos, and held a menacing perspective of the Soviets and communist activists on that archipelago, U.S. intervention became the only sensible policy, despite America's having given the Philippines its sovereignty a few years before.[12] If Max pursued a constructivist hypothesis, he could use Doty's work as an example and examine the ways in which Russia conceived of itself, its role in world politics in general and in Eurasian (former Soviet states') affairs in particular, and its relationship to Ukraine. Did the language change in ways that might account for the intense intervention in 2014? A discourse analysis would expect that Russia's sense of its importance, place in the world, and need or desire to control Ukraine would be communicated clearly in elite as well as more popular communications and make the later intensive intervention almost automatic when an opportunity, such as political turmoil there, arose.[13]

In conclusion, while all my instructions and analogies might seem reasonable as you are reading through them, actually writing your own design might still seem difficult. To aid you in your efforts, I offer you a "Designing Your Project" worksheet in the online resources that will be invaluable in planning your research. It reminds you of the medical analogy and walks you through each stage of the RD. This worksheet should be as helpful in completing the RD as writing the Annotated Bibliography was in finishing your Literature Review.

FINISHING TOUCHES ON THE RESEARCH DESIGN

As you turn to writing this section, remember that it should be able to stand alone as an essay yet be integrated into the rest of the text. Consider this the place where you explain exactly how you will conduct your research and why your research strategy will help you answer your question as accurately as possible. Thus, the section answers the query, How should I proceed for the truest assessment of my thesis? It should be set off from the rest of the text with a heading and include introductory and concluding sections. The body of the essay must accomplish the three tasks identified at the start of this chapter.

To name this section, remember that the focus is on communicating what you will do and why. Something like "Planning a Comparative Study of American Polarization" for Gabriela or "How to Explore the Impact of Media on the MENA Uprisings of 2011" for Kevin would be appropriate. Again, the heading both sets off this section from the others and informs the reader of its purpose. In the Research Design, you are performing four or five rather involved tasks—concept definition and operationalization, case selection, data identification, information generation, and a brief discussion of methodology. Because of these many different requirements, you may want to use subheadings here if some parts are particularly long, but you'll notice that Kevin was able to complete this section successfully without them. Still, he has signal words in the text so that a reader can tell precisely which task he is fulfilling at any given time.

How to Explore the Impact of Media on the MENA Uprisings of 2011

Access to old and new media among citizens of the Middle East enabled the uprisings of 2011, and in fact, the greater the access to media, the more likely did the revolt succeed in ousting the longtime leader. To test that relationship, I will perform a *comparative case study* of Egypt and Algeria in the years prior to and including 2011. These instances provide *variation* in the dependent variable, as Egypt successfully removed its leader after a massive uprising, and Algeria remained rather quiet and its regime stayed

(Continued)

(Continued)

in place. This pairing, then, allows me to investigate the extremes in pressure on the regime and its fall. By *choosing these cases*, I am also able to *control* for factors that other scholars deem important, such as the international system, socioeconomic conditions, and domestic structures. Regarding the international system, I am examining both states at the same time, so they are confronting the same arena. In terms of economic conditions, while their situations are not precisely the same, they are closely similar on many important factors. Egypt and Algeria are relatively poor and suffer from similar levels of unemployment, have rentier states with great involvement in the economy, and are ethnically homogenous. In terms of domestic structure, both are regimes where the military dominates, although some may argue that in recent decades, the Mubarak regime has become more personalist than has the Algerian one. Still, if that were the case, this difference in domestic structure would mean that Egypt would be less likely than Algeria to have a successful revolt, which is clearly not supported by the data.

Perhaps some areas of concern in terms of control relate to the role of elites (societal and regime) in negotiating the outcome or in the role of activists in each case. As I have pursued my research, I see that my argument about the role of media subsumes within it the importance of elites' and citizens' mobilizing and working toward the collapse of the regime. At times, success will require societal and regime elites (such as the military) to cooperate, and will mean that people take to the streets in protest. Thus, my argument requires and incorporates the importance of these factors, and my case selection, therefore, provides my study with variation (very different outcomes on the dependent variable) and control of alternative explanations, as summarized in Table 7.3.

Regarding *operationalization*, I will capture the causal factor, access to the media (traditional and social), using three indicators: media freedom in the society, the influence of independent (i.e., non-regime-controlled) cable TV, and the availability of new media sources, such as Twitter and Facebook. Freedom House, a well-respected organization that evaluates democracy and liberty around the world, provides a ranking for media freedom on a 1–100 scale, where a score of 1 indicates full media freedom and a score of 100 indicates the least amount of media freedom. To determine the influence of old media, I will look at television ownership, assuming that citizens with TVs have access to independent cable news, as networks such as Al-Jazeera were broadcasting an independent (of the regime) interpretation of politics into the MENA households. Last, the Arab Social Media Report provides information about the use and availability of new media outlets,

Table 7.3 Controlling for Competing Explanations

Variable	Egypt	Algeria
GDP (in billions)	$525.6	$267
Unemployment rate	12.2%	10%
GDP PPP	$6,600	$7,400
Government role in economy	Highly centralized	Highly centralized
Population	83,688,164	37,367,226
Culture	99.6% Egyptian	99% Algerian
Percentage below poverty line	20%	23%
Percentage of labor force in agriculture	14.5%	14%

Source: CIA *World Factbook*, 2012, https://www.cia.gov/library/publications/the-world-factbook/geos/eg.html. Accessed November 15, 2012.

Note: GDP = gross domestic product; PPP = purchasing power parity.

such as Twitter and Facebook, in the relevant countries. It is a product of the research of the Governance and Innovation Program at the Mohammed bin Rashid School of Government. Together these three indicators help me conceive of the level of citizen access to media. My strategy here is both *valid* and *reliable*. Freedom House seeks to quantify the very concept of media freedom, and it is an organization that is respected and performs careful research, so most observers accept its evaluation as unbiased and an accurate representation. Nation Master, the source of TV ownership, is also a trusted source of basic information. Last, the Arab Social Media Report, although it is funded by Dubai, seeks to capture the penetration of social media in the Arab world. The problem, of course, is that aggregate figures of access do not tell us what channels or sources any individual is experiencing and how often. It also can't tell us, as Lynch (2012) asserts regarding cable news, that this information creates a different identity from, for instance, the regime-produced sources. Thus, in that sense, my measures could have some validity problems. Of course, these data are reliable, because anyone can read the figures from the relevant charts.

Together, these three indicators will give me an estimate of the level of access to media that citizens in Egypt and Algeria had. If the Freedom House ranking is relatively high, TV ownership is broad based, and social

(Continued)

(Continued)

media use and cell phone ownership are significant, then I can conclude that the population is knowledgeable and connected. If these are low, then I cannot expect that the media would have a significant effect, for a biased official media will not provide citizens with the truth about what is going on in the country, citizens won't have access to broadcasts if they don't have TVs, and similarly, they won't be able to use new media if they are not on the Internet or can't connect via calls, texts, and pictures sent on their mobile phones.

While there is an easy way of conceiving of the dependent variable—did the regime fall or not—here I will look at how the opposition that was produced by the media led to an ouster, seeking to include not only the toppling but also some of the mechanism of why the revolt succeeded or failed. Again, I have a *multi-indicator approach to finding the value of the proxy*, by looking at not only the size and intensity of the demonstrations but also the geographic and social expanse of the opposition's popularity, determining whether it includes supporters around the country and from different types of groups. Together, I will assess whether the strength was great (large and frequent demonstrations, growing geographic and social expanse) or small (sparsely attended and few demonstrations with limited geographic and social appeal). This measure is also *valid* and *reliable*, because I will use news reports of crowd estimates and locations for demonstrations, as well as accounts of the negotiations and agreements between different groups participating. Of course, greater accuracy will have to wait for historians to dig up more information, but this approach to knowing the pressure that brought about the government's fall is adequate for now.

In each comparative case, first Egypt and then Algeria, I will assess the values of the variables as well as look for links between the role of the media and the government's fall. Can I see particular coverage of events or social media requests leading to an increase in the opposition, not only in terms of presence at demonstrations but even discussions between societal and regime elites that show that together they were pressuring the leadership? If that is the case, then I feel confident that a causal connection, not simply a correlation, exists between my proposed independent variable and the fate of the regime.

In sum, this design provides me with a sufficient test of my hypothesis. I have sampled cases that provide both variation (very different outcomes for the leadership) and control (as Egypt and Algeria are relatively similar on the alternative factors), and finding such a pairing is not easy. There are no nearly identical states in the region that experienced the Arab spring in different ways. My strategy for operationalizing the concepts is carefully thought out to capture the essence of these factors, depends on information that comes from reliable sources, and is not subject to interpretation. However, I am leaning on news sources, which may be found to be incomplete or inaccurate in the future when scholars have more access to now closed document sources, can perform interviews, and are able to do more thorough information searches. Still, given the importance of these events, doing this preliminary research is useful, particularly because through my comparative case approach, I am seeking not only to uncover correlation but to examine the connections between the variables, investigating whether media access influences what happens on the streets and the kind of pressure that can be brought to bear on a government.

Kevin has done an excellent job on his RD, as it contains each of the required elements (case selection, including a discussion of variation and control; operationalization, with explicit mention of validity—even potential problems—and reliability; sources; and methodology). I have added italics—which you won't do in your text—so that no one can mistake that he has accomplished all he should. While he is confident of his choices, he does mention some weaknesses. For other projects, in which the cases are less comparable or the data would require more judgment, a writer would have to spend more time on these issues and what effects they might have. But once mentioned, now the student moves forward.[14]

A few characteristics of this section are likely also notable to you. First, Kevin uses "I" and other first-person pronouns here, and he does so because I ask students to use direct language rather than the passive voice. Your professor might rather see you avoid "I," so pay attention to your instructor's usage preferences. Second, the table about control is not required for everyone, but in this case, Kevin wanted to show any skeptics that these countries were comparable, so including the data helps disarm critics. Whether you need a full table depends on how controversial your case selection is. Also note that Kevin tells us here what he is going to do, but he doesn't actually go out and begin to find the raw values for his indicators or determine the variable values over the course of the relevant time period. That job of filling in the values and actually analyzing the hypothesis on the basis of the data is the work of the next section, the Analysis and Assessment. He has, however, made sure that the information he hopes for exists, so he knows that his plan is workable. Fourth, Kevin never tells us that he is "proving" his hypothesis. Again, banish that word from your vocabulary throughout this paper. Last, this section is relatively short, but yours might be longer. For instance, if you needed to develop a questionnaire, you would discuss its logic and goals and prepare a draft of it to share (although you would include it as an appendix).

After you have finished the design, you are ready to move forward and perform your research—you know what you need to do, and now the only issue is enacting your plan. At this stage, you should feel happy that you are now heading into what most students see as the best phase of the project—when you have the chance to investigate whether your ideas about your concept of interest are confirmed.

PRACTICAL SUMMARY

The Research Design is the section of the paper in which you provide the plan for your research—how to choose cases, define and operationalize concepts, identify information sources, generate data (at times), and explain your methodology. Typically, you cannot define or conduct a true experiment to evaluate your hypothesis, so you have to make well-informed choices about how to proceed. As long as you are aware of the concerns about methods—minimizing bias, controlling for other explanations, choosing cases that maximize variance in either the dependent or the independent variable—you can come up with a good plan. Such a program, however, is likely not to be perfect, so you must be explicit about the possible imperfections and their effects on your research. After you admit them as possible weaknesses and defend them as acceptable compromises, you move on, because conducting perfect social science research is nearly impossible. You will return to consider how the design choices might have affected your analysis in the concluding section of the research paper.

RECIPE 6: RESEARCH DESIGN

INGREDIENTS

- Your Model and Hypothesis section
- Your Research Question
- The "Designing Your Project" worksheet (download a copy)
- Your Literature Review
- Access to Kevin's Research Design example
- Access to all of chapter 7

INSTRUCTIONS

1. Download the "Designing Your Project" handout with the goal of filling it out.

2. Return to the conclusion of your Literature Review, and look closely at which school of thought you believed was the most important. Look carefully at your model and think to yourself, Have I come up with the best pairing? Do I need to make any changes to either one? If you are pleased, copy and paste

your hypothesis into the spot on the handout for the hypothesis. Otherwise, make the necessary changes and type in the hypothesis.

3. Then, copy and paste your question into the appropriate slot. Turn to the case selection section of the worksheet. Try to identify the universe of cases. If you have already defined your cases, double-check that they provide variation (the outcomes are different) and control (hold other factors constant). If not, think through the case selection criteria. Perhaps you can keep one of your cases? Mimic the processes of Gabriela and Kevin provided for you in this chapter as you proceed and fill in the table to help you think through the specifics of your case selection and justification. As you consider sampling, also consider what type of research (comparative cases, statistical analysis, discourse analysis) might be required and whether you would find it appealing. Those judgments should also enter into your selection decision. If you are sampling:

a. *To find cases that include variation*, you want to find instances of your phenomenon (for Gabriela, polarization; for Kevin, MENA revolt in 2011; for Max, Russian intervention; and for Zoe, women's issues legislation) in which the outcomes are different (higher or lower polarization, strong revolt or little revolt, intense intervention or less intense intervention, more women in the Senate or few women in the Senate). Here you need to consider whether you want to compare different time periods (like Gabriela or Max) in the same country or different places (Kevin) or different legislative sessions (Zoe, which is like different time periods). If you know little about your concept or independent variable, then you need to read up to find out what might be good comparisons that provide very different conditions. What would be a case for you? In medical science, it is an individual who has had a heart attack; for Kevin, it is a MENA country. Try to write down some cases that have different outcomes on your dependent variable.

b. *To find cases that provide control*, you must determine which cases you are going to study. Go back to your LR and list the alternative factors. While also considering what Gabriela and Kevin did, ask yourself, In the cases I thought gave me variation, are the alternative factors relatively stable? Think through what was happening on each of the alternative factors for your cases. Do a little research if necessary to find out whether those other potential causes stay constant across your possible cases. Eliminate any cases in which the other factors change greatly. Remember, you likely won't be able to find cases with perfect control. Ultimately, pick those that give you the most variation with the most control. Fill out the chart as appropriate. If you are stuck, write down the factors that need control, put down some possible cases and the issues involved with choosing them, and move on to the next step. Return later.

4. Discuss precisely how you will translate your concepts (independent, intervening, and dependent variables) into knowable entities. Here, turn to the operationalization portion of the worksheet. This is often a multistep process that includes finding an operational definition (i.e., one that helps you think about what your concept means in concrete terms) and then determining the strategy for knowing its value for your cases. If you have seen research that operationalizes concepts similar to yours, use those ideas, but modify them to make them doable. Otherwise, you can think through your issues yourself, as Kevin has done. Remember that you might need a few indicators (parts of the whole concept) that you can look at to understand different pieces, and then you have to find a way of thinking about how these parts fit together. I encourage students to brainstorm first about what they would need to know to capture the concept, writing down everything they can think of. Then, I have them go back and think, which one(s) is (are) truly essential? As a general rule, never use more than three indicators for a concept; otherwise your task becomes too complex. Think about validity and reliability as you operationalize, and discuss why your strategy captures the essence of your concept (is valid) and is reliable (doesn't introduce bias). Also remember, you have to operationalize every variable in your model—independent, intervening, and dependent. Fill out the table to explain your strategies and make your justification for each concept.

5. As you are working on operationalizing and narrowing down how you will know your variables' values, you will likely have to start looking for sources of information. If you do an Internet search, be sure that any source is reputable, subjecting the site to the five-criteria test. If you cannot get access to the data you wanted, you need to rethink the decisions you made in the first and second subsections. Remember, finding perfect data is next to impossible; make the best of the data you have and admit any weaknesses when you discuss operationalization and data sources in your RD. Go back to your cases. Does your strategy make sense of those cases? Can your work on operationalization help you make better decisions about your cases? Fill in this information in your data chart.

6. For those of you conducting surveys or interviews or using other methods for creating a scale, include a discussion that clearly specifies how you will generate data. If you need to design an interview questionnaire or survey, describe your goals for writing it and any concerns you had in developing the instrument, and include a copy of it. Also, fill out the necessary paperwork and submit this questionnaire to your institution's review board for approval for using human subjects in your research.

7. Finally, think about the methodology you will use. Perhaps you have already done this because questions of exactly how you are going to evaluate your thesis came up as you thought about the cases and operationalization. But if you haven't, think explicitly about the steps you will take to evaluate whether your argument holds.

8. Consulting your worksheet and Kevin's example, write your RD, complete with a heading and a concluding paragraph. Again, you should feel free to mimic Kevin's organization and even his style and sentence structure. Move through each of the five tasks, without skipping one (except, of course, if you are not generating data). Be sure to explain and justify your choices. In addition, notice Kevin's conclusion, which specifies his choices and acknowledges potential problems. Like Kevin, you do not perform your research here, just make your plan and justify your decisions in preparation for that next phase.

EXERCISES

1. Determine strategies for selecting cases and operationalizing one of the following two theses:

- In the United States, areas with more highly engaged citizens are more highly polarized.
- The more the imbalance of power favors postcommunist Russia, the more likely Russia will be to intervene in former Soviet states.

Be sure to discuss variation, control, validity, and reliability.

2. Imagine that Kevin decided to study the universe of cases in understanding the Arab spring. How might he now write his Research Design if his hypothesis were "The lower the standard of living, the stronger the revolt in the MENA countries in 2011"? Please note that he would have to perform statistical analysis, most likely a regression of the data. (We will talk more about this method in the next chapter. If you're not sure what to write about method here, don't worry. Do the best you can writing everything else in the RD for now.)

3. Develop a questionnaire for surveying students at your school about polarization. Remember, as you develop the questionnaire, you should be trying to determine whether there are data to evaluate at least one of the arguments Gabriela examined.

4. Develop an interview schedule for talking to elites (local, state, national, or all) about polarization. Identify which types of elites you would survey and consider how your chosen group might affect the questions you ask. Then develop your interview questions, realizing that you are doing so in an effort to evaluate at least one of the arguments Gabriela examined.

NOTES

1. To repeat, the research paper–writing process is iterative. In a marathon, you wouldn't go back and run mile 10 again, but in this endeavor, you might rethink a decision you made earlier. However, you need to be aware that (1) a clock is ticking (you usually have a due date for your paper), and (2) you have made important forward progress. Keep thinking and writing, realizing that as you take new steps, you may have insights you need to incorporate or ideas you need to adjust in older parts of the paper.

2. For detailed and methodologically sensitive discussions of research design, see Donald T. Campbell and Julian C. Stanley, *Experimental and Quasi-experimental Designs for Research* (Boston: Houghton Mifflin, 1963); Janice Buttolph Johnson and H. T. Reynolds, *Political Science Research Methods*, 7th ed. (Washington, DC: CQ Press, 2011); W. Phillips Shively, *The Craft of Political Research*, 7th ed. (Upper Saddle River, NJ: Pearson, 2009), 74–96; and W. Laurence Neuman, *Social Research Methods: Qualitative and Quantitative Methods*, 7th ed. (Upper Saddle River, NJ: Pearson, 2011).

3. Shively, *The Craft of Political Research*, 7th ed., 17.

4. The medical community now generally thinks that daily moderate exercise is better; if I were deciding to proceed with this research (and hoping for external funding), I would have to show a good reason for thinking that this consensus is flawed. My apologies that I have not selected a medical example that reveals awareness of the cutting edge of current research on cardiovascular disease; I do know something about political science, though, and I recommend that you pursue a hypothesis you have good reason to believe (because of your literature review and knowledge of politics) could be correct.

5. Of course, people who are in the position to be in this study might not be thrilled about their choices. They might enroll in the research as a last resort, and they might not enjoy the long (in our example, three years!) commitment or what they have to do. Often, individuals drop out, so researchers have to make sure that sample sizes are large enough to be able to overcome this attrition.

6. It is not, of course, a perfect one. You need to determine whether your participants are likely voters. In 2012, when overall turnout was about 57.5 percent, only about 49 percent of Oklahoma voters cast ballots, with 66.8 percent of them choosing Romney and 33.2 percent selecting Obama. (For election details, see Bipartisan Policy Center, "Detailed Charts: Turnout Charts: Presidential Race," http://bipartisanpolicy.org/sites/default/files/Turnout%20Detailed%20Charts.pdf, and "Election 2012: President Map," *The New York Times*, http://elections.nytimes.com/2012/results/president, November 29, 2012.) Pollsters have found that if you ask a participant directly whether she or he plans to vote, you are likely to get the answer "yes." Most Americans know that they are supposed to vote to be considered good citizens. So to get at likelihood more accurately, you may want to ask, "For whom are you going to vote?" first and then ask when was the last time your respondent voted. For more on the importance of careful case selection, see Arend Lijphart, "How the Cases You Choose

Determine the Answers You Get," *Journal of Policy Analysis 2* (1975): 131–52. Also, Shively noted that the *Literary Digest* made a huge sampling error in 1936 when it polled telephone and car owners on their preferences for president. Taking those who returned their surveys, the publication predicted a defeat for Franklin Delano Roosevelt, who ultimately won convincingly (Shively, *The Craft of Political Research*, 7th ed., 50–51).

7. They may perform a single case study for other purposes, for instance, considering the plausibility of their thesis (plausibility probe) or as a heuristic case study, to determine how multiple perspectives account for what happened. See Alexander L. George and Andrew Bennett, *Case Studies and Theory Development in the Social Sciences* (Cambridge, MA: MIT Press, 2004).

8. Robert D. Putnam, with Robert Leonardi and Raffaella Y. Nanetti, *Making Democracy Work: Civic Traditions in Modern Italy* (Princeton, NJ: Princeton University Press, 1993).

9. Please realize that Zoe was writing a yearlong senior thesis. I could not imagine that a student could complete this detailed an analysis, with so many cases, in a semester-long course project.

10. Reference librarians have created these particular terms and helpful ways of assessing sources. See "Evaluating Web Sources," First-year Seminar Library Modules, Saint Joseph's University, http://librarytoolkits.sju.edu/content.php?pid=103334&sid=776924.

11. Many research methods textbooks provide excellent advice on designing surveys and performing interviews. See, for example, Janet Buttolph Johnson and H. T. Reynolds, with Jason D. Mycoff, *Political Science Research Methods*, 6th ed. (Washington, DC: CQ Press, 2005), 297–350.

12. Roxanne Lynn Doty, "Foreign Policy as Social Construction: A Post-positivist Analysis of U.S. Counterinsurgency Policy in the Philippines," *International Studies Quarterly* 37, no. 3. (1993): 297–320.

13. In the Web Resources, I have included a version of a student paper that performs a discourse analysis of a pope's impact on activism in Poland during the communist era.

14. I hope that you can see that Kevin has taken his filled-out Designing Your Project worksheet (available in the online resources) and used it to write this section.

Evaluating the Argument

The Analysis and Assessment Section

You're about two-thirds of the way through the research paper–writing marathon, and you are feeling pumped because the course is now downhill and there's a wind at your back. The most fun part of the project (in most people's opinion) is about to begin: you are ready to investigate the actual phenomenon in which you are interested, and all the work that you have done so far in your Literature Review, Model and Hypothesis, and Research Design (RD) will help guide and protect you during this evaluation. The goal of this section is to *analyze* relevant information to *assess* your thesis.

Briefly, there are two main forms of analysis—*qualitative* and *quantitative*. With qualitative analysis, an investigator assesses evidence in the form of words, images, and numbers to determine where the weight of it lies—on the side of the thesis or against it. This judgment is based on the researcher's ultimate consideration of the factors and how they account for the relationships in question. With quantitative analysis, the evaluation of the argument is based primarily on statistics. A researcher rejects a hypothesis if the numerical data show that the relationship posited among the variables is not statistically significant. Here, the analyst's independent assessments or impressions do not matter: the statistics are decisive, and that calculation determines whether to accept or throw out the thesis.[1] Oftentimes, however, scholars combine qualitative and quantitative forms of analysis in their work, so do not be surprised to see a mixture.

Regardless of which type of analysis you pursue, you need to remember that (1) your thesis or hypothesis allows you to concentrate on what is important, and (2) your Research Design specifies exactly what you need to do. In other words, you continue your laserlike focus on your argument and your plan for evaluating it. Although you might be enticed to add additional, interesting, yet extraneous information, resist that temptation! That tendency is an old habit developed from your report-writing days. Now you are beyond that; you know that a research paper consists of the careful analysis of a thesis, not simply a broad story about some political event, phenomenon, or idea. To put yourself in the proper mind-set for this section, think back to the many courtroom dramas you have seen. The Analysis and Assessment (A&A) section is the trial phase of your research project. You've done the background work, and now you are ready to present your case. What do lawyers do at the trial? They present the logic of their arguments and then the evidence that supports their interpretations of events. They do not, for instance, recount all the details of the various interviews they conducted prior to their court date or bring witnesses to the stand who do not add something substantial to their cases. In this section of the paper, like an attorney, you lay out the pertinent facts. For case studies, you examine the fit of your thesis for each case, uncovering the values of your variables as specified in your RD and seeing if they relate as you expected. Often, you can't judge fully the quality of your hypothesis until after you have performed all your case studies, because to have confidence, your argument should hold across cases. If you are performing statistical analysis, this focus means that you present your data, perform your test(s), and interpret the results. Unlike a lawyer in a trial situation, you have no vested interest in whether your thesis holds or not; you are not an advocate for a position (remember, you're not "proving" anything!) but an investigator in search of knowledge.

QUALITATIVE ANALYSIS

Political science undergraduates are most likely to be familiar with qualitative analysis. Many of us become interested in political science because we like reading newspaper, magazine, or policy articles that make arguments (based predominantly on logic, values, and historical evidence) about political ideas or phenomena. Most of the readings you have done in your introductory courses are and even many of your upper-division classes primarily assign qualitative studies. But what is this as a form of analysis? Isn't it just description and argumentation? Yes, there are descriptions and arguments included in these assessments, but remember that the evaluation is focused, concentrating on the thesis and using the methods you determined in your Research Design.[2]

The most dangerous misconception about qualitative analysis and case studies, in particular, is that they are "simply" histories or stories of particular incidents. As any historian, journalist, and political scientist knows, whenever writers provide versions of events, they are including some information and leaving out other elements. How to decide what belongs in the account, and how to organize it? Well, the RD determines exactly what the building blocks of the case are, as well as what information you need to assess your thesis. The Analysis and Assessment section is where you walk your reader through the values of the variables, and that information helps you know whether your contention (your hypothesis) holds. You have identified the parameters (time period, place, etc.), the operationalization strategy, sources, any data creation rubrics, and a methodology for knowing what to do with your information. Your job now is to amass this precise information, using your stated method, think carefully about the meaning of all these data with respect to the variable values as well as the hypothesis, and then make a judgment about your contention. All this takes time (prior to writing and then in crafting an easily understandable and organized narrative) and is best done methodically. Various writers approach the task differently. Some start with the dependent variable, but others find starting with the independent variable to be the "natural" way (in English, we read from left to right, after all). There's also the question of whether all the cases should be evaluated in one big section or each in its own part. That decision is a judgment call based on the lengths of the case studies as well as the author's feel for what seems right. If there is one big section, the introductory portion should provide an overview of the entire A&A. Otherwise, that first paragraph can simply introduce the case. No matter the order, headings provide the reader with important signposts, not only conveying the substance of the section (e.g., this is about the independent variable) but also indicating the values or findings. As with introductory sections, give the punchline to the reader early. There should be no surprises, because keeping the reader waiting can be confusing, and using those signposts to state exactly what a section is about can help you, too, to know what you're writing and how it relates to the larger picture. Again, the purposes of the A&A are to subject the hypothesis to the RD-specified test. When you write the section, your account centers on your hypothesis and variable values, so you are telling a kind of story, but it is a special one, indeed.

Because we are very familiar with Kevin's work by now, let's look at what he has done for his Analysis and Assessment. Here is an excerpt, as the whole A&A is too long to include. Try to identify what he is doing, generically, and look to see how well he enacts the plan he set out in his RD (at least for this portion). Are there inconsistencies between the RD you read previously and the A&A? If so, any differences will have to be eliminated in the final draft.

Accounting for the Arab Spring: Media Access Makes Some Difference, but There Must Be More to the Story . . .

The world watched in awe in 2010 and 2011 as long-time dictators in Tunisia, Egypt, and Libya were toppled, and other repressive regimes in the Middle East and North Africa (MENA) faced challenges to their domination. Comparing the experiences of Algeria and Egypt shows that there was only a small variation in citizens' access to old and new media, with the

(Continued)

(Continued)

advantage in access tilting slightly toward the Egyptians. Yet the difference in outcomes was great. Algeria had demonstrations and food riots, but its people were ultimately intimidated and pacified, while Egyptians kicked out their ruler. Apparently, memories of the violence of the 1990s, when earlier demonstrations rocked that state, affected Algerians' demands (asking not for the regime's departure but for more reasonable prices) and willingness to go home when the regime turned to brutality and agreed to give in to economic demands. In Egypt, on the other hand, protesters called for the ouster of Mubarak, and over time, the military began to side with the opposition. Thus, this case analysis suggests that the MENA uprisings depended on more than the media. Yes, cable TV and social media helped spread the truth about the regime's abuses and protest strategies, but access to these sources doesn't appear enough to explain whether the opposition was successful in toppling the dictator. Important, too, seems to be whether the regime's concessions convinced people to go home and whether the elites stayed united in their commitment to keeping the leader in power. The differences in media access alone can't account for why the Algerian regime held on while Mubarak fell.

Assessing the Levels of Media Access in Algeria and Egypt

Because much of the data on media access is provided on relative scales or for the region as a whole, I will look at the values of media access in Algeria and Egypt simultaneously, and then make judgments about their differing impacts.

While Egypt's population (83.7 million) is a little more than twice that of Algeria's (37.4 million), the latest available data (which are admittedly old, from 2002) show that both countries have about the same percentage of televisions among their households, 88.6 and 88.06 percent, respectively. The regimes in both try to control the messages broadcast, and during the period in question, they did a good job of it, according to Freedom House. That organization gave Algeria and Egypt very close ratings, on the borderline between partly free and not free, with Algeria never achieving the "partly" designation but Egypt's media repression getting slightly worse as the uprising approached and then unfolded, improving *after* Mubarak fell.

The data show that the media situation in Algeria was worse, but only marginally so. Algeria had been operating under a state of emergency from 1992 until February 2011, which gave the government enormous powers to punish those who engaged in what it defined as "threatening" public speech (Freedom House 2012a). Regarding outside outlets, Al-Jazeera was kicked out of the country in 2004, but that did not prevent it from broadcasting back

Table 0.1   Freedom House Media Rankings, Algeria and Egypt, 2009 to 2011

Year	Algeria's Press Freedom Ranking	Egypt's Press Freedom Ranking
2009 (2010 report)	64 = not free	60 = partly free
2010 (2011 report)	62 = not free	65 = not free
2011 (2012 report)	63 = not free	57 = partly free

Sources: Freedom House, *Freedom of the Press* reports from 2010, 2011, and 2012 at http://freedomhouse.org/report/freedom-press/2010/algeria, http://freedomhouse.org/report/freedom-press/2011/algeria, http://freedomhouse.org/report/freedom-press/2012/algeria, http://freedomhouse.org/report/freedom-press/2010/egypt, http://freedomhouse.org/report/freedom-press/2011/egypt, and http://freedomhouse.org/report/freedom-press/2012/egypt.

in via satellite, and 60 percent of citizens owned these devices, so they could hear and see this unsanctioned news. The difference was that the channel couldn't provide its own reports from within Algeria. Still, independent media (print and electronic) did their best to provide a clear picture, but the vast majority of television, radio, and print journalism was largely controlled by the regime and provided the state's view only (Freedom House 2011a).

Ironically, in the run-up to Egypt's November 2010 parliamentary elections, the state limited media freedoms, and officials engaged in all forms of intimidation of journalists and bloggers. Freedom House makes clear that in late 2010, the regime was brutal against those trying to disseminate information about politics and the regime. These behaviors continued into the revolutionary period of January and February 2011. Citizens with TVs could often get cable news outlets, sources that experts like Marc Lynch believe were very important in providing more accurate information to the Arab publics about politics. In the critical period, cable news reported on the revolts and provided discussions and analysis of these events, both providing an alternative narrative to the official one and helping create a sense of unity among the people of this region (Lynch 2012: 8–9). This external perspective was very important, because as Freedom House (2011b) asserted, despite an apparent diversity of outlets (more than 500) in Egypt, the state owned or acted as a sponsor of most.

Regarding new media use, data from the Arab Social Media Report (ASMR) show that during the period in question, Egyptians were using social media at a proportionally much higher rate. For instance, while 0.15

(Continued)

(Continued)

percent of the Egyptian population had Twitter accounts, only 0.04 percent of Algerians did (ASMR, Twitter Penetration). There were other Arab countries, particularly in the Persian Gulf, with far more users in total and certainly as a percentage of the population, in places such as (in descending order) the United Arab Emirates (UAE), Qatar, Saudi Arabia, and Kuwait. Moreover, those in Egypt who used their accounts were responsible for almost one-tenth of the entire MENA region's tweets, whereas Algeria was not even ranked independently (ASMR, Volume of Tweets).[3] In addition, Egyptian-themed tweets, particularly #Egypt and #Jan25, were the top two trends in the first quarter of 2011, coming in at 1.4 million and 1.2 million, respectively. Algerian-themed tweets numbered about 620,000.

Egypt also led Algeria in Facebook use, but not by much. One potentially important difference is that Egypt's Facebook use was less concentrated in cities than was Algeria's. But perhaps not surprising (because of their greater wealth) was that the top Facebook-using MENA citizens (as with Twitter) were in the Persian Gulf (the UAE at 50 percent, Bahrain at 37 percent, and Qatar at 31 percent), while Egypt had a penetration rate of 7.66 percent, and 5.42 percent of Algerians used this social networking site. In terms of Internet use (which could lead people to all sorts of information), the International Telecommunications Union (ITU), an agency of the United Nations, gives Egypt an almost three-to-one advantage (39 percent to Algeria's 14 percent in 2011) in access (International Telecommunications Union 2013b). Freedom House (2011b) reported that just prior to the uprising, almost 27 percent of Egyptians used the Internet regularly, with comparable data from Algeria not available. The organization said that 12.5 percent of Algerians "accessed the Internet" in 2010 (Freedom House 2011a). One last way people can contact one another, obtain information, and spread it is with cell phones. Here again, the ITU found an advantage among Egyptians, but only a slight one. In 2011, the rate in Egypt was 105 lines for every 100 people, compared with 94.31 in Algeria (International Telecommunications Union 2013a Mobile Cellular).

In considering all the indicators for Algeria and Egypt, then, the differences between the states in media access seem relatively small. With respect to traditional media, Egypt has a very slight edge in terms of freedom, but the regime clamped down during the most raucous times of protest, so that slight difference in media freedom disappeared during the crucial period. At that point, perhaps satellite broadcasts were effective, and reliable estimates of access are unavailable. Based solely on TV ownership, the impact of Al-Jazeera's reports in Algeria and Egypt would seem to be similar. The data also show that Egypt has an advantage in social media, with the ITU reporting Egypt's significant margin in overall Internet access and greater Facebook and Twitter use. Interestingly, however, Egypt is not one of the leaders in social media among the MENA countries, and remember, too, that the regime tried to shut down access to the Internet and cellular technology at crucial points in the protest (Lynch 2012: 89–90). One would think—for the hypothesis to hold—that Egypt would have far more social media use compared not only to Algeria but also to other regional states that didn't have significant uprisings. On the other hand, technology access is often correlated with income, and because the Middle East has many rich, not populous countries, finding that those wealthy states have very high proportions of citizens who use various forms of technology regularly is not surprising. Finally, with respect to cell phones, Egypt certainly has an

Table 8.2 Summary of Independent Variable Values in Algeria and Egypt

Indicator	Algeria	Egypt
Old media	About the same in terms of FH ranking (though always NF) and TV penetration. Not clear whether proportions of population with access to cable (unbiased information) is similar.	About the same in terms of FH ranking (though PF before and after the uprising) and TV penetration. Not clear whether proportions of population with access to cable (unbiased information) is similar.
Social media	Fewer Internet users, including Facebook and Twitter.	Far more Internet users, in general, by percentage. More Facebook and Twitter users. Penetration is less concentrated in cities than in Algeria. Still, relative to other MENA countries, proportions (and absolute numbers) are moderate.
Phones	Smaller percentage of the population than in Egypt (94.31 percent penetration).	Higher percentage of the population than in Algeria (105.08 percent).
Composite	Slightly less access.	Slightly more access.

Note: FH = Freedom House; MENA = Middle East and North Africa; NF = not free; PF = partly free.

(Continued)

(Continued)

advantage over Algeria, but by only about 11 percent. (Note that Saudi Arabia's and Bahrain's rates were far greater than Egypt's.)

Thus, in assessing the difference in social media access, Egypt did have an advantage, but the difference wasn't that great. Regarding old media, the two populations are about tied in their repression (lack of access to free information), and Egypt has the advantage in social media and mobile phones. Given the importance of the Internet and phones in helping publicize and organize people (PBS 2012), I have thus determined that Egyptians had a slightly higher level of access than did Algerians. Still, these values of the independent variable would suggest that both countries had similarly significant protest movements and regime outcomes because of the relative closeness of the levels of media access.

Assessing the Strength of Opposition to the Regime: Widespread Protests Bring Regime Violence and Concessions in Algeria, Massive Turnout Topples Mubarak

. . .

Kevin's excerpt is an excellent example of keeping the focus on the hypothesis and walking through the values of the variables for the case(s). His introduction to the whole section previews what he found (as does his title), and the first paragraph communicates that Kevin is not confirming his hypothesis, but will have more thinking to do at the end. That conclusion is OK, because Kevin has carefully enacted his plan (and it was a good one). In the first subsection, devoted to the independent variable, Kevin again provides the reader a sense of what he found. Then, he presents the values for each of the indicators and sums them up (figuratively) to come up with the composite value. Slightly different from what Kevin had originally planned, he didn't evaluate Algeria and Egypt separately (in distinct sections). When he found his data, much of the information appeared in graphs or charts, so he decided to find the relative values of media access for both countries in the same section. Also, because this information often listed values for the whole region or world, Kevin could see that Egypt's ratings were not extremely high, which he expected given his hypothesis. Thus, he began to raise questions about the veracity of the hypothesis, even as he was determining the values of the independent variable.

Also noticeable in this section is that Kevin uncovers the values for each of the indicators, and then he explicitly discusses how they come together to create a value for media access. For some information (Freedom House Press Rankings), he presents the data in a table, as readers (and writers) generally have an easier time understanding and seeing patterns in numerical information if it is displayed in this way. He is able to do this because he created a data chart based on the "Raw Data Chart," which is also available to you in the companion site for this book. This device is an excellent mechanism for keeping you organized and helping you focus on the information you need (and what it all means). Likely, Kevin could have included additional tables or graphs, too. His summary chart in Table 8.2 for the independent variable is very helpful to both him and the reader, as it lays out the weight of all the indicators and the relevant data and allows him, then, to make a final judgment on the values, giving the advantage (even if it is slight) to Egypt. I recommend that you use a similar table if you have multiple indicators, if only just for your notes, although it can also work in the text, as you see here. Perhaps a bit confusing is Kevin's mention of social media access in other countries. Here he is straying a bit from his plan, and he could perhaps use this more effectively in a later discussion or concluding section. This information does provide him with additional reasons to question his contention that the greater access to media, the higher the likelihood that a regime would fall, because citizens of these wealthy states used more media, but their governments stayed put.

Finally, the excerpt ends with the subheading for Kevin's next section, in which he will determine the values for the dependent variable in Algeria and Egypt, according to the plan he determined in his Research Design. I wanted you to see how Kevin will continue, particularly because the title again gives you a sense of what values he found, and in the new section itself, he will repeat the process he engaged in before, although this time, because much of the information is separate, he will uncover the story of the uprisings (focusing on the indicators he deemed important: size, intensity, and geographic and social expanse) in each country over the relevant course of time (December to May 2011 in Algeria and December to February 2011 in Egypt). Remember, you are not done when you know the value of the independent variable. Your hypothesis links at least two factors, so your evaluation must examine both parts of it. To save space, I have not included it here, but both Kevin and you will provide a full accounting of all of the variable values in your finished paper.

Kevin has done a great job, and his excerpt provides you with a fine model for writing your own Analysis and Assessment section, especially if you are using qualitative analysis.

QUANTITATIVE ANALYSIS

As you would expect, much of quantitative analysis deals primarily with numbers and statistics, which is particularly useful for assessing contentions that can apply to many cases. When you begin contemplating quantitative analysis, you need to (1) identify what kind of data you will be using—continuous or discrete—and (2) be sure you have sufficient cases to make the statistical analysis valid.

Consider the following hypothesis, which was inspired by Gabriela's early interests:

> Democrats are more likely than Republicans to support immigration reform (making the path to citizenship easier), and independents or members of other or no parties would have an intermediate level of support.

What type of information is involved here? To evaluate this hypothesis, you would be putting people into categories reflecting both their party affiliations and their attitudes toward immigration reform. Imagine that you decided to evaluate this contention by studying students on your campus. In compiling your data, you were allowed to survey virtually all freshmen in introductory political science classes.[4] You asked them to provide some basic demographic information and then asked them to check off answers to the following items:

I consider myself a

☐ Republican

☐ Democrat

☐ Independent/other

My attitude toward comprehensive immigration reform is

☐ Favorable

☐ Unfavorable

☐ Don't know/none

Your results are presented in Table 8.3.

This matrix shows you how party affiliation lined up with attitudes toward immigration reform. If partisanship affects attitudes as hypothesized, with Democrats more likely to support reform and Republicans more likely to oppose it, then we would expect the data to reflect a pattern: more supporters in the upper right and very few in the lower left. While we may be able to discern a pattern simply by looking at the results, we can calculate the precise nature of the relationship by using something called the *chi-squared statistic* (χ^2). This statistic will tell you the extent to which your observations are different from what you would expect to see if there were no relationship between the independent (party affiliation) and dependent (attitude) variables. Moreover, if the results are significantly different, the χ^2 statistic will let you know at what *confidence level* (or *probability level*) you can uphold your hypothesis. In other words, if your statistic holds at the .01 confidence level, that means you can be 99 percent sure the results you found could not have occurred by chance. In other words, you can be 99 percent sure that you have found a relationship between your independent and dependent variables.

Table 8.3   Party Affiliation and Support for Immigration Reform

		Party Affiliation			
		Democrat	Independent/Other	Republican	Total
Attitude toward immigration reform	Favorable	90	40	40	170
	Unfavorable	20	10	80	110
	Don't know/ none	40	50	30	120
	Total	150	100	150	400

There are a number of *statistical packages* that will perform this computation for you. (A statistical package is a software tool that comes ready to perform all sorts of functions, as long as you supply the data and tell the program exactly what you want it to do.) Below I use SPSS, which is a Windows-based program. There are many other packages you can use, so feel free to use one with which you are already familiar or the one your professor recommends.

In this particular example, the relationship between party affiliation and support for immigration reform is incredibly robust. It is significant at greater than the .001 level, and this means that you can be confident 99.9 percent of the time that party affiliation is an excellent predictor of attitudes toward immigration. In this case, the numbers are overwhelmingly good. But imagine that we had a different dispersal of answers from our respondents, so that even when looking at the table we could see little difference between the opinions of Democrats, Republicans, and others. If that were true, when we calculated the χ^2 value, we would find that our confidence level was higher than .10. In other words, we would be less than 90 percent sure that there was a relationship between our variables. In that case, we would conclude that the relationship between party and attitude toward immigration was not strong enough, and we could not confirm our hypothesis. In general, you need a 90 percent or better confidence level to accept your contention.

The χ^2 statistic is useful in evaluating relationships between sets of discrete data (information that comes in categories), but there are other tools to use when understanding the relationship between continuous or interval data (information that spans a continuum). The last type of quantitative analysis we will consider is what is called a *simple linear* or *ordinary least squares (OLS) regression*. Please note that there are other statistical tests you can use. I am simply demonstrating one I have found useful for my students. You should consult a reference book and/or ask your professor as you determine precisely which type of statistic you should calculate. OLS regression will evaluate whether your independent variable affects your dependent variable in a predictable way, in a linear relationship. While there are other types of regression you can perform, we will assume that a linear relationship is adequate for many types of research beginning students will be evaluating.

If Kevin had decided to look at the universe of cases[5] and come up with numerical values for his level of media access and pressure on the regime, he could have used OLS regression to test his hypothesis that the greater the citizens' media access in MENA countries in 2011, the stronger the pressure on the regime. Of course, he would need a different strategy for operationalizing his concepts, but that approach would still need to capture the same factors. This time, his variables would have final numerical representations. In fact, let's imagine that for media access, he took new media penetration data from the ITU (Internet use and cell phones) and then the Freedom House Media Freedom Rating,[6] but reordered them (literally, 100 minus the Freedom House ranking) so that higher ratings were associated with more freedom, just as the new media data increase with more ability to connect or have access to information, and then averaged them. So, for instance, for Egypt, the value would be $59.97 = [39.83 + 105.08 + (100 - 65)]/3$. Then, using the BBC Web site and Marc Lynch's *The Arab Uprising*, he came up with rankings of the level of pressure in each state that were sensitive to the intensity and geographic expanse of the protest, the geographic and social (i.e., did many different groups, including privileged regime members, support the protest) expanse, and whether the regime actually fell or not. A score of 100 was very high (including a toppled dictator), with 0 being very low. Of course, Kevin would have to justify his operationalization scheme and talk very seriously about how he was creating the data for his independent variable. In fact, this would be a case in which he would create a kind of questionnaire to use as he read his sources, filling it out in a manner similar to how a respondent completes a survey. He could make those raw data available to his reader in an appendix so that anyone could assess their validity and reliability.[7] For our purposes, we will trust that Kevin has done a good job and look at how the analysis turns out.

Kevin's next step (after determining the values for his data across all his cases) would be to use one of the statistical packages to perform regression, because he has two continuous (or interval) variables and he wants to see if they are related. What regression analysis does is fit a line through the points, not by connecting the dots but by capturing the trend of the direction and slope of the data. Then, the program computes a statistic called R-squared (R^2), which tells us something about how close the line is to the actual data. When R^2 is 1, the calculated line fits the data points exactly, which means that the independent variable accounts for all the variation in the dependent variable. As R^2 decreases, it shows our independent variable as less powerful in explaining the dependent variable. In other words, the closer R^2 is to 0, the worse the line fits. For a low R^2 value, the points are scattered throughout the diagram with seemingly no pattern to them, and at zero, they are arrayed in a band around a horizontal line. If we see no pattern, we can guess intuitively (and see visually) that the independent variable has no effect on the dependent variable. Also intuitively, when our eyes can see a line (assuming we're performing a linear regression), then we are likely to find a relationship when we have the software perform the calculation. In the social sciences, an R^2 value of .40 (an R value of about .63) is decent. If our calculations give us those values, then our cause explains 40 percent of the variance of our effect.

What follows is an excerpt of a hypothetical Analysis and Assessment of these data that we will attribute to Kevin. SPSS computes charts, which he includes and explains. Just as in the earlier selection, Kevin is evaluating the appropriateness of the hypothesis, and while statistics can be definitive, you'll see him preparing to discuss more than just the "bottom line" (i.e., "my hypothesis is confirmed" or "my hypothesis must be rejected").

Accounting for the Arab Spring: Media Access Appears Inconsequential

To what extent did the level of access to old and new media affect a country's experience in the "Arab spring?" After generating the data according to my method spelled out above (see the Appendix for raw data), I ran a regression to evaluate my hypothesis; unfortunately, the R^2 value was low (.226), meaning that the level of media access explains only 22.6 percent of the variance in the protest levels across the Middle East during the period of uprising. In other words, the link between the variables is weak, and other factors account for the balance of the variance, which is more than three quarters of the total (77.4 percent).

Table 8.4 Model Summary

Model	R	R Square	Adjusted R Square	Std. Error of the Estimate
1	.475[a]	.226	.178	29.684

a. Predictors: (Constant), MediaAccess.

b. Dependent Variable: ProtestLevel.

(Continued)

(Continued)

Looking directly at graph of the data, we can see the fragility of the relationship, as the points (one for each country case) are scattered all around the box, showing a faint negative-sloping pattern.

Figure 8.1 Level of Media Access and Strength of the MENA Uprisings

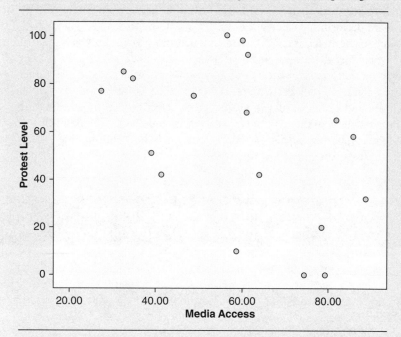

Here, the results from the regression help us understand more:

While the *F* statistic tells us that the line calculated through these points is significant at the 5 percent (4.6 percent) level, the problem is that this line is actually negatively sloping. If Y = protest level and X = level of media access, the model tells us that

$$Y = 103.544 - .806X.$$

However, the fundamental argument was that the more the media access, the more the protest (and the more likely the regime would fall). This line means the opposite. Eyeballing the data does not suggest that another type of curve might be a better fit or help me save the hypothesis. Moreover, because of that basic negative slope, I must conclude that given my data,

Table 8.5 Analysis of Variance, Media Access and Protest Levels

ANOVA[a]					
Model	Sum of Squares	Df	Mean Square	F	Sig.
Regression	4,116.069	1	4,116.069	4.671	.046[b]
Residual	14,098.209	16	881.138		
Total	18,214.278	17			

a. Dependent Variable: ProtestLevel.

b. Predictors: (Constant), MediaAccess.

Coefficients[a]					
	Unstandardized Coefficients		Standardized Coefficients		
Model	B	Std. Error	Beta	T	Sig.
1 (Constant)	103.544	23.353		4.434	.000
MediaAccess	−.806	.373	−.475	−2.161	.046

a. Dependent Variable: ProtestLevel.

level of media access does not account for the level of Arab spring activity, as I thought.

Along with that basic conclusion, these results leave me with two broad sets of questions. First, is the problem my operationalization scheme? In other words, do my values have severe validity and/or reliability problems that have prevented me from accurately capturing the essence of these concepts? Second, have I overestimated the role of the media, and do I need to consider other factors, as Lisa Anderson (2011) warned soon after the fall of Mubarak?

In this except of Kevin's quantitative analysis, we see him being driven by the hypothesis (as in the qualitative analysis example), while presenting the values without discussion. However, he spent a good deal of time figuring out those values (looking up data for the independent variable from the three sources) and then reading, evaluating, and calculating the index for the dependent variable. Kevin would provide those data in the appendices, along with his questionnaire or rubric (and the intermediate value judgments he made) for the level of protest. The focus of the section is the statistical results. Notice that he does not just copy and paste the output in his text, but he explains and interprets the figure and graphs for you. The essay helps you understand what the scatterplot and statistics mean, even if you are not familiar with these techniques, and keeps you focused on the hypothesis.

What should jump out at you are the structural similarities between the two Analysis and Assessment sections, regardless of the type of analysis. The big question is, does the hypothesized relationship describe and explain reality? In a qualitative analysis, an author spends more time explaining what the values are, whereas in a quantitative analysis, these can be presented in a table or scatterplot. Then, regarding whether there is a relationship between the factors, in a qualitative analysis, the analyst needs to explain the logic of whether and how there appears to be a causal relationship and what pieces of evidence are convincing. In the quantitative analysis, the researcher can go immediately to the statistics and discuss what the calculation means for the hypothesis. Interestingly, both evaluation styles lead the researcher to ask more questions, particularly when the relationships between the variables aren't robust or are unexpected.

As you know, neither A&A is complete; however, both provide excellent examples of how to present your analysis, regardless of which type you use.

PRACTICAL SUMMARY

The Analysis and Assessment section of the paper is where you decide whether (and sometimes to what extent) your hypothesis describes and explains reality. You make this decision on the basis of evidence that you carefully assemble according to the method you set out and the sources you identified in your Research Design; thus, your case or statistical analysis is focused on only the factors you earlier deemed important and is presented in the manner you explained in the RD. In writing your A&A, you should not feel pressure to reach a positive finding. Social and natural scientists are constantly learning by being wrong about what they originally thought. What is important is that you accurately assess your contention using appropriate data. Depending on your Research Question, the type of information that is available, and the number of cases that make sense to study, you will perform qualitative or quantitative analysis. Sometimes, you may be able to mix the two. For instance, Kevin could have had a very interesting paper presenting both the case studies and the regression. With each method, he learned something important and could have asked great additional questions. Frequently, however, a student has time for only one approach, and regardless of which you use, you want to gather evidence carefully and, where appropriate, assess the relationship between the variables. Remember not to get distracted by extraneous information. While other experts or commentators may have interesting opinions about related subjects, what is most important here is to keep your attention on your hypothesis and your plan. Develop your own set of evidence and interpret its meaning on your own. You may use scholarly and even journalistic information to help you determine variable values, as Kevin did in both examples. Notice that Kevin didn't repeat Marc Lynch's argument in his qualitative section or copy and paste some scholar's statistical analysis of all the cases in the quantitative section. Instead, he developed the methods—whether in qualitative or quantitative analysis—for assessing the composite values. In this section, you follow the plan that you set out in the Research Design. The data are so important here; your hunch about your hypothesis should not guide you. Analyze the information, and make your assessment of the thesis or hypothesis on the basis of those data alone.

When you have finished the A&A, you are almost done. Truly, the hardest part is over, and you can turn toward the happy business of making your final paper a coherent and well-organized one by writing your Conclusion, Introduction, and title next and then making one final (and very resolute) effort at revising and editing.

RECIPE 7: ANALYSIS AND ASSESSMENT

INGREDIENTS

- Your Research Question and hypothesis
- The "Raw Data Chart" (see the Web Resources and download a copy so that you can fill it in)
- Your various data sources
- Access to all of chapter 8
- Access to additional student examples (see Web Resources)

INSTRUCTIONS

1. Download the "Raw Data Chart" and begin adapting it to your needs. For instance, if you are performing quantitative analysis, you likely want to create a Microsoft Excel file as suggested. For either qualitative or quantitative analysis, you should fill out the chart so that you have the appropriate number of cases, variables, and indicators, and you understand how you will determine the composites. These big decisions are all based on your Research Design. Students sometimes find at this stage (or at the next step) that they must make adjustments, that elements of their design are inappropriate or unworkable. Make changes where you see fit (thinking through the consequences for the overall design) or consult your instructor with problems.

2. Go to your appropriate data source(s) and find the information to fill in your data chart. Depending on the type of data you have and the

sources available, you may want to work through one case at a time or find all the values for one indicator. How you proceed is your choice, but stay focused on precisely the data you need. Work methodically—through one case or through all the independent or dependent variable values—so that after a reasonable amount of time, you will know something useful in analyzing you data. The example of Kevin's moving through the independent variable data for both Algeria and Egypt is a good model for qualitative data, as is his effort to calculate the composite for the independent variable. Also helpful: use the examples provided to understand the notion of values here.

3. If students are doing more than one comparative case (qualitative analysis) or multiple statistical tests, I advise them not to wait to complete all their analyses before they start writing. You can see this in the examples provided. Although your section introduction will necessarily be incomplete (because you don't know the whole story yet), you can begin to write up your case (or a partial version of it), as Kevin did. In qualitative analysis, for each case, you must discuss the values of your independent variable, as well as those of your dependent variable and, if relevant, whether you can see the cause exerting an impact on the effect. Please realize that in first drafts, many students forget to discuss the dependent variable, and they assume that the reader "knows the story." Don't make that mistake. Enact your whole plan and explain the full case, because you might be surprised (as Kevin was) that your understanding of what unfolded was not accurate. As you write, use the relevant Kevin example to guide you, but realize that these excerpts are incomplete. In fact, in the first one, I haven't provided his discussion of the dependent variable. Still, both are great models to follow (if you remember that you have to also work through the effect and linking mechanism), and I encourage you to follow his structure carefully and even feel free to mimic some of the devices he uses as you write your case. The focus is on presenting (and explaining where necessary) the values of the variables and then examining whether they are related as the hypothesis says. If you are using quantitative analysis, this is the time to input your data into SPSS (or another program) and run the appropriate test. The ultimate statistic, as well as a scatterplot and other information, can provide interesting information. You must always convince your reader that your judgment about the nature of the relationship is correct. This job is easier to do with statistical analysis, but it can still be done through evidence and argumentation in qualitative analysis.

4. Be as thorough as you can, and begin to think through any "funny," unexpected patterns you see. In other words, you may want to do a residual analysis (consider outliers—cases that are very different from expectations) or begin to raise questions about some of your data here. (Again, consult Kevin's examples. His mention of the Persian Gulf states in the qualitative study is an example.) Do not worry if you can't confirm your hypothesis.

If your data and method have been approved and you have enacted your Research Design, then your professor will commend you for working honestly and diligently.

5.   When you have filled out your data chart completely and been able to test your hypothesis across all your cases and performed all the tests you planned, you are ready to write the full data analysis as well as to complete an introduction and conclusion to this section. Look to Kevin's and the other student papers available on the companion site for more guidance. Zoe's is included there, and she does a more complicated statistical analysis that might be more useful for some of you. There's also a paper that relies on discourse analysis that will help others. Remember to include an introduction to prepare the reader for the whole section and a conclusion to help the reader move on to new ideas and questions you will address in the last section of the paper. Learn from any and all of the provided student examples. They are all great, but different models.

EXERCISES

1.   Finish writing the text for Kevin's quantitative A&A, in which he discusses his potential operationalization problems and alternative explanations. What paths for future research do you think are appropriate?

2.   Consider the hypothesis and the data provided in this chapter that link party affiliation and attitudes toward immigration reform at your school, along with actual national data available from the report "What Americans Want from Immigration Reform in 2014," at http://publicreligion.org/site/wp-content/uploads/2014/06/Final-Immigration-Survey.pdf. Write up a subsection for the Analysis and Assessment section of a research paper whose author had access to both sets of data. How would you title this part (and any other subsections), and what additional research do you think would be useful if you wanted to write a strong research paper on immigration reform and party affiliation today?

3.   Imagine you were seeking to evaluate the hypothesis that higher levels of human development are associated with higher levels of female empowerment. Imagine that you used the United Nation's Human Development Index scores to capture human development and the ability of women to be elected to the lower house of parliament as the way to operationalize female empowerment. Consulting these Web sites (http://hdr.undp.org/en/content/table-2-human-development-index-trends-1980-2013, http://www.ipu.org/wmn-e/world.htm, and http://www.ipu.org/wmn-e/classif.htm), write an A&A either by eyeballing the data (clearly not a precise evaluation, but this method gives you some practice in analysis and assessment) or, if you have more time, by plugging the information into a statistical program.

NOTES

1. Note that with statistical analysis, there is always some probability that the relationship you find to be significant is not. If we accept a hypothesis at the 99 percent confidence level, that means there is still a 1 percent chance that the relationship occurred by chance.

2. An excellent resource about a form of qualitative analysis, case studies, is Alexander L. George and Andrew Bennett, *Case Studies and Theory Development in the Social Sciences* (Cambridge, MA: MIT Press, 2004).

3. Kuwait, Qatar, the UAE, and Saudi Arabia were all ranked higher than Egypt in tweet volume, but these countries (except the UAE) had approximately the same number of users as Egypt. The range of those considered similar was 113,000 to 133,000 Twitter accounts (with Egypt at about 131,000), and the UAE topped out the group at 201,000 (ASMR, Active Twitter Users).

4. You might choose this sample because it is one to which you could get easy access at your school. In your Research Design section, you would want to discuss the significance of using this sample, of course, and consider what impact it could have on your findings.

5. I found the universe of cases by going to the World Bank's Web site, which defined the MENA region. I excluded Djibouti, however, because it was not listed in the Freedom House rankings for MENA, and Israel because it is not an authoritarian state. Granted, 17 cases is a small set, but for the purposes of illustration and learning at the undergraduate level, I decided to continue and would have allowed Kevin to do so too. Typically, I would like to see at least 30 cases, but I would make 15 the minimum for an undergraduate paper. Because many of my students are intimidated by statistical analysis, particularly on large data sets, I make exceptions.

6. I took the rankings from 2010 because some states, such as Egypt, opened up after the uprisings, but citizens faced a much less friendly environment during the protests.

7. To generate the data, I gave a maximum of 20 points on five factors: success in toppling the regime, disunity among the elite, social and mass solidarity in favor of toppling the regime, geographic expanse of the protests, and size and intensity of the protests.

chapter 9

Bringing the Paper Together in Three Essential Ways

The Conclusion, Introduction, and Title

When you have performed your analysis and written all of the substantive parts of your paper, you are at the equivalent of the home stretch of a race; the crowds are cheering, but you might have hit the wall. Like the marathoner in the last few miles, the research paper writer who has finished all of her or his paper except the first and last sections is also very tired at this point. Still, you—whether runner or writer—want to end strong as you complete these crucial and related parts of the paper—the Conclusion, Introduction, and title.

You might be surprised that I am mentioning them in the reverse order from how readers will encounter these sections. The reason for this seemingly backward approach is that to write the Introduction well, you need information from the Conclusion, and the best titles reflect the Introduction. So bear with me as we proceed in this sensible sequence.

These kindred parts of the paper help you sum up what the research has been all about as well as point you forward to potential additional work, create positive initial and final impressions, and entice someone to pick up and read your paper. The Conclusion reminds readers of what you argued and why, as well as what you learned. In addition, it steps back and makes sense of your results, interpreting them in light of any methodological challenges you had; suggests ways these findings might improve our understanding of other phenomena or incidents; and charts paths for further research, showing your vast (and now enhanced, after undertaking the study) understanding of the area of inquiry in which you have been engaged. The Introduction, though separated from the Conclusion by many pages, performs related functions. First, however, it must both introduce the reader to your question and convince that person to keep reading. Typically, you can accomplish those goals by explaining why your topic and query are important and interesting to multiple audiences, stating your thesis, and providing an overview of the whole paper. When the Introduction is drafted, you can turn to perfecting the title. You have put forward earlier working titles, but for the last version, you want to expend some serious brainpower on coming up with a great title for the paper. Why? The title captures, to the best of your ability, the argument and cases of your paper, and it creates that very first impression on the reader. The title, then, is the equivalent of a firm handshake, while the Introduction compares with appropriate and engaging initial conversation with a new acquaintance, and the Conclusion is a satisfying end to your meeting that creates confidence in you, underlines the initial positive first impression, and makes your interlocutor want to see or hear from you again.

CONSIDERING THE SIGNIFICANCE AND LIMITATIONS OF YOUR FINDINGS: THE CONCLUSION

Your Conclusion accomplishes several tasks. First, it ties the whole paper together by restating your thesis and where the weight of the evidence came down. Second, the Conclusion discusses why the argument and the particular findings (across your cases) are important and what your results mean for various audiences. Third, the Conclusion is a critical assessment of what you accomplished. Here, you return to those best decisions you made in the Research Design section and consider what impact they had on your findings. What, if anything, would you do differently if you could do this study over? Fourth, it assesses the versatility of your thesis, considering the extent to which you can apply your argument to other cases or, conversely, whether you need to limit its applicability. Last, the Conclusion is a jumping-off point for the future, for you or other researchers who might like to pick up where you left off. This is where you can set out questions to pursue to continue this line of research in a fruitful manner.

As you know by now, the research paper consists of several sections that appear before the Conclusion. When you first started writing this paper, you probably could not adequately conceive of how these parts were related to one another and what the logical flow between them would be. At this point, you have, I hope, mastered the interrelationship among the segments and, through your section introductions and conclusions, have provided smooth transitions between the different parts of the paper. The Conclusion also helps you accomplish this task by tying the paper together one last time: very briefly reminding the reader of your question, why it was important, what you thought the best answer to it was, how you were going to evaluate this contention, and what the assessment of the evidence showed. The concluding section walks the reader through the significance of the research, the argument, and the evidence.

A vital part of this discussion is to remind the reader why anyone should care about what you found. Why was your Research Question so important?

Why are the instances that you studied significant? Remember, you want to answer these questions from the perspective of several audiences. For the social scientific community, your findings say something about a theoretical debate in the field. Remind your reader of the scholarly controversies and what you have learned about the merits of a particular line of reasoning. In addition, your results also have significance for the interpretation of a particular set of cases. For practitioners, your findings might provide advice about appropriate behavior when dealing with comparable situations, and for citizens, your work might be important for understanding the world or being better members of a local, national, or global community. Don't ignore the normative implications of the work, which enlighten us about what ought to be and how we ought to behave.

Your Conclusion likely engenders feelings of both humility and pride. While this section itself is polished to finalize the beautiful "package" that is your paper, you should not feel that the "ribbon-tying" has to be neat and that once assembled, you are done with your discussion. In fact, research is often quite messy, and despite our best efforts to find uncomplicated support for our original contentions, we often cannot reach such a nice conclusion. Turning back to our discussion of medical research, you do not have to confirm your assertions to do well; you simply need to evaluate them honestly. This section is where you come back to the compromises and the lines of logic you pursued— whether you found support for your thesis or not—to consider whether your choices had both a significant and possibly a detrimental impact on your study. In the Conclusion, you might want to suggest that a different school of thought appears stronger now or that you would alter the plan for conducting the study (whether in selecting cases, operationalizing variables, choosing sources, and/ or generating information) in certain ways. Of course, you should explain why you want to make these changes as well as assert why you think these modifications would lead to a better design and outcome.

As you consider what you did and found, you should think about the extent to which your findings provide insight into other cases. Take pride if your results help you understand any other political phenomena. But perhaps you need to scale back your earlier claims, finding that your thesis only partially applies or is relevant to a smaller subset of cases. Consider whether some of the limitations may have resulted from faulty decisions you made at earlier stages in the research (Literature Review or Research Design), from which you could never recover.

Finally, regardless of how tired you are of this paper, the concepts involved, and the cases, you should discuss how you would proceed if you had the resources (and stamina) to continue. In doing this, you reinforce to the reader that you understand the significance of your findings for this area of scholarship. Moreover, you indicate what you would do differently or which new paths you would pursue to enhance the field's understanding of this debate and these sets of cases (or even related instances). By charting a hypothetical next course, you impress the reader with your enthusiasm and command of the discipline, and you help yourself on any future research paper assignments. Next time, you won't have to agonize about your Research Question. It will be set out for you in this Conclusion!

For an example of a Conclusion, let's turn again to Kevin and look at the Conclusion for his hypothetical quantitative study, which we viewed at the end of chapter 7. Remember, his statistical analysis contradicted what he expected. There was a very weak but negative relationship between media access and the success of the revolts in toppling their governments. Kevin's section heading reminds readers of his argument and indicates (after the colon) that his research leaves him with many questions. Then, as you read, look how systematically Kevin accomplishes each of the requirements for this section, reminding the reader of his question, the literature, his hypothesis, and the outlines of his Research Design. He presents his results, and then Kevin faces head on some of his weaknesses. In fact, he grapples with something many students face: the realization that some element(s) of his Research Design was (were) faulty. Thereafter, Kevin makes suggestions about how to carry on the research, discusses realistically the nature of the uprisings in the Middle East and North Africa (MENA), and assesses the value of his research to scholars, practitioners, and observers. Kevin has done a fantastic job racing, not limping, to the finish line and turning in an excellent performance.

The Role of Media in the Recent MENA Uprisings: More Questions Than Answers

In December and February 2011, Tunisians and Egyptians shocked the world when popular uprisings against long-serving dictators quickly forced those leaders out of power. Unrest spread throughout the region, and the potential for removing authoritarians from the Middle East and North Africa seemed great. After so many years of oppression and different attempts to overthrow their rulers, why did these revolts succeed? Scholars suggested multiple reasons, some focusing on the nature of the international system, the socioeconomic conditions within societies, the ability of opposition and regime elites to negotiate pacts, the role of activists, and the variation in the dictatorial regimes, but the one that appeared most appealing was the role of old and new media. This new period of unrest (beginning with the Iranian uprising in 2009) seemed to coincide with the enormous growth in communications technology that allowed ordinary citizens to know things their leaders wanted kept secret and to contact one another, spreading news, information, and, at times, horrifying pictures. Access to the media, then, seemed to be the most compelling factor in accounting for the revolutions, with greater citizen access to the media meaning more opposition (and success) in toppling the regime.

I chose to evaluate that argument by examining the universe of cases in MENA and determining values for media access and level of opposition. Because I believed in the importance of both old and new media in affecting the outcome, I used the Freedom House Freedom of the Press Rankings (scaled so that larger numbers reflected greater freedom levels) to capture conditions in old media as well as United Nations figures for Internet and cell phone penetration rates in countries. As these were all calculated on 100-point scales, I took the average to come up with an access rating for each country. Then, I determined another 100-point score for the level and success of opposition, looking at not only whether the regime fell but also if the opposition presence in the streets was large, widespread, and socially diverse. In addition, my index also took into account whether the regime was united or whether some political elites began defecting. All of these data came from respected news sources (BBC) and Professor Marc Lynch's (2012) account of the uprisings. Finally, I ran a regression to investigate the relationship.

The regression analysis indicated that I could not sustain my hypothesis. In fact, my data were negatively related, and the relationship was very weak. These findings led me to consider whether my operationalization scheme was appropriate, as well as to rethink my initial argument. With respect to calculating my variable values, I have some concerns about my independent variable. Although the building blocks came from well-respected organizations whose ratings are considered robust, my focus on access only might have been misguided. Looking at Lynch's argument, access to cable outlets was supposed to transform identities, but raw figures that look at openness of the media system don't capture the effects on those consuming the media. In addition, having a cell phone or Internet access and Facebook or Twitter accounts is insufficient for understanding whether people are connected and politically engaged. Thus, these quantitative measures were convenient and perhaps captured access, but maybe my model would have been best served to highlight the impacts of watching and being wired. Potentially my assessment of the dependent variable was problematic, as my knowledge and understanding of the Middle East are not expert. I did rely on good sources and was careful in filling out my questionnaire, although I may have needed different categories. Still, I believe that my full accounting gave me an excellent sense of the uprisings, and as I was encountering these data and making my assessments of the dependent variable, I began to question my original argument. Many states had sizable uprisings, but then they used some combination of repression and enticement to demobilize the crowds. Thus, I began to think that in

(Continued)

(Continued)

arriving at my hypothesis, I was too affected by the euphoria over Tunisia and Egypt (as well as the initial joy and hope regarding Libya and Syria, which were soon dashed) and that even if my values of the dependent variable were more precise, media access wouldn't tell the whole story. Of course, the regression results confirmed my negative impression.

When I began researching the subject, one of the first pieces I encountered was by noted Middle East expert Lisa Anderson (2011), who reminded readers that observers a century earlier had touted the role of new technology (the telegraph) in promoting Middle East uprisings. She cautioned readers that other factors were likely more important. As I proceeded in my research on my dependent variable, I began to think more about Anderson's warning, especially the roles of social (ethnic, religious, and sectarian) diversity and domestic structures. In countries with sizable and distrusted minorities, leaders were often able to blame the uprisings on them and defuse popular demands, especially with a mix of rewards and punishments (Anderson 2011; Lynch 2012; Gause 2011). In addition, the role of regime elites in deciding to abandon or stay loyal to the leader seems important in determining the outcome. Here, whether structure matters (Geddes 2004) or more emphasis should be placed on social pressure and pacts (Karl 2005) is not clear. Thus, while my project presents a definitive answer about the role of media access (it wasn't important), this research raises more questions about the recent MENA uprisings.

In the past twenty-five years or so, analysts have noted a new type of revolution that some have called velvet (Ash 2009) and others have deemed color (Bunce and Wolchik 2006). Their key features are that they are generally nonutopian in their ideology, liberal in their espousal of human and individual rights and assertion of the dignity of ordinary people, mass based, and nonviolent. The MENA uprisings are part of this class of rebellion, but many turned brutal, and even in those that apparently succeeded in toppling a dictator, that success hasn't guaranteed a more liberal system. Perhaps more sensitivity to these other velvet and color cases might help us better understand 2011. The sobering fact that many regimes have seen challenges and have allowed dictators to be dumped, and then elites clambered onto a new oppressive bandwagon suggests that tempering euphoria as we watch revolts unfold would be wise.

Thus, this investigation underlines that revolution is a process that only seldom succeeds. Perhaps trying to characterize the revolts' outcomes in 2011 and 2012 was a big part of the problem in this research, because rarely is a political and social transformation complete in two years. Still, these findings teach theorists to be wary of crediting new technology for political change and to take more time to understand the internal politics of the states under siege. Moreover, political scientists should be more cautious about claiming victory for revolution in its early days. Yes, the dictator has to be overthrown, but true liberal democratic change encompasses institutional and cultural reforms too. For policy makers, while encouraging the dissemination of information is important for giving people access and hope, this research suggests that knowledge and linkages can't bring about political change if a regime is bent on violence and/or its major elements are united in preventing reform. Thus, we need more research to understand what does lead to lasting and liberal political change and what policy makers and citizens can do to encourage these transformations.

In sum, this research answers one question, but leaves me with many more. My efforts also give me great respect for the research process itself and the complexities of both bringing about the toppling of a dictator and translating that ouster into a stable and free political system.

WRITING A GOOD INTRODUCTION

With the Conclusion completed, you can turn to the Introduction. Although the Introduction comes first in the paper, one of its most important functions (and one that many students overlook) is to provide an overview of the whole work. Thus, writing this piece at the end—when you have written all of the sections, and the logic, arguments, evidence, and conclusions are clear—makes sense. Very basically and obviously, your Introduction introduces the reader to your research paper.

What most students know about the Introduction is that it should grab a reader's attention; it should entice the reader into wanting to continue. In attracting the reader, you need to introduce her or him to your topic and why it is so interesting and important to multiple audiences (scholars, policy makers, and citizens). Does this sound familiar? It should, because you thought through these issues at the beginning of the process. Your recipes, worksheets, and checklists from the question development and Annotated Bibliography phases will come in handy here. In the Introduction, you provide basic background and content so that the reader—whether she or he knows much about your issue at the outset or not—can follow your argument and learns to care about it because you and important others think it is significant.

After enticing the reader, the Introduction provides that overview of the paper so that the reader knows what you are arguing and why, how you are performing the study, what you actually found, and what is notable about these results. In other words, you provide a kind of road map to the paper, with your thesis prominently stated early on. Some students chafe at the idea of the overview because they think it is repetitive. True, you should avoid needless redundancy in a paper, and you should never copy and paste your own words from section to section. Still, in discussing complex issues, reminders and reinforcement are good. They help the reader understand better. So don't be that mystery or joke writer—holding your thesis or punchline and key evidence until the end—when writing research papers or essays. Give your reader the necessary previews to enhance her or his understanding and your paper's clarity. Here, also realize that your ultimate thesis has two parts. It contains not only your original contention (what argument you subjected to an empirical test) but also your finding (to what extent was your contention confirmed). Stating both at the outset is important for a good paper, and as you know, good writing always contains a clearly stated, prominently placed, and easy-to-find thesis. You will likely include yours at either the end of the first or second paragraph of your Introduction.

Writing this first section shouldn't be too difficult for you, because you have already had experience writing a good introduction that includes an overview. In chapter 4, we explicitly discussed how to write this part of the Literature Review. (You saw this again in Kevin's example of qualitative analysis in chapter 8.) As before, you want to communicate your query (here it is your Research Question; in the Literature Review it is how scholars have answered your Research Question and which response is most compelling). Moving forward to the road map part of the Introduction, you want to do something like you did in the Conclusion, recapping the essential elements of your paper. In other words, you want to summarize what you have done in each of the subsequent sections of the paper in a way that links each element of this larger process smoothly and logically. Perhaps a difficulty will be to make the Introduction different enough from the Conclusion. Here, you can simply preview the research results, methodological concerns, and additional questions you need to ask, and spend more time on them in the final section.

An important metaphor to think about when you write the Introduction is that of a contract between you and your readers, and you want to write it to your advantage. You start by attracting readers to your paper (so they will sign on the dotted line and keep reading), and you keep that attention because, in the overview, you promise only what you deliver. You are careful not to mention extraneous information or overstate what you have accomplished, because otherwise readers will wonder where those ideas or assertions are. Also, like a contract, you want to lay everything out clearly. Neither you nor readers want surprises, so everything of consequence that follows in the paper is mentioned in the Introduction.

Again, let's see how Kevin handled this task. This time, however, we will look at his Introduction to his actual paper, which was the comparative case analysis. Again, I want to underline that while these two sections (the Conclusion for the hypothetical quantitative study and this Introduction to his qualitative paper) are related, Kevin could not use them in the same paper, because his Research Design and precise findings are different. Still, each shares the same foundation of the Annotated Bibliography, Literature Review, and Model and Hypothesis, and discussions of those parts should seem familiar. As you read this one, again pay attention to the structure of the section and think about how the form of this Introduction is similar to and different from the Conclusion. Also make sure that Kevin has not literally repeated himself, using the same phrases or sentences. One other point to note: the Introduction is the one section for which a heading is optional. Typically, because this section follows directly after the paper's title, a distinct heading is not necessary. There are occasions, however, when a writer (or your instructor) will want to (or want you to) include one.

On December 17, 2010, Mohamed Bouazizi, a fruit vender in Tunisia, set himself on fire in an act of frustration and desperation. His self-immolation ignited a regionwide protest movement that has been called the Arab spring. While many observers had long thought that Arab publics wouldn't or couldn't revolt against their leaders and had no interest in liberal ideals, these protests proved them wrong. The challenges indicated that popular dissatisfaction with repressive regimes was widespread in the Middle East and North Africa (MENA), that Arab and/or Islamic populations were just as interested in political freedom as other peoples, and that political actions (symbolic and otherwise) in one place can have effects around a region as well as across the world.

Understanding why these uprisings succeeded is therefore a compelling and important question, and scholars have offered six different explanations to account for them. Some arguments stress structural factors—the distribution of power in the international system (Skocpol 1979) or national socioeconomic conditions (Huntington 1997; Moore 1967; Ross 2001)—while others focus on the role of agents, including the interaction of opposition and regime elites (O'Donnell and Schmitter 1986; Karl 2005), or citizen dissatisfaction (Havel 1978; Kuran 1991). Still a fifth school of thought combines this interest in structure and agents to emphasize the role of domestic institutions in determining whether elites hang together or are willing to negotiate with the opposition and enable protests to succeed (Geddes 2004). Yet as the first decade of the twenty-first century came to a close, an important new factor seemed to be the most compelling: the access to information provided by cable television that the regimes couldn't control and the ability of citizens to connect via social media (Lynch 2012).

To evaluate the importance of access to media (old and new) in toppling regimes and bringing about political change in 2011, I performed comparative case studies of Algeria and Egypt. This pairing provides variation and control, as Algeria had a relatively smaller and ultimately unsuccessful revolt, while Egypt had a massive uprising that unseated the

(Continued)

(Continued)

long-time dictator, Hosni Mubarak, and the countries faced similar international and domestic socioeconomic conditions, as well as roughly equivalent social and domestic political structures and citizen activism. To capture the levels of activism, I used data on media freedom from Freedom House and information from the International Telecommunications Union (Internet and cell phone penetration), and to understand the success in bringing down the government, I looked at not only whether the regime fell but to what extent it faced popular challenges and how broad based that opposition was.

My case analysis found that while there was a different ultimate outcome in each state, the role of media access is likely not the best factor for accounting for the variation.[1] In fact, old and new media access in both states was similar, with Egypt having a slight advantage. Moreover, the opposition in both countries was strong, with Algeria's citizens rioting and making demands. Important differences, however, were that Algerians didn't call for their regime's ouster, but for better food prices and conditions. Moreover, regime violence intimidated the Algerians more than the Egyptians, just as the state's concessions were more likely to buy the Algerians off. Perhaps my findings regarding the role of media would have been different if I had chosen a better pairing. In making this sample, I underestimated the level of opposition in Algeria, and thus I wasn't comparing highly different outcomes.

Still, the research provides some interesting insights. First, while it could not confirm the importance of media access, it did suggest other potential causes for examination, including ones that scholars have already noted as important, such as the unity or disunity of elites and domestic structure. In addition, these case studies pointed to another factor: the role of a recent, traumatic past that created a political culture of intimidation. Algerians experienced terrible violence in the 1990s when they tried to stand up for the integrity of elections Islamists had won but the regime erased. Some observers suggest that this violence helped demobilize them. Egyptians did not have a similar, recent trauma.[2]

Thus, the study leads to more questions than answers, and continued research would serve scholars, policy makers, and ordinary citizens. The scholarly debate about what causes political challenges and when they succeed is not resolved, and we have an inadequate understanding of why the events in 2011 unfolded as they did. Because MENA is an important region of the world, policy makers and citizens have an interest in better understanding the politics there. With this research, we begin to see that new developments are interesting, but attention to traditional, causal factors in political science (such as elite politics, domestic structures, and political culture) remains important.

As you would expect, given what I've told you about the Introduction and the Conclusion, the structure of these two sections is similar, as is the information provided. (Although given the difference in the content of the data analysis, these two sample sections vary. Again, remember, I provided the Conclusion for the hypothetical quantitative paper and the Introduction for the qualitative analysis.) This kind of positive reinforcement helps the two serve as attractive bookends to the material in the paper. The Introduction spends more time enticing the reader by talking a bit about the context that inspired the question. In addition to laying out what is to follow in each section (and notice that the discussion proceeds in the order that the reader will meet this information), the Introduction explains why different audiences would find this research interesting and important—again part of its effort to sustain attention. Kevin has done a fine job, as each section of the paper is carefully represented, including the Conclusion, and while the whole section is similar to the Conclusion, the language does not mirror it. The Introduction, however, spends little time discussing the data analysis, potential problems with the method, and future research, although it does mention these things. The Conclusion devotes less space to the earlier sections of the paper, focusing more on the issues related to the Research Design and Analysis and Assessment. Also notice that in both cases (quantitative and qualitative), these sections consist of several paragraphs. You have too much to accomplish in each to adequately wrap up, consider and offer remedies for any weaknesses, and point to new directions for research (Conclusion) or entice and preview (Introduction) in one or even two paragraphs. Kevin has understood the requirements well and has struck the right balance here. Excellent!

A LAST ELEMENT IN ATTRACTING READERS: DEVELOPING AN APPEALING TITLE

Kevin has one more job to do before his draft is complete: he needs to come up with a title for the paper. Your title should do at least three things: communicate your question or puzzle, identify your cases or the specifics of your study, and summarize your argument or thesis. Yet you have a limited number of words—if the Introduction is the paper in brief, the title is the microscopic view. Because you're trying to accomplish so much in so few words, you'll often need to use a colon to separate the ideas. Successful titles, in addition, express the question, cases, and argument in an appealing way. Be careful, though, that your attempts at cleverness don't introduce confusion. The title's main goal is to communicate the basics of the paper. From the title, readers should understand in a nutshell what you have learned and how.

Taking a careful look at some great titles from published works can help you see how to strike that balance of finding something creative that accomplishes these goals:

Deborah Gordon Brooks, *He Runs, She Runs: Why Gender Stereotypes Do Not Harm Women Candidates* (Princeton, NJ: Princeton University Press, 2013).

Christine Chinkin and Freya Baetens, *Sovereignty, Statehood, and State Responsibility: Essays in Honour of James Crawford* (New York: Cambridge University Press, 2014).

Tom Clark with Anthony Heath, *Hard Times: The Divisive Toll of the Economic Slump* (New Haven, CT: Yale University Press, 2014).

Carolyn W. Lee, *Do-It-Yourself Democracy: The Rise of the Public Engagement Industry* (New York: Oxford University Press, 2015).

Christopher S. Parker and Matt A. Barreto, *The Change They Can't Believe In: The Tea Party and Reactionary Politics in America* (Princeton, NJ: Princeton University Press, 2013).

Bruce Riedel, *What We Won: America's Secret War in Afghanistan, 1979–1989* (Washington, DC: Brookings Institution Press, 2014).

Richard J. Semiatin, *Campaigns on the Cutting Edge*, 2nd ed. (Washington, DC: CQ Press, 2012).

Yuhua Wang, *Tying the Autocrat's Hands: The Rise of the Rule of Law in China* (New York: Cambridge University Press, 2014).

Stephen J. Wayne, *Is This Any Way to Run a Democratic Election?* 5th ed. (Washington, DC: CQ Press, 2013).

These titles succeed because they communicate key information in an attractive way. Notice how authors use their imaginations most on the first part of the title, and that is no accident, because this phrase makes the initial impression. When the title is shortened, the second half—after the colon—is dropped, so you want your opening to be clever.

Looking more carefully at the first title, you conjure up a picture, but also think about a pop-culture book and an expression (*He Says, She Says*). Several other titles also use those devices (creating an image or harking back to culturally relevant phrases). Another popular device for catchy names is to use alliteration. After the colon, however, authors tend to communicate the information about the subject matter and cases in a more prosaic manner. Once you start looking, you'll see titles that borrow creatively from movies, songs, and other types of literature. In sum, by finding a beginning that is evocative, alliterative, suggestive of another famous work, or even surprising or provocative, you will be on track to writing a successful title, as it will likely jump out at readers, attracting them to the work. Then, finish up by providing more information so the reader can be clear about your argument. Of course, not all authors succeed in communicating the argument and focus instead on case and subject, but you should strive to be catchy, clever, and clear about your contention.

I counsel students to write down a basic title (one that captures the key elements) first, and then take some time—perhaps half an hour or even a few 10-minute attempts over the course of a few days—to play with ideas for making it a more appealing one. Your friends or classmates are often great helpers here. Just be careful not to settle on a title that is too silly or difficult to understand. You are looking to strike a balance between appeal and clarity. If you have to choose, I advise you to be clearer rather than too cute.

For Kevin, here are some basic options: "Understanding the Arab Spring: Why Media Access Alone Can't Account for the Uprisings in Algeria and Egypt" (qualitative version) or "The Uprisings in the Middle East and North Africa: A Statistical Analysis of the Relationship between Old and New Media and the Fall of Regimes." Now, how might Kevin adapt these to be more appealing? In fact, he offered "You Say You Want a Revolution: Why Media Access Alone Can't Account for the Uprisings in Algeria and Egypt." Another possibility for the first part—for those of you very familiar with Theda Skocpol's highly influential work *The State and Social Revolution*—might be "The Media and the 2011 Revolutions," followed by the same basic information. Both of these are fine titles in that they are interesting but they also communicate the most important information about his paper—argument, cases, and findings. Do you have other ideas to offer Kevin?

ARE YOU DONE? THE JOY (AND CONTINUED RESPONSIBILITIES) OF FINALIZING YOUR DRAFT

If you have proceeded in writing this paper as I have recommended, after you write the Conclusion, Introduction, and title, you have completed a first draft. That is an accomplishment to celebrate. While I know this is easy for me to say, try to finish your draft in time to get some distance from it so that you can ultimately turn in an excellent paper. As you know from chapter 6, revising and editing gives you that polished *final* product. Again, assuming that you've been writing the paper in sections, rethinking and rewriting as you've gone along (e.g., always consulting Recipe 5, "Revising and Editing," using the "10 Rules (and Then Some) to Write By" handout, and integrating your own and your readers' comments into your revisions and edits) and spiraling back as you sharpen or adjust your ideas, this end-stage task won't be too hard. It is very important for both the overall quality of the paper and your satisfaction with the process.

In our marathon analogy, it's mile 25.[3] Your feet are hurting, and your legs are aching, but you feel excited because you have a whole paper. As numerous authors have noted, writing a complete version of a paper is hard, and a full draft is a great accomplishment. Take some time, celebrate, and stop thinking about this work for a little while (preferably a few days or at least several hours, not just a few minutes) so you will be in a better position to finish your research paper. Your mind should be fresh when you revise and edit for the last time.

While I have encouraged you to circle back and make adjustments as you move forward, the first completed full draft is seldom perfect. In fact, this version can often be quite awkward and problematic in places.[4] Therefore, you have a little more work to do (maybe another mile to run) before you can cross the finish line. Still, working with a complete draft—particularly one that has already been revised and edited in places—is much easier than starting from scratch. But you can always make it better. Because you have been pushed throughout this book to write, often before you felt ready, you now have many pages of text to consider for their overall coherence and methodological soundness as well as basic grammatical and usage problems. In other words, you need both to revise and to edit your paper with the goal of producing a final draft of which you can feel enormously proud.

So go back to chapter 6 to remind yourself of what you need to do to make the logical and rhetorical flow of the paper the best you can. Also be concerned with the formatting and appearance of the paper. Don't put your fabulous ideas in a substandard package! Follow the guidelines there and, at the very last, when you are truly satisfied, print out your work. Feel proud as you hand it in; your accomplishment in writing this research paper has been great. And see—you have completed a task that initially seemed so formidable. Like the tortoise—moving slowly, steadily, and wisely, I might add—you have run a great race and written your research paper. Hooray!

PRACTICAL SUMMARY

The last jobs of your paper involve writing some very important elements: the Conclusion, Introduction, and title. The concluding and introductory sections are not short if your paper is long, and you need to give them significant attention. Although they are bookends for the material that comes within your paper, they are not identical. Be sure to avoid reusing exact phrases or sentences in these sections. While both are comprehensive, in the Conclusion, focus more on the significance of your findings, any ways you could have improved this study, and directions for future research. In the Introduction, concentrate more on the background, the appeal of your Research Question, scholarly perspectives and your Research Design, although you will also reveal your findings and suggest future plans. When these are complete, turn to the title. It is short, but a good one is creative and attracts readers to the paper. Your title seeks to convey these same first elements (question, answer, and cases) as briefly and memorably as possible. Typically, your title will have two parts to it, separated by a colon, and the clever phrase will come first.

RECIPE 8: CONCLUSION, INTRODUCTION, AND TITLE

INGREDIENTS

- Conclusion, Introduction, and Title Worksheet (see Web Resources and download a copy so that you can fill it in)
- Access to all of chapter 9
- Access to additional student examples (see Web Resources)

INSTRUCTIONS

1. Download the Conclusion, Introduction, and Title Worksheet, which asks you to summarize each section of the paper, and fill it out.

2. To write your Conclusion, open chapter 9 to Kevin's example and have your filled-in worksheet available. Then, mimicking the structure and even some of his language, write your Conclusion, being sure to include every element of the worksheet, but providing more detail on the last five elements (consideration of the findings, what you would do differently in your design, how you might apply your research to other cases or why you must restrict its application, and directions for future research). You may want to consult other student examples in the Web Resources too.

3. To write your Introduction, open chapter 9 to Kevin's example and have your filled-in worksheet available. Then, mimicking the structure and even some of his language, write your Introduction, being sure to include every element of the worksheet, but providing more detail on the first six elements. Remember not to use the same words or even sentence structures as you did in your Conclusion. For additional ideas, consult other student examples in the Web Resources.

4. In writing the title, sometimes a creative idea pops into mind right away. If that's the case for you, work with it, but remember that you need to communicate what you found and what you studied, too. (See the worksheet for guidance.) If you have no immediate inspiration, write out a basic title that communicates the question, cases, and findings. Think about what you have, and then try to advance an alliterative, evocative (of a picture or instance), or culturally connected idea for the first phrase. Look at the examples provided in the textbook for additional inspiration. Write down any and every title you create. If, after about half an hour, you don't have one you like, come back to this job later and try again. Work with a friend or classmate if possible; you can help each other out.

EXERCISES

1. With the information you have, write a Conclusion and an Introduction for Gabriela's project assuming that she found that the changes in party and election systems did account for the higher polarization today than in the 1980s. Develop a title for the paper.

2. Develop clever titles for both of Kevin's papers (quantitative and qualitative), as well as catchy first parts of the title for Gabriela, Max, and Zoe.

NOTES

1. I've added italics here so that you can find the thesis. You don't need to italicize yours, but you should make a point of finding it and being sure it is clearly and prominently stated.

2. It is interesting to consider whether Egyptians as of this writing (fall 2013) would have a sense of trauma after revolution given what has happened since the fairly elected leader Mohammed Morsi was deposed and the military has clamped down on freedoms and made thousands of arrests. [This footnote was Kevin's reflection on this case.]

3. As I mention in chapter 6, if this is a yearlong (or greater) thesis, you will likely need more time to revise and adjust. Making sense of all your data after such a complex process takes time, so give the revisions significant attention.

4. Eviatar Zerubavel, *The Clockwork Muse: A Practical Guide to Writing Theses, Dissertations, and Books* (Cambridge, MA: Harvard University Press, 1999) provides many quotations from famous authors who discuss the inadequacies of their first drafts. Please note, however, that Zerubavel does not advocate revising carefully throughout the process, as I have.

Bibliography

Abramowitz, Alan I. *The Disappearing Center: Engaged Citizens, Polarization, and American Democracy*. New Haven, CT: Yale University Press, 2010.

Anderson, Lisa. "Demystifying the Arab Spring." *Foreign Affairs* 90, no. 3 (May 2011): 2–7.

Arab Social Media Report, Dubai School of Government. "Twitter Usage in the MENA Region." June 8, 2011. http://interactiveme.com/index.php/2011/06/twitter-usage-in-the-mena-middle-east/.

Ash, Timothy Garton. "Velvet Revolution: The Prospects." *New York Review of Books*. December 3, 2009. http://www.nybooks.com/articles/archives/2009/dec/03/velvet-revolution-the-prospects/.

Baumer, Donald C., and Howard J. Gold. *Parties, Polarization, and Democracy in the United States*. Boulder, CO: Paradigm, 2010.

Bipartisan Policy Center. "Detailed Charts: Turnout Charts: Presidential Race." http://bipartisan policy.org/sites/default/files/Turnout%20Detailed%20Charts.pdf.

Bishop, Bill. *The Big Sort: Why the Clustering of Like-minded America Is Tearing Us Apart*. New York: Houghton Mifflin, 2008.

Boix, Carles, and Susan C. Stokes, eds. *Oxford Handbook of Comparative Politics*. New York: Oxford University Press, 2009.

Boyd, Richard. "Thomas Hobbes and the Perils of Pluralism." *Journal of Politics* 63 (2001): 392–413.

Bratton, Kathleen A. "Critical Mass Theory Revisited: The Behavior and Success of Token Women in State Legislatures." *Politics & Gender* 1, no. 1 (2005): 97–125.

Breuning, Marijke, Paul Parker, and John T. Ishiyama. "The Last Laugh: Skill Building through a Liberal Arts Political Science Curriculum." *PS: Political Science and Politics* 34, no. 3 (2001): 657–61.

Brooks, Deborah Gordon. *He Runs, She Runs: Why Gender Stereotypes Do Not Harm Women Candidates*. Princeton NJ: Princeton University Press, 2013.

Bunce, Valerie, and Sharon Wolchik. "Favorable Conditions and Electoral Revolutions." *Journal of Democracy* 17, no. 4 (2006): 5–18.

Campbell, Donald T., and Julian C. Stanley. *Experimental and Quasi-experimental Designs for Research*. Boston: Houghton Mifflin, 1963.

Childs, Sarah, and Mona Lena Krook. "Critical Mass Theory and Women's Political Representation." *Political Studies* 56, no. 3 (2008): 725–36.

Chinkin, Christine, and Freya Baetens. *Sovereignty, Statehood, and State Responsibility: Essays in Honour of James Crawford*. New York: Cambridge University Press, 2014.

Clark, Tom with Anthony Heath. *Hard Times: The Divisive Toll of the Economic Slump*. New Haven, CT: Yale University Press, 2014.

Dahlerup, Drude. "The Story of the Theory of Critical Mass." *Politics & Gender* 2, no. 4 (2006): 511–22.

Deans, Thomas. *Writing and Community Action: A Service-Learning Rhetoric with Readings*. New York: Longman, 2003.

Doty, Roxanne Lynn. "Foreign Policy as Social Construction: A Post-positivist Analysis of U.S. Counterinsurgency Policy in the Philippines." *International Studies Quarterly* 37, no. 3 (September 1993): 297–320.

Doyle, Michael W. "Liberalism and World Politics." *American Political Science Review* 80, no. 4 (1986): 1151–69.

Edwards, Mickey. *The Parties versus the People: How to Turn Republicans and Democrats into Americans.* New Haven, CT: Yale University Press, 2012.

"Election 2012: President Map." *The New York Times,* June 10, 2014. http://elections .nytimes.com/2012/results/president.

Fiorina, Morris P., with Samuel J. Abrams. *Disconnect: The Breakdown of Representation in American Politics.* Norman: University of Oklahoma Press, 2009.

Fiorina, Morris P., with Samuel J. Abrams and Jeremy C. Pope. *Culture War? The Myth of a Polarized America.* 3rd ed. New York: Pearson Longman, 2006.

Gause III, Gregory F. "Why Middle East Studies Missed the Arab Spring." *Foreign Affairs* 90, no. 4 (July 2011): 81–91.

Geddes, Barbara. "Authoritarian Breakdown." Los Angeles, CA: UCLA Center for Comparative and Global Research, January 2004. http://www.international.ucla.edu/ media/files/authn_breakdown.pdf.

George, Alexander L., and Andrew Bennett. *Case Studies and Theory Development in the Social Sciences.* Cambridge, MA: MIT Press, 2004.

Goldstone, Jack. "Toward a Fourth Generation of Revolutionary Theory." *Annual Review of Political Science* 41 (2001): 139–87.

Goldstone, Jack A. "Understanding the Revolutions of 2011." *Foreign Affairs* 90, no. 3 (May 2011): 8–16.

Goodin, Robert E., ed. *The Oxford Handbook of Political Science.* New York: Oxford University Press, 2011.

Hacker, Diana. *A Pocket Manual of Style.* 4th ed. Boston: Bedford/St. Martin's, 2004.

———. *A Pocket Manual of Style.* 5th ed. Boston: Bedford/St. Martin's, 2009.

Havel, Vaclav. "The Power of the Powerless." 1978. http://history.hanover.edu/courses/ excerpts/165havel.html.

Huntington, Samuel P. "After 20 Years: The Future of the Third Wave." *Journal of Democracy* 8, no. 4 (1997): 3–12.

International Telecommunications Union. "Mobile-cellular Telephone Subscriptions per 100 Inhabitants." June 2013a. http://www.itu.int/en/ITU-D/Statistics/Pages/ stat/default.aspx.

———. "Percent of Individuals Using the Internet, 2000-2012." June 2013b. http://www. itu.int/en/ITU-D/Statistics/Pages/stat/default.aspx.

Johnson, Janet Buttolph, and Richard A. Joslyn. *Political Science Research Methods.* 3rd ed. Washington, DC: CQ Press, 1995.

Johnson, Janet Buttolph, and H. T. Reynolds with Jason D. Mycoff. *Political Science Research Methods.* 6th ed. Washington, DC: CQ Press, 2008.

———. *Political Science Research Methods.* 7th ed. Washington, DC: CQ Press, 2011.

Jones, Robert P., Daniel Cox, Juhem Navarro-Rivera, E. J. Dionne, Jr., & William A. Galston. "What Americans Want from Immigration Reform in 2014: Findings from the PRRI/Brookings Religion, Values, and Immigration Reform, Survey, Panel Call Back." Washington, DC: Public Religion Research Institute and Governance Studies, Brookings Institution, April 2014. http://publicreligion.org/site/wp-content/uploads/2014/06/Final-Immigration-Survey.pdf.

Kanter, Rosabeth Moss. *Men and Women of the Corporation.* New York: Basic Books, 1977.

Karl, Terry Lynn. "From Democracy and Democratization and Back: Before Transitions from Authoritarian Rule." Working Paper No. 45. Palo Alto, CA: Center on

Democracy, Democratization, and the Rule of Law, Stanford University, 2005. http://lls-db.stanford.edu/pubs/20900/Karlsep03.pdf.

Katznelson, Ira, and Helen V. Milner, eds. *Political Science: State of the Discipline.* Centennial ed. New York: Norton, 2005.

Kennan, George. "The Sources of Soviet Conduct." *Foreign Affairs* 25, no. 4 (1947): 566–82.

Kuran, Timur. "Now Out of Never: The Element of Surprise in the East European Revolution on 1989." *World Politics* 44, no. 1 (1991): 7–48.

Lee, Carolyn W. *Do-It-Yourself Democracy: The Rise of the Public Engagement Industry.* New York: Oxford University Press, 2015.

Liebell, Susan P. *Democracy, Intelligent Design, and Evolution: Science for Citizenship.* New York: Routledge, 2013.

Lijphart, Arend. "How the Cases You Choose Determine the Answers You Get." *Journal of Policy Analysis* 2 (1975): 131–52.

Lowi, Theodore J. "American Business, Public Policy, Case Studies and Political Theory." *World Politics* 16 (1964): 677–715.

———. *The End of Liberalism: The Second Republic of the United States.* 2nd ed. New York: Norton, 1979.

Lynch, Marc. *The Arab Uprising: The Unfinished Revolutions of the New Middle East.* New York: Public Affairs Press, 2012.

McCarty, Nolan M., Keith T. Poole, and Howard Rosenthal. *Polarized America: The Dance of Ideology and Unequal Riches.* Cambridge, MA: MIT Press, 2006.

Mearsheimer, John. "Back to the Future: Instability in Europe after the Cold War," *International Security* 15, no. 1 (1990): 5–56.

Merton, Robert K. *Social Theory and Social Structure.* Enlarged ed. New York: Free Press, 1968.

Moore, Barrington. *Social Origins of Dictatorship and Democracy: Lord and Peasant in the Making of the Modern World.* Boston: Beacon, 1967.

Morgenthau, Hans, and Kenneth W. Thompson. *Politics among Nations: The Struggle for Power and Peace.* 6th ed. New York: Knopf, 1985.

Mutz, Diana C. *Hearing the Other Side: Deliberative versus Participatory Democracy.* New York: Cambridge University Press, 2006.

National Commission on Writing in America's Schools and Colleges. *The Neglected R: The Need for a Writing Revolution.* New York: College Entrance Examination Board, 2003. http://www.collegeboard.com/prod_downloads/writingcom/neglectedr.pdf.

Neuman, W. Laurence. *Social Research Methods: Qualitative and Quantitative Methods.* 7th ed. Upper Saddle River, NJ: Pearson, 2011.

O'Donnell, Guillermo, and Phillippe C. Schmitter. *Transitions from Authoritarian Rule, Vol. 4: Tentative Conclusions about Uncertain Democracies.* Baltimore, MD: Johns Hopkins University Press, 1986.

Parker, Christopher S. and Matt A. Barreto. *The Change They Can't Believe In: The Tea Party and Reactionary Politics in America.* Princeton, NJ: Princeton University Press, 2013.

PBS. "Revolution in Cairo." *Frontline.* 2012. http://www.pbs.org/wgbh/pages/frontline/revolution-in-cairo/.

Penn State Libraries. "Choosing a Citation Manager." http://www.libraries.psu.edu/psul/lls/choose_citation_mgr.html.

Pitkin, Hanna Fenichel. *The Concept of Representation.* Berkeley: University of California Press, 1967.

Putnam, Robert D. "Bowling Alone: America's Declining Social Capital." *Journal of Democracy* 6, no. 1 (1995): 65–78.

Putnam, Robert D., with Robert Leonardi and Raffaella Y. Nanetti. *Making Democracy Work: Civic Traditions in Modern Italy*. Princeton, NJ: Princeton University Press, 1993.

Rabinow, Paul, and William M. Sullivan, eds. *Interpretive Social Science: A Reader*. Berkeley: University of California Press, 1979.

Reus-Smit, Christopher, and Duncan Snidal, eds. *Oxford Handbook of International Relations*. New York: Oxford University Press, 2010.

Rhodes, R.A.W., Sarah A. Binder, and Bert A. Rockman, eds. *The Oxford Handbook of Political Institutions*. New York: Oxford University Press, 2008.

Richmond, Oliver P. "Critical Research Agendas for Peace: The Missing Link in the Study of International Relations." *Alternatives* 32, no. 2 (2007): 247–74.

Riedel, Bruce. *What We Won: America's Secret War in Afghanistan, 1979–1989*. Washington, DC: Brookings Institution Press, 2014.

Robinson, Michael, and Susan Ellis. "Purple America: The Country Is Really an Even Mix of Blue and Red." *Weekly Standard* 9, no. 46 (2004): 27–29.

Ross, Michael. "Does Oil Hinder Democracy?" *World Politics* 53, no. 3 (2001): 325–61.

Rubin, Jennifer. "Immigration Polling Tells Congress to Act." *The Washington Post*, July 9, 2014. http://www.washingtonpost.com/blogs/right-turn/wp/2014/07/09/immigration-polling-tells-congress-to-act/.

Saint Joseph's University. "Evaluating Web Sources." http://guides.sju.edu/webevaluation?p=285388.

Semiatin, Richard J. *Campaigns on the Cutting Edge*. 2nd ed. Washington, DC: CQ Press, 2012.

Shively, W. Phillips. *The Craft of Political Research*. 5th ed. Upper Saddle River, NJ: Prentice Hall, 2002.

———. *The Craft of Political Research*. 7th ed. Upper Saddle River, NJ: Prentice Hall, 2009.

Shrag, Peter. *Paradise Lost: California's Experience, America's Future*. New York: New Press, 1998.

Skocpol, Theda. *States and Social Revolutions: A Comparative Analysis of France, Russia, and China*. New York: Cambridge University Press, 1979.

Smith, Daniel A., and Caroline J. Tolbert. *Educated by Initiative: The Effects of Direct Democracy on Citizens and Political Organizations in the American States*. Ann Arbor: University of Michigan Press, 2004.

Swers, Michele L. *The Difference Women Make: The Policy Impact of Women in Congress*. Chicago: University of Chicago Press, 2002.

Stossel, Scott. "Subdivided We Fall." *New York Times Book Review*, May 18, 2008. http://www.nytimes.com/2008/05/18/books/review/Stossel-t.html?pagewanted=all&_r=0.

Tamerius, Karin L. "Sex, Gender and Leadership in the Representation of Women." In *Gender Power, Leadership, and Governance*, edited by Georgia Duerst Lahti and Rita Mae Kelley, 93–112. Ann Arbor: University of Michigan Press, 1995.

Taylor, Charles. "Interpretation and the Sciences of Man." In *Interpretive Social Science: A Reader*, edited by Paul Rabinow and William M. Sullivan, 25–71. Berkeley: University of California Press, 1979.

Telequest. *Across the Drafts: Students and Teachers Talk about Feedback*. Cambridge, MA: Expository Writing Program, Harvard University, 2005.

Toal, Gerard. "Could Crimea Be Another Bosnia?" March 14, 2014. http://www.open-democracy.net/od-russia/gerard-toal/could-crimea-be-another-bosnia-republika-srpska-krajina.

Tremblay, M., and R. Pelletier. "More Feminists or More Women? Descriptive and Substantive Representations of Women in the 1997 Canadian Federal Elections." *International Political Science Review* 21, no. 4 (October 2000): 381–405.

Tsygankov, Andrei. *Russia and the West from Alexander to Putin: Honor and International Relations.* New York: Cambridge University Press, 2014.

Waltz, Kenneth N. *Theory of International Politics.* Reading, MA: Addison Wesley, 1979.

Wang, Yuhua. *Tying the Autocrat's Hands: The Rise of the Rule of Law in China.* New York: Cambridge University Press, 2014.

Wayne, Stephen J. *Is This Any Way to Run a Democratic Election?* 5th ed. Washington, DC: CQ Press, 2013.

Wendt, Alexander. "Constructing International Politics." *International Security* 20, no. 1 (1995): 71–81.

Wolff, Stefan. "Consociationalism: Power Sharing and Self-Governance." In *Conflict Management in Divided Societies: Theories & Practice*, edited by Stefan Wolff and Christalla Yakinthou, 23–56. New York: Routledge, 2012.

Yglesias, Matthew. "The Great Divider." *American Prospect* 18, no. 4 (2007): 47–49.

Zerubavel, Eviatar. *The Clockwork Muse: A Practical Guide to Writing Theses, Dissertations, and Books.* Cambridge, MA: Harvard University Press, 1999.

Index

CQ Press, an imprint of SAGE, is the leading publisher of books, periodicals, and electronic products on American government and international affairs. CQ Press consistently ranks among the top commercial publishers in terms of quality, as evidenced by the numerous awards its products have won over the years. CQ Press owes its existence to Nelson Poynter, former publisher of the St. Petersburg Times, and his wife Henrietta, with whom he founded *Congressional Quarterly* in 1945. Poynter established CQ with the mission of promoting democracy through education and in 1975 founded the Modern Media Institute, renamed The Poynter Institute for Media Studies after his death. The Poynter Institute (*www.poynter.org*) is a nonprofit organization dedicated to training journalists and media leaders.

In 2008, CQ Press was acquired by SAGE, a leading international publisher of journals, books, and electronic media for academic, educational, and professional markets. Since 1965, SAGE has helped inform and educate a global community of scholars, practitioners, researchers, and students spanning a wide range of subject areas, including business, humanities, social sciences, and science, technology, and medicine. A privately owned corporation, SAGE has offices in Los Angeles, Boston, London, New Delhi, and Singapore, in addition to the Washington DC office of CQ Press.

$SAGE research**methods**

The essential online tool for researchers from the world's leading methods publisher

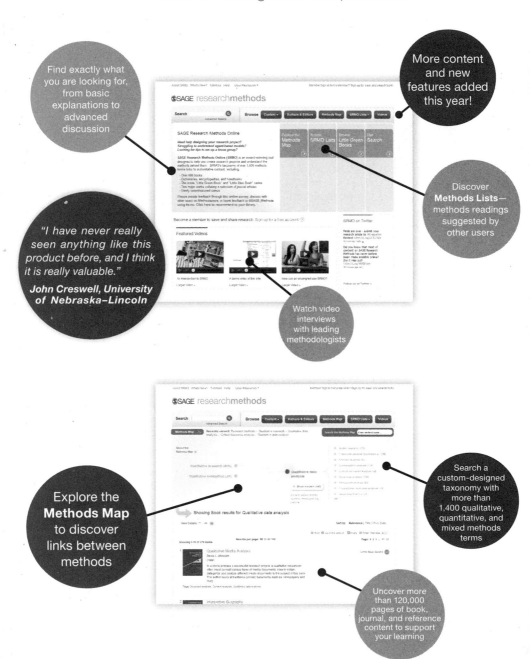

Find exactly what you are looking for, from basic explanations to advanced discussion

More content and new features added this year!

Discover **Methods Lists**— methods readings suggested by other users

"*I have never really seen anything like this product before, and I think it is really valuable.*"

John Creswell, University of Nebraska–Lincoln

Watch video interviews with leading methodologists

Explore the **Methods Map** to discover links between methods

Search a custom-designed taxonomy with more than 1,400 qualitative, quantitative, and mixed methods terms

Uncover more than 120,000 pages of book, journal, and reference content to support your learning

Find out more at
www.sageresearchmethods.com